M000102162

Elder Mountain:
A Journal
of Ozarks Studies

Issue 10

Missouri State University-West Plains ·

ISSN 1946-0511

C. D. Albin, Founder
Phillip Howerton, General Editor
Morgan Blanck, Associate Editor and Intern
Leigh Adams, Assistant Editor
Jason McCollom, Assistant Editor
Frank Priest, Assistant Editor

Editorial Advisory Board
Drew Beisswenger, Missouri State University-Springfield
Brooks Blevins, Missouri State University-Springfield
Erika Brady, Western Kentucky University
Rachel Gholson, Missouri State University-Springfield
Gene Hyde, Radford University
Howard Marshall, University of Missouri-Columbia
Gordon McCann, Independent Scholar
Lynn Morrow, Missouri State Archives (Retired)
J. Blake Perkins, Williams Baptist University
Bonnie Stepenoff, Southeast Missouri State University
Terrell Tebbetts, Lyon College
Tom Williams, University of Central Arkansas

Editorial Board
C. D. Albin
Leigh Adams
Phillip Howerton
Jason McCollom
Matt Meacham
Frank Priest

Elder Mountain: A Journal of Ozarks Studies is published
once a year by the Department of English at Missouri State
University-West Plains.

Submission Guidelines

A juried journal, *Elder Mountain* seeks Ozarks-focused manuscripts from all disciplinary perspectives (particularly anthropology, economics, folklore, geography, geology, history, literature, music, and political science) as well as interdisciplinary approaches. In addition, high-quality, Ozarks-oriented short stories, poems, and works of creative nonfiction are of keen interest, as is visual art that examines the Ozarks.

Only electronic submissions are accepted and may be sent as a Word attachment to PhillipHowerton@MissouriState.edu. Deadline for first consideration is April 1.

Well-crafted, thesis-driven articles free of discipline-specific jargon have the greatest likelihood of acceptance. Articles should use the documentation style appropriate to the discipline.

Carefully wrought short stories and essays free of common Ozark stereotypes will receive appreciative consideration. Creative prose pieces should be a maximum of 5000 words.

Poems may range in style from formal to free verse. Strong imagery and intelligently rendered content are attractive qualities.

For visual art we seek images (photography, paintings, ink drawings, etc.) suitable for reproduction in black and white. We prefer that images be sent electronically as a JPG, PNG, or TIF file. Include a one- or two-page artist's statement.

Simultaneously submitted or previously published work will not be considered.

Elder Mountain reserves first North American serial rights only. All other rights revert to the authors and artists upon publication in *Elder Mountain*.

Table of Contents

Poetry

Photography

Reviews

Contributors /

Editor's Note

Welcome to this double issue celebration of a decade of *Elder Mountain*. Since its founding by Dr. Craig Albin, *Elder Mountain* has steadily published a wide array of outstanding work in the field of Ozarks Studies. In the previous nine issues, *Elder* presented more than 1196 pages of work, including 51 essays, 137 poems, 21 short stories, 21 reviews, and a total of 102 authors.

This issue of *Elder* celebrates both past and present scholarship by reprinting selected material from earlier issues and presenting more than 200 pages of new work. Some of the topics explored within are storytelling, loft barns, drug addiction, cancer, caves, stereotypes, fishing, Hollywood in the Ozarks, placenames, true crime, a Civil War road, environmental disasters, and beekeeping. This material is supplemented with numerous photographs and is followed by reviews of eight recent books.

Several writers in this issue are appearing in *Elder Mountain* for the first time, including a Missouri State University-West Plains student, Faith Collins, who provides an overview of the growing challenges to honeybees in the Ozarks.

Much of material from this current issue and from issues eight and nine is posted on the *Elder Mountain* website online at *https://blogs.wp. missouristate.edu/elder-mountain/*. The website has now had more than 5000 views, and it is proving to be an excellent platform for making the research published in *Elder* easily accessible to scholars every-where.

The future of the field of Ozarks Studies is largely dependent upon the few journals and magazines, such as *Arkansas Historical Quarterly, Arkansas Review, Cave Region Review, Elder Mountain, Missouri Folklore Journal, Missouri Historical Review*, and *OzarksWatch*, that welcome scholarly and creative work focusing upon the Ozarks. Please support these and other such publications--several of which are truly a labor of love.

Phillip Howerton

The First Day

John Mort

I hadn't driven that little Nissan for almost five years, but it ran nice. My brother kept it for me while I was away. She took the big Ford SUV and it was a fine car, all right, but nothing I wanted. The little Nissan was economical and never caused any trouble.

An hour after sunset I parked between two big trucks and walked slowly through the entrance. The greeter, an old woman, had her back turned. I grabbed a cart even though I didn't need one. Push a cart, you're invisible. I walked past the dairy counter, then the meat. Same old crap in the same places.

A teenaged girl in a tight red sweater and jeans that might as well have been skin threw her big, brown eyes at me, and I raised from the deep that old way of thinking, not like a memory but like something I read somewhere. It's easy to get into trouble with young women. Say, "Hello, there," and you're in trouble.

The girl returned to her mother, six inches shorter, thirty pounds heavier, but they shared the same springy, black hair. The mother glanced at me almost in sympathy, then wearily contemplated her daughter, who held high her frozen chicken, twirling it like she was some model on a runway. The girl reached her mother's cart and turned for a final, fulsome glance my way—well, I can't honestly say so. I had already grabbed my package of salami and headed for the checkout.

I walked between the pallets of rock and dirt, slipped past Automotive, and found a path in the field behind. The moon scuttled under dark clouds and I felt the tug of wind from the north. Rain, I thought, but not yet.

I weaved around piles of asphalt slag and busted-up lumber, then dodged a campfire where a homeless person sat on a ruined couch, smoking. I reached the drainage ditch behind the row of houses. Coming this way, I didn't need to walk down the street, causing neighbors to wonder about the strange man out there in the dark, maybe even recognizing me from the old days. Those neighbors of mine would call 911 if you spat gum on the walk.

The wind blew stronger in my face. That meant dogs couldn't smell me.

Pete and Maggie Yates, if they were the people who still lived there, raised chickens now. The birds had settled for the night into a collective murmur, but one hen clucked nervously as I passed.

She'd put up a privacy fence, so I went down to the drainage ditch and brought up old tires to make steps. Just as I slid into the yard, lightning flashed, and twenty feet to the east I spotted a gate. All right, I thought, story of my life. But the gate made it simple to leave.

The moon darted half out of the clouds again and I reached the storage shed in a few steps. The latch was rusty and squeaked some before I could make it work. A light came on in the bedroom and I panicked, but then I heard the faint whoosh of the toilet and realized the light was a coincidence.

No one had entered the shed since I went away. Lightning flashed again but I didn't need to see. I reached above the workbench and found my grandfather's hand saw. It was a Disston saw with an apple wood handle. Five inset, ornate screws. Swedish steel. Nobody's made a saw like that in fifty years.

Up there, they had me building handy little stools they put around everywhere. I took pride in my work, but when it came to the trim, there wasn't a decent saw in the entire place. It always made me think of Grandpa's beautiful old Disston.

Why would she care about the saw? She wouldn't. She took out that restraining order but the saw wouldn't matter. You forget what it was all about. You stop caring.

She'd care about Lucky, though.

I unfolded a lawn chair and sat in the opening, waiting. He'd figure it out pretty soon just from the little sounds a human can't hear.

I could see over the deck and through those glass doors right into the kitchen. She could have taken up with another man by now but it didn't seem so. She walked around in that same old, green housecoat and her hair was a mess. Just like me, she wasn't getting any younger.

She spread what looked like peanut butter on dark bread and came toward the deck, munching slowly like she was in deep thought.

I sat directly in front of her, fifty feet away, and didn't move. She slid open the door and held one hand high, feeling for rain. She returned to the kitchen, drew a glass of water, and slouched off to bed again. No TV, that woman. She always hated television.

I heard a thump as he jumped off the bed and hit the floor. Old fellow, almost twelve now. I brought him home when he was a pup.

He walked through that dog door I had so much trouble installing and came steadily across the deck, barking once. "Hush," I whispered, and he dropped to the grass and slid forward on his belly. I gave him a slice of salami just as the rain began. We'd get soaked but I had towels and blankets in that little Nissan. I figured we could make Ft. Smith.

"C'mon, Lucky," I said. "Let's go."

The Future of Beekeeping in the Missouri Ozarks: Lack of Forage and the Proliferation of Pests and Pesticides

Faith Collins

After a tour of almost 3000 miles through the Missouri Ozarks, Michael Myer, a commercial beekeeper for 47 years, reported that he saw "no backyard beehives." The basic reason for few beehives in the Ozarks, according to bee experts George S. Ayers and Jay R. Harman, is that "the somewhat drier Ozarks landscape supports a less diverse native flora, with correspondingly fewer bee plants" (422). Beekeeping in the Ozarks is an increasingly difficult undertaking because of the lack of forage and the abundance of pests that destroy bees and beehives, yet the region currently exhibits lower levels of pesticide use due to the limited presence of mono-culture farms.

Lack of forage is a long-term problem that will continue in the coming years due to the eradication of plants that are beneficial to honeybees. Although the Bee & Butterfly Habitat Fund has "established 284 habitats on 3,122 acres of land" since 2015, honeybee forage is still minimal (Coleman 767). The lack of forage for honeybees cannot be corrected easily. Forage for honeybees include such plants as dandelions, thistles, goldenrod, and clover. Many of these plants are considered useless weeds and are destroyed; however, these weeds are far from useless in the eyes of bees and beekeepers. In addition, many farmers do not like white Dutch clover because they think that the clover causes their cows to bloat, but clover and alfalfa "are responsible for about 55% of the total honey production" (Morse 131). According to John Jacob, founder and president of Old Sol Apiaries, "[p]ollinator habitat is rapidly disappearing because of changes to conservation acres in the Farm Bill, suburban and exurban development, and fence post to fence post farming practices" (451). In the 1900s, the largest beekeeper in the U.S. "produced great quantities of buckwheat honey," and the area he lived in had very little woods, and buckwheat was common on the farms (Morse 133). Today that same area is virtually abandoned in respect to farming and is roughly 50% wooded, which obstructs bee flight. This example shows how bee forage has deteriorated over the years. Efforts are being made to restore pollinator habitat, but, even if it is possible, it will take many years to restore it to previous levels.

The lack of forage in the Ozarks often weakens beehives to the point that they will die of starvation during winter. Morgan French, a beekeeper for many years in Mountain Grove, Missouri, states that the "biggest challenge to beekeeping is keeping the bees alive in the wintertime." Bees depend on their natural foods of nectar, honey, and pollen to survive. Although synthetic foods created for bees are better than nothing, bee feed is less beneficial for bees than their natural foods. Bees require ten essential amino acids in their diet or they will suffer from malnutrition. Bees are also able to sense when the hive is deficient in any of these amino acids, and when they have a wide variety of forage to choose from, they will select a plant that contains the missing amino acid. Ozarks beekeeper, Jeff Maddox, says that there is not a great variety of forage in the Ozarks, and bees will get only one type of pollen for up to two weeks. Forage is often scarce due to the rough terrain and the worn-out soil in many areas. Stephanie Pain, writing in the *American Bee Journal*, the leading bee journal in the U.S. today, says "[m]alnourished bees are smaller and weaker, less fertile and shorter lived" (195). For centuries bees had their choice of many types of flowering plants and were able to ensure that the hive received all the necessary amino acids, proteins, and fats needed for survival. Currently there is an extreme lack of diverse forage and the bees are suffering the consequences.

The lack of forage in the Ozarks, due to dry conditions during July and August, often requires beekeepers to ship their beehives out to a nectar flow, which boosts bee populations. According to beekeeper, Rick Bledsoe, "the second week of July dries up for a while." The queen bee is solely in charge of bee production, and she is the only bee that lays fertile eggs. The eggs will mature into larvae and pupae, and then a young bee will emerge. However, the queen will lay eggs only when there is a nectar flow and food, so if there is no nectar flow, the queen will not lay, and the bee population will dwindle. During mid-summer droughts in the Ozarks, most plants stop producing nectar and the bees have nothing to eat for extended periods of time. Morgan French, Rick Bledsoe, and fellow beekeeper Carl Fry agreed that one of the greatest challenges in the Ozarks is the unpredictable weather. During the dry season, beekeepers will anxiously await rain, but if it rains for a week, they will anxiously await the day it stops. The rain is beneficial, but it must be interspersed with days of sunshine. Rain washes away the nectar from many flowering plants and forces bees to remain in the hive where they will begin to eat the honey reserves. Drought places immense stress on bees, but too much rain can be just as detrimental.

Pests in the Ozarks are also a great problem in beekeeping due to their ability to kill and weaken bees, which causes hives to decline. Most people, who try to keep bees, give up after a couple years because it is too difficult to keep bees alive due to pests and viruses. According to Rick Bledsoe, the paramount problem in beekeeping is the varroa mite which carries viruses and feeds on the bees' fat. To put size into perspective, a varroa mite on a bee is comparable to a tick the size of a softball on a five-foot human. However, the mite itself is not the primary problem. Randy Oliver, a commercial beekeeper who conducts research on the varroa mite, says that mite-transmitted viruses, particularly Deformed Wing Virus, are the leading problem (69). Deformed Wing Virus prevents the host bee from being able to fly by damaging wing formation and body structure when bees are in the pupae stage. Although a naturally mite-resistant bee would control the problem, such mite-resistant breeding stock is not available on a large scale or affordable to non-commercial beekeepers. Another pest that is very destructive is the small hive beetle (SHB) which can kill a weakened hive relatively quickly. Carl Fry, who keeps hives in West Plains, Missouri, says that if he could change one thing about beekeeping it would be "getting rid of the pests, specifically small hive beetle." The pest problem is prevalent all over the world, but in the Ozarks, warm weather during winter increases pest populations.

Due to the multiplicity of pests and viruses, beekeeping in the Ozarks is a relatively expensive hobby and a financially unprofitable occupation. Mite medication varies in price, but the most effective, and still affordable, medication costs an average of $4.57 per treatment for one hive. Multiplied over millions of hives, the treatment becomes extremely costly to the industry. In 2018 alone, beekeepers in the U.S. spent roughly $17,788,000 on mite medication (USDA 5). The small hive beetle is another destructive pest, and in this case a trap rather than medication is the remedy. Hive beetles are an invasive pest that mate and complete part of their reproductive cycle in a beehive. Naturally, bees attempt to remove hive beetles themselves by herding or carrying the beetles out of the hive. However, since hive beetles are very small, they can hide well and are difficult for the bees to remove. In time, the hive will be taken over by beetles and both the honey and wax will be destroyed. Therefore, when a beekeeper sees any hive beetles, she or he must add a trap to the hive to capture and kill most of the beetles, and such traps are yet another expense. Morgan French stated that he keeps bees because of the "interest level," and he adds that he has spent more money on beekeeping than he will ever earn from this hobby.

Due to relatively warm winters in the Ozarks, pest larvae seldom freeze and thus pests that are harmful to bees grow more prevalent each year. When Roy LeGrande, president of the beekeepers' club in Poplar Bluff, was asked whether the warmer winters in the Ozarks were more beneficial for the beehives or for pests, he replied "it is more beneficial for the pests." During a cold winter, bees will get in a small cluster in order to stay warm and will eat a minimum quantity of food. However, in a warmer winter the bees will come out of the hive and fly looking for food to take back to the hive, but in the winter there is no food to find, and the bees will return to the hive hungry and will eat the reserve food. A warm winter will often cause bees to consume more food than is necessary for survival and will begin the process of starvation. In time, the bees will become weak and pests will capitalize on the opportunity to decimate the hive. During a cold winter, pest larvae outside the hive will be frozen, and inside the hive the bees will stay strong and will control the pests.

Another problem in beekeeping is the overuse and misuse of pesticides which destroy entire beehives and apiaries, resulting in the declining bee populations across the U.S. Most row-crop farmers rely heavily on pesticides to protect their crops and often to save time will mix many various sprays together. However, this mixture is untested by chemical companies or by federal and state regulatory agencies. Fipronil and imidacloprid are systemic insecticides, meaning they can be taken in by any plant and incorporated into pollen and nectar

(McArt 281). Since pollinators gather both pollen and nectar, they will also gather insecticides that harm the pollinator, and bees will take the contaminated food back to the hive, which, in turn, weakens the hive. The hive will be weakened because bees will feed their young contaminated pollen which does not always kill the young bees instantly but often weakens them and thus weakens the whole hive. According to Daniel Collins, who keeps roughly 200 hives in the Ozarks, the effects of systemic insecticides on beehives are "similar to a human being having a continuous cold or the flu." Furthermore, the "[l]ack of information on the effect of all pesticide ingredients makes them appear safer than they are" ("Commercial Pesticides" 492). Pesticide companies are required to test the active ingredient in a pesticide on honeybees to see if the ingredient harms them, but they are not required to test the complete product on honeybees. According to Michelle Colopy, representative of The Pollinator Stewardship Council, in 2014 the "poisoning of more than 80,000 honeybee colonies . . . was linked to a tank mix of fungicides and insect growth regulators" in the almond groves of California (27).

However, most of the time there is not a significant pesticide problem in many areas of the Missouri Ozarks due to the lack of row-crops, vegetable crops, or fruit crops. These particular mono-culture crops cannot be grown on a large scale in much of the Ozarks because the soil is thin and rocky. Having replaced many extensive tracts of forest with a mono-culture crop of fescue, farming mostly consists of raising cattle. As a result, there are fewer sprays and less area that needs sprayed compared to areas with mono-culture crops, such as corn, cotton, almonds, and apples. To many beekeepers, the presence of sprays is one of the most detrimental factors in beekeeping. Roy LeGrande says that there are row-crop farmers in his area and he has "many problems with pesticides." But Rick Bledsoe, who keeps bees in a more remote portion of the Ozarks, states that he doesn't "have many problems with pesticides in his area" because "there is no mono-culture farming." There are many different types of sprays, but most beekeepers view neonicotinoids as the worst because, after application, they are secreted in the pollen and nectar of the plant sprayed and are taken by pollinators back to their hives. When Jeff Maddox was asked what he would change about beekeeping if he could, he replied it would be "eliminating neonicotinoids." Another solution to the problem would simply be notification. Many farmers notify their local beekeeper, and the bees are removed from the area to be sprayed. But some farmers do not think of notifying the local beekeeper until it is too late. Farmers and beekeepers must work together. According to Bryan Walsh in *Time* magazine, almonds rely 100% on an outside pollinator, apples 90%, asparagus 90%, avocados 90%, blueberries 90%, cucumbers 80%, and plums 65% (30-31). Farmers need bees to pollinate crops and beekeepers need farmers' crops for a nectar and pollen source.

The absence of neonicotinoids in many areas of the Ozarks makes it a refuge for some beekeepers. Pesticides are everywhere, but in the Ozarks some areas have fewer sprays due to the lack of crops other than fescue. However, the relative lack of pesticides is accompanied by a lack of forage, unpredictable weather, and an abundance of pests. The national pesticide problem is grave indeed if a small group of beekeepers are still willing to risk pests, weather, and, most of all, an extreme lack of forage in the Ozarks to simply find refuge from sprays. According to Rusty Berlew, who has studied agriculture, honeybees, and the environment for thirty years, "[i]n terms of acreage, the largest irrigated crop in America is lawn" (78). Berlew further states that "U.S. lawns require 3 trillion gallons of water, 200 million gallons of gas, and 70 million pounds of pesticide annually" (79). The use of sprays on lawns is unnecessary as well as costly, and it is harmful to all pollinators. It is not just the farmers who forget momentarily about the helpful bee, but it is also the average homeowner who forgets. But perhaps they do not forget. Perhaps people do remember and care; they go to the store and look at the label on a pesticide. The label says that the pesticide is not toxic to bees. What the label actually means is that the active ingredient is not toxic, and that the finished product might be. Unless drastic changes happen soon, we may be facing a world without bees.

Considering the many challenges, why do a few dedicated people still keep bees in the Ozarks? When five Ozarkian beekeepers, Carl Fry, Rick Bledsoe, Morgan French, Jeff Maddox, and Roy LeGrande, were asked why they keep bees, they did not point out the relatively low level of pesticides or the hope of earning a profit. They answered simply that they enjoyed it, and Fry added, "[b]eekeeping is not an exact science" and noted that there is a lot to know about bees and that one can never learn it all. Perhaps a deeper reason people keep bees in our region, despite the difficulties, is the same reason people keep them in other regions: the fascination of witnessing creatures that are organized, harmonious, and intricate work together for the benefit of the hive. Bees are not only fascinating and marvelous; they are essential to all life on this planet, and the miracle of bees should be recognized and nurtured by us all.

Works Cited

Ayers, George S., and Jay R. Harman. "Bee Forage of North America and the Potential for Planting For Bees." *The Hive and the Honey Bee*, edited by Joe M. Graham, Dadant & Sons Inc., 2015, pp. 371-461.

Berlew, Rusty. "The Curious Beekeeper: The Pesticide in Our Own Backyards." *American Bee Journal*, vol. 159, no. 1, January 2019, pp. 77-79.

Bledsoe, Rick. Personal Interview. 7 March 2020.

Coleman, Katie. "Seed a Legacy Pollinator Habitat Program Expands to 11 Midwestern States." *American Bee Journal*, vol. 158, no.7, July 2018, pp. 767-769.

Colopy, Michele. "Federal Agencies Could Help Ensure Pollinator Health." *Bee Culture*, August 2014, pp. 25-27.

Collins, Daniel. Personal Interview. 17 March 2020.

French, Morgan. Personal Interview. 7 March. 2020.

Fry, Carl. Personal interview. 7 March 2020.

Jacob, John, and Rob Davis. "Flowering Solar Farms: 'Agrivoltaics' a Powerful Sweet Synergy." *American Bee Journal*, vol. 159, no. 4, April 2019, pp. 451-456.

LeGrande, Roy. Personal Interview. 12 March 2020.

Maddox, Jeff. Personal Interview. 7 March 2020.

McArt, Scott. "Notes from the Lab: The Latest Bee Science Distilled." *American Bee Journal*, vol. 159, no. 3, March 2019, pp.561-562.

Morse, Roger A. *The Complete Guide to Beekeeping*. The Countryman Press, 1997.

Myer, Michael. Personal Interview. 2 November 2019.

"News Notes: Commercial Pesticides Not As Safe As They Appear." *American Bee Journal*, vol. 158, no. 5, May 2018, pp. 491-492.

Oliver, Randy. "The Varroa Problem Part 14: Virus Dynamics and Treatments." *American Bee Journal*, vol. 158, no. 1, January 2018, pp. 69-74.

Pain, Stephanie. "The Whole Food Diet for Bees." *American Bee Journal*, vol. 158, no. 2, February 2018, pp. 193-198.

United States Department of Agriculture: NASS, *Honey Bee Colonies*, 2019, https://usda.library.cornell.edu/concerns/publica tions/ rn301137d?.

Walsh, Bryan. "The Plight of the Honey Bee." *Time*, 19 Aug. 2013, pp. 26-31.

Artifacts of Absence

C. D. Albin

I learned the story as a boy, how my
Great-grandfather strolled home on Christmas Eve
To fall dead of a heart attack, torso
Draped over the front gate like a sweater

Tossed onto an armchair. Light snow dusted
His back until school children found him
And raced to tell of the tiny, bent man
Who still held Christmas gifts crooked in an arm

As if Wall Street's crash left him little else.
Somewhere in his clothing was a wallet
He had inked with date and place of purchase:
Fourteen January, nineteen-nineteen,

Crider, Missouri. The wallet has come
To me. From pockets parched by dust I lift
Receipts, news clippings, a darkened tintype
The size of a stamp, the face that looks back

Eerily like my own. The last item
Is a letter from my father's father,
A neat cursive in blue ink, legible
After ninety-one years though the paper

Brittles on fingertips. I read as fourth
Generation, my grandfather penning
The tale of his father's death for his son,
My father preserving by happenstance

Random artifacts of absence for me.
I consider again the tintype face,
The odd bequeathals of brow, lip, and bone
Wrought by the riddling alchemy of genes.

The wallet itself has transformed with time,
The hurly-burly of use abrading
Dark leather with a crosshatching of scars—
Evidence of episodes forever

Unknowable to me. I am taken
By the stark irony of tangibles,
Mere material queerly redolent
Of the old, abiding griefs of the heart.

Letter and tintype, all else I return
To folds of the wallet, store them away
At the back of the hickory bureau
Where my father's hand left a final print.

Origin Stories

C. D. Albin

Like images engraved upon both sides
Of a coin, the historical marker
Outside the Ozark Heritage Center

Tells dual tales of home town history.
Facing west, the marker greets visitors
With a narrative of modest founding,

Josephus Howell having thought to open
A post office inside his home, circa
1850. The Civil War requires

A separate paragraph to recount
Rebels who fled Union troops, and raiders
Who burned the town in 1863,

Resettlement impeded for two years.
Facing east, the marker's back side informs
Visitors of an ancient north-south trail

Running through the county and professes
More than a thousand prehistoric mounds
Remain in the region. The town resides

In territory Osage seceded
In 1808, although the Shawnee
And Delaware continued to visit

Through the 1840s. Highway 63,
Now running north-south across the county,
Assails the Ozark Heritage Center

With incessant sounds of passage, drivers
Migrating from place to place at sixty
Miles per hour, road dust marking their absence.

Magic Kids

Steve Wiegenstein

The change in the sound was almost imperceptible, with the radio playing and the traffic noise, but somehow they all knew from the disappearance of that one note—the baritone hum that they could never even have said they heard—that they had run out of gas.

Dad was at the wheel and instantly at the edge of something, crying or shouting or what, couldn't tell yet. Mom sat in the passenger seat with her arms folded. She was always at the edge of crying so being at the edge of crying was nothing new. In the back seat, Will didn't much care. Being out of gas was just as interesting as having gas.

"I knew we should have got gas at that last place," Mom said. Dad hit the wheel with the heel of his hand. Nobody wanted to mention that the last place, Warsaw or Clinton or wherever, was where they had changed drivers, and she could have filled up the car just as easily as anybody. Besides, miracles abounding, the exit ramp was a down slope and Dad, hauling against the dead power steering, got them to the light and managed to switch with Mom while the light was red, shoving against the back of the car while she steered, and this place being almost like the country, far enough west of Kansas City to feel like something more or less rural, people jumped out to help him push and within a minute they were in a station and miracles abounding, the hotel was just across the way.

Dad was again at the edge of something, although now it was joy or singing or whatever, his clothes dirty as they checked in, but his face filled with a smile at the kindness of strangers. Magic Kids had gotten them a suite, so Will had sort of a room of his own, at least with its own TV set, which was cool. Dad took a shower while Mom called Magic Kids to let them know they had arrived. Will wanted to check out the TV but first there was the round of pills.

"Am I going to have to come in there and remind you to take your pills?" Mom said. Will was already halfway done.

"No," he mumbled through a mouthful. Will didn't mind the pills. They just took practice.

Then there was time for PlayStation. Dad and Mom stayed in their room and made phone calls, called Grandma and uncles and aunts, called the radio stations and the TV stations, the people back home who had raised money. Everything looked good for tomorrow. The weatherman said it was going to be a nice day. He spoke in hard, flat syllables as though his voice were bouncing off a metal roof; Will had never heard anything like it, even though Kansas City wasn't all that far from Mountain View. Will wondered whether the guy was making it up, but Mom said they all talked that way up here.

"There's no plug-in for my clock," Mom said. "Dennis, find a plug-in."

"There's a clock here."

She gave him her look. "You know how I hate those cheap clock alarms. That nasty buzzy sound. Scares me to death. Besides, they don't work half the time. You want to sleep through this?"

Will didn't feel much like eating that night. Everybody thought he was too excited, and he let them think that. Truth was he was having a bad day.

The lady from Magic Kids came over later. She was a sharp-faced woman with dyed black hair, and she didn't look at Will with that moony expression so many people took on. Will liked her for that.

"How old are you, young man?"

"Fourteen."

She sized him up. Of course he was small for his age. All his food, all his energy, had been going to The Thing for years.

"I think you'll fit in the seat okay. You realize," she said, turning to his parents, "that there is risk involved anytime you step onto a racetrack." His father nodded, almost too eager. "You'll need to sign some releases. After you're done at the track, I have some passes for the National Agricultural Hall of Fame, if you like." She laid them on the side table and glanced at Will, whose face must have revealed something. "It's very interesting."

Will watched while they went through the paperwork. Finally, it was over.

"You a big NASCAR fan?" the woman said.

Will nodded. "Yes, ma'am."

It wasn't true. The races on TV bored him, but his dad liked them, and they were a good way to spend time with his dad in a way that didn't end up in shouting or crying. When they got approved by Magic Kids, he figured what the heck, nothing else he really wanted to do. Dad would get a kick out of being in the pit area.

Another round of pills, and Will lay on his bed watching TV with the sound down while Mom and Dad slept. He could feel his insides working. Maybe it was just his imagination, but it seemed like as soon as he got sick he became able to feel what was going on in all his internal organs—his stomach, his kidneys. He could feel his heart working, not just the beats, but all the separate movements of the muscle. He felt fluids running in and out of his liver.

Will put on his clothes and slipped out the door, blinking in the unexpectedly bright light of the hallway. He could see two doors open at the far end and heard the sound of voices—kids his age, it sounded like, on a field trip or something. He thought about going down to say hi, but didn't. With his bald head and wasted face he'd just freak them out.

He ended up at the vending machines by the front desk. The desk clerk was a stout woman, maybe thirty-five, with bobbed brown hair and a pair of thick glasses.

"You need anything, honey?" she said.

"No, ma'am," Will said. He'd forgotten to put any change in his pants, so there was no point in standing at the vending machine. Nowhere else to stand, though.

"You here for the Kansas Speedway?"

"Yes, ma'am. I'm—" Not much to say. He let it run out.

"We get three or four of you fellas a year," she said. "No girls. Guess they all want to go to Disney World or somewhere."

"Guess so."

Will walked to the door. The parking lot was quiet. The highway seemed empty, although he could see headlights and taillights tracing its path.

"What you going to do there?"

He turned back to the desk. "One of the drivers said he was going to take me on a few laps."

"Which one?"

"Mark Sharp."

"Oh, honey, he's cute! Wish he'd take me on a few laps."

"That's my dad's favorite driver."

The woman was rustling papers, clicking on her computer mouse, tearing sheets off the printer from time to time. She perched on a padded stool, giving Will an occasional glance.

"You say you get a lot of kids like me?"

"Mm, like I said, four or five. Our chain is a national partner with Magic Kids," she said, with a momentary note of pride in her voice. "Some of 'em come in, they are in ba-ad shape. One little boy, couldn't hardly even talk. He was in a wheelchair, kinda leaned over all the time." She seemed about to say more, but then thought better of it. From a mount in the far corner of the room, a shopping channel danced silently. "Now you, you look pretty good."

"Yes, ma'am, I feel okay." And it was true. Whatever it was that had kept him awake had gone for now. "You got any kids?"

Her face seemed to open and then shut. "One, but he has passed away. He had a heart defect. Passed away at two and a half months."

"Oh. I'm sorry."

"Thank you."

For a couple of minutes their silence was broken only by the clicking of her mouse. The woman lowered her eyes to her computer screen and Will, embarrassed, leaned against the front desk and looked out the door. He'd known this silence himself. Friends would come by, his friends, his parents' friends, and they would accidentally say something painful. And then the silence, or worse, the rush of apologies, more words trying to cover the earlier words, but never succeeding.

He looked back over his shoulder at her. Her name tag read "Ruby Simmons."

"Mrs. Simmons?"

She looked up, her face composed.

"I'm very sorry about your son," Will said.

"Thank you again." She smiled. "It was ten years ago next month."

"What was his name."

"Aaron. His daddy and I picked it out together."

"That's a good name."

Ruby Simmons turned back to her work, and Will thought he should probably quit talking. He felt sleepy.

His father woke him in the morning dressed in his Mark Sharp jacket complete with advertiser patches. Mom was already down in the breakfast room.

"At least somebody got some sleep," she said when they brought their trays. "I don't see how you do it."

Soon the Magic Kids lady was there, shiny in black and red polyester, and they were checking in at the speedway. A knot of people waited at an entrance.

"We're from Mr. Sharp's team," someone said. "And you must be William."

Then before he knew it they were standing at the edge of the racetrack, patting themselves in the crisp air, one of the team off apart with her back turned, talking on a cell phone. A black car gleamed nearby.

"He's not going to stand us up, is he?" Mom said. "It's three hundred miles."

Someone had a souvenir Mark Sharp jacket for Will, and he put it on, grateful for the warmth. And then there he was, the celebrity, striding out from a door Will had not noticed before, big smile, fast walker.

Dad made a strange noise like a moo. Then they all began to talk at once.

Mark Sharp was a small man, wiry and muscular, not much taller than Will himself. In their jackets, Will felt as if he and his dad were badly drawn cartoon versions of the real Mark Sharp, who stood relaxed, letting the effusions of his parents wash over him. At a pause in the talking, he stepped over to Will.

"So what do you say, buddy? Ready to roll?" And poof, they were in the car.

"Now this is not my real car, you understand," Mark Sharp said. "My real car, you have to climb in the window. This here's the pace car. But you know that."

He eased the car though the first few gears. "So how fast does your dad drive?"

"I don't know, eighty maybe on the interstate."

Mark Sharp smiled a practiced smile. "Okay, here's eighty."

Scenery flew past, advertising signs, fences, people. As they made a curve, invisible hands pressed him into his seat.

"Now here's a hundred," Mark Sharp said. "Now ten."

Will knew he should respond—whoop, or yell, or something—but he just felt content to watch it all go past.

"This is twenty."

Will watched his parents flash by. They seemed to be clapping or waving.

"You ever worry about getting killed out here?" Will said after a while.

"God, yes. All the time. Can't let it mess you up, of course, but still. Especially nowadays, with some of these new drivers they've let in. Bunch of ignorant motherfuckers—" He shot Will a glance. "Oops. Sorry about that. We're supposed to watch our mouths, too. No more cursing."

"It's okay."

"You should hear me after the races. 'Well, gosh darn it, if it hadn't a been for that doggone tire going out on me on 42, I would been in the doggone top ten.'"

They shared a laugh, and then Will said, "Listen, would you mind giving my dad a few turns around the track? He's the real racing fan of us two. He's been wanting to come up here for the Richard Petty Driving Experience, but we never could afford it."

Another glance. "Okay, sure. Just as well. They throttle you down on that Driving Experience. Hell, more thrills on the L.A. Freeway than that thing." He poked Will in the side, gently, with the knuckle of his index finger. "Now if you see Mr. Petty, don't tell him I said that."

They rolled to a stop by the knot of people. Mom was clapping her hands and Dad was making big windmill motions with both arms.

"How about you, poppa? Want to take a turn?" Mark Sharp said.

"Um, the release forms—" began one of the assistants, but the driver cut her off.

"Heck with the release forms, we're just gonna take a turn. Test out this new asphalt they put on. Come on, what do you say?"

And he and Dad were off, sweeping through the curves like before. Mark Sharp was probably saying "Here's eighty." They flashed past, his dad a blur of waving hands. Will thought he heard a whoop.

The air had begun to warm up. Will was about to unzip his jacket when he caught his mother looking at him out of the corner of her eye. She would just make him zip it up again. The small talk had trailed off, and they stood quiet, the sound of the car faint as it sped down the backstretch.

"You get all the cars in here on race day, and it is loud, loud, loud," the assistant said. "But you know."

"No," Mom said. "Never been to a race. Meant to, but with Will—" She stopped herself, and the silence returned.

After a couple more rounds, the car pulled to a stop again and the men got out. Dad had a look of goofy pleasure on his face like a drunk. They all shook hands again, standing in a small circle, and Mark Sharp's crew turned to their cell phones again and stepped off to the side.

"So you heading back home?" Mark Sharp said.

"Yes," Mom said. "Tomorrow. Tonight we'll have a nice dinner and rest."

"So buddy, what you gonna do once you get back home?" Mark Sharp gave his shoulder a soft punch.

"I don't know," Will said. "Die, I guess."

In the silence that suddenly deepened and surrounded them, silence that reached all the way out into space, Will could feel the others rearranging themselves, reallocating their positions in the small circle they had formed at the edge of the pavement, an edge, he noticed looking down for the first time, that was cracked and invaded by tendrils of crabgrass and chickweed. Will didn't know whether to take that as a sign of hope or one of disheartenment, the stubborn persistence of life or the inevitable victory of chaos. He could feel his body at work, its ceaseless labor, blood flowing in and out of The Thing, his nerves firing, electrons jumping from synapse to synapse.

"Well, fuck," Mark Sharp said.

"My beautiful son," said Mom.

And then the moment was past, they all talked at once again, just as at the beginning, covering as best they could the embarrassing truth. Mark Sharp jumped to join his crew, who were ready with new sheets of paper, new public relations events. They disappeared as fast as they had arrived. Mom and Dad and Will stood on the concrete apron of the track, aware of the Magic Kids lady waiting for them at the gate and the National Agricultural Hall of Fame in the near distance. But none of them moved to leave, not quite yet.

Remembering Yonder Mountain: Storytelling as Cultural Survival

Brian Hardman

Storytelling is often thought of, first and foremost, as entertainment, but in many regions, it is a key to preserving cultural history and memory. In the Ozarks, for example, storytelling goes by many humorous names. If you have spent much time in the region, you have likely heard someone spinning a windy, telling a tall tale, or stretching the blanket, and the seriousness of storytelling is often overshadowed by the entertainment value found in listening to (or reading) a grand storyteller. Beneath the playfulness found in many stories, though, there is something vitally important at work, and that is the subject of this discussion. Storytelling, both the oral form and the print form, allows for marginalized cultures and regions to maintain their traditional values and beliefs, while still negotiating the broader world. Such storytelling has been essential to the survival of Native American cultures, and its significance is largely the same for the Ozarks and its inhabitants, especially in a world of rapid urbanization and increasing technology, where the possibility of losing the storytelling tradition is a significant threat to cultural survival and regional identity. By drawing parallels between the storytelling traditions found in Native American cultures and the Ozarks (particularly in the work of Leslie Marmon Silko and Donald Harington), we may see how storytelling ensures a continuity in cultural and regional memory. In short, storytelling for Native Americans is the most important way to maintain cultural and regional identity and to ensure cultural survival. This is also true for the Ozarks.

In an introductory poem to her celebrated novel *Ceremony*, Leslie Marmon Silko, a Laguna Pueblo author and expert on the oral tradition and storytelling, says:

I will tell you something about stories,
They aren't just entertainment.
Don't be fooled

They are all we have, you see,
All we have to fight off illness and death.
You don't have anything
If you don't have the stories. (2)

Silko goes on to say that "if you think about it, nearly everything of consequence that we tell one another involves narration or story" (*Storyteller* xvii). She means that when we explain ourselves or our reasoning in a situation, when we describe what we remember of an experience, we organize that experience in a narrative structure to communicate our vital information: we are telling stories. The development of language and storytelling go hand in hand. The need to share our experiences, to tell our stories to another person, is so strong, Silko argues, that we invented language, in part, to be able to communicate our most important experiences to each other.

Imagine for a moment what some of the first words we spoke to each other must have been. I like to think that our first utterances might have conveyed love or even hunger. Silko, however, suggests those first words must have served a safety or survival function and likely were the earliest versions of "help!," or "hide!," or "run!" (*Storyteller* xvii). She goes on to explain that the moment the danger passed the desire to communicate what had just happened would have been so strong that stories began to develop to re-create the experience.

From this perspective, it is most likely that humans first swapped stories to acquire knowledge as an individual survival strategy, to learn to anticipate the many threats and dangers in a still wild world. This, Silko believes, is the heart of storytelling's origins: "Considerable details and vivid descriptions—the lifeblood of an entertaining story, if you will—must have been essential to the telling. The most important details and actions were likely repeated and emphasized so that listeners would know what to do to survive in a similar situation" (*Storyteller* xviii). We can imagine that those early storytelling listeners took a great deal of pleasure in hearing stories told by survivors. These would have been hair-raising adventure tales, but with happy endings. Such stories give courage to others who might face similar dangers, and the hope and faith that if they did exactly what the survivor had done, they, too, might survive. For obvious reasons, the earliest audiences for these stories must have paid close attention to the details, and thus, the stories with the richest descriptions and most vivid details were the ones most sought after, and the ones that brought the most pleasure, because they conveyed the most useful and necessary information. For reasons of individual survival, the connection between storyteller and audience begins here. In fact, Silko concludes that the connection between knowledge and power also begins here (*Storyteller* xviii).

Now, if we expand the importance of storytelling between individuals to that of families, cultures, and regions like the Native American reservations west of the Ozarks, we find that the essential point remains the same. Silko, to use her own experience as an example, says that "Storytelling among family and clan members served as a group rehearsal of survival strategies that had worked for the Pueblo people for thousands of years" (*Storyteller* xviii). In most Native American cultures, all the knowledge, experience, and beliefs were kept in tribal memories in the form of stories that were told and retold from generation to generation. Moreover, Silko says that her people, like many other Native American tribes, view themselves in a changing world as part of an ancient continuous story composed of innumerable bundles of other stories (*Storyteller* xviv).

And, of course, the earliest accounts of a marginalized culture in North America (think Native Americans, like the Pueblo people) encountering and being threatened by a dominant culture that seeks to subsume it appear in the stories told between family members and from tribe to tribe. Such a story, on a different scale, is parallel to the experience in the Ozarks region, a region also under the threat of being subsumed by a mainstream American society that is eroding cultural and regional boundaries. For Native Americans, storytelling became a way of maintaining cultural identity, and it was a way of gauging the relative sickness or health of their own culture. To more fully explain how this works, it will help to consider an example in fiction from the Native American tradition, Silko's *Ceremony*.

Silko's novel is a case study in this regard, and it is instructive in our discussion of the Ozarks to first consider some details from this novel. The hero of the book, Tayo, a Laguna Pueblo Indian, has just returned from World War II and is suffering from Post-traumatic

Stress Disorder (PTSD) and a sense that he has lost all connection to or understanding of his Native American heritage. In effect, Tayo is caught between two worlds—his isolated native tribe and mainstream American society. After all, in the world of the novel, he has just returned from fighting for America only to find that America still views him as a Laguna Indian, a marginalized figure, and Tayo himself doesn't know where he fits in. Tayo's mental health problems have literally led him to forget much of his upbringing and almost all of his family and tribal history. Storytelling, however, is the medicine that begins to heal Tayo. As he hikes, hunts, and rides horseback across the Laguna reservation, he begins to remember stories that his grandmother used to tell about the mountains and the people and the animals.

Tayo's healing begins with stories, stories about place. In Tayo's case, the place is his Laguna reservation, and settings like this play central role in many Native American stories, just as place is one of the defining characteristics of the Ozarks, and stories like Tayo's are most frequently recalled as people are passing a specific geographical feature or the exact location where other stories have occurred (Silko, *Ceremony* 185). In addition, the turning point of a story often depends upon a special quality of the landscape, a special rock or tree, an important creek or mountain. It sometimes becomes difficult to determine which comes first, the incident or the geographical feature that stirs the imagination. Whatever the case, each story that rushes back to Tayo heals him just a bit more, and eventually these stories reconnect him to the land, to his people, and to his own sense of identity. More importantly, Tayo's journey to heal himself mentally and to reclaim his tribal identity itself becomes a story that is passed down from generation to generation to remind the community of the sacred power of stories and storytelling, and to remind them of the continuity between their past and their present (Silko, *Ceremony* 257). For Silko and her tribe, as we find in the example of Tayo, storytelling has the ability to heal, to comfort, to connect people and places. For Native Americans, it is the most important way to maintain cultural and regional identity and to ensure cultural survival. As we will see, this is also true for the Ozarks.

In the Ozarks region, storytelling follows a similar path in that it allows us to preserve our collective memories and unique cultural history and many of our folk traditions. It also allows our region, which historically has been marginalized, not only to just preserve but to keep alive traditional values and beliefs, while still allowing us to participate in a contemporary world where urbanization and new technology make it increasingly difficult to find, let alone define, distinct regions like the Ozarks any more. Storytelling is an antidote to such homogenization, and key examples of this are found in *Yonder Mountain: An Ozarks Anthology*, a collection of Ozarks literature published in 2013.

The primary example of Ozarks literature in this context is Donald Harington's "Telling Time," a short story first published in *Yonder Mountain*. Harington is best known for his many novels dealing with the fictional but familiar-feeling town of Stay More, a small village in a rural and rugged part of the Ozarks in northern Arkansas. "Telling Time" is at its heart about the desire for towns like Stay More to endure, even though they are set in a historical period on the cusp of major change. The plot of the story is fairly simple: There is a growing rivalry between the town's two main storytellers, Lion Judah Stapleton (with humorous confusion over the name Lion/Lyin' Judah) and Harry Tongue (with the same humorous confusion regarding Harry/Hairy Tongue).

There are two general stores in the fictional, and representative, town of Stay More, and each of our storytellers sets up on the porch of one of the stores from which he can hold forth to the whittlers, loafers, and other idlers that hang about the place. Many in the audience are there just to pass the time, to be entertained, but the audience also gets the town news and the latest gossip from those front porch sessions. In fact, as the rivalry between storytellers escalates, listeners are getting quite a lesson about the history and people of the region, too, and the significance that Harington invests in the idea of storytelling grows along with the Lion Jude/Harry Tongue rivalry. Although the plot centers on the storytelling competition between Lion and Harry, the story eventually becomes less about the storytellers and more about the significance of storytelling itself.

Now the types of stories and the style of storytelling are quite different between Lion Jude and Harry Tongue, and the difference between the two storytellers contains the serious message that flows below the playful surface of Harington's story. In terms of style, we hear that "Jude was a taker-outer and Harry was a putter-inner," and that any story of Jude's always began with "One time," no matter whether that time was yesterday or a hundred years ago (Harington 84). This phrase is one of the keys to unlocking the story. Harry, in contrast to Jude's way of beginning a story, might start off with any offhand introductory phrase so that you weren't sure when he was starting a story or when he was just talking. But it's in the matter of substance and subject matter that Harington's two storytellers differ the most.

Harry's tall-tales became known as "master histories" because one of his stories first began, "Now it happened that there was dwellin in Stay More a certain ole boy who wasn't good for nothing, but come the shank of evening around the porch of Miz Latha's store he shore could charm the peepers down outen the trees with the masterest histories. . . ." (Harington 84). These master histories, the narrator explains, might be about the James Gang's exploits in the Ozarks, or "the incredible battle of Whiteley's Mill, during the Civil War, in which Newton County soldiers on opposite sides fought each for two hours with rifle and cannon without one single battle death occurring" (Harington 84). Harry's stories, we soon find out, are taken from the history of Newton County, and especially the town of Stay More, and its neighboring counties in northern Arkansas and southern Missouri. Harry would tell legends of the founders of many towns in the Ozarks, stories that not even the locals had heard before, and he would take incidents that had just happened or just been reported and convert them into dramatic and sometimes humorous narratives.

The narrator of "Telling Time," who sure sounds like Harington himself, calls these stories "memorates," a term he learned in a folklore class at the local university (82). The narrator explains that these memorates are narratives of actual events that have occurred or even events which the storyteller himself has witnessed (82). These "memorates," and the few examples of them we are given in "Telling Time," seem like the ideal type of story to ensure that the cultural memories and the history of the Ozarks and its people would endure, but Harington complicates this view of Harry Tongue's stories and their function in preserving our most important memories. Harington reveals that the problem with Harry's stories, if we want to phrase it that way, is that they are always tragic, that there is always a clear end to the stories and usually an unhappy end to the people in those stories. The narrator says that it boils down to Harry's stories being pessimistic, while Lion Jude's stories are optimistic (Harington 86). While everything in Harry's stories supposedly actually happened and was therefore "real," Harry could not avoid converting all of his stories into tragedies in which the seemingly ordinary people in them become larger than life heroes and heroines who fall prey to extra-ordinary ends, quite out of keeping with the Ozarkers in Jude's tales. Due to this difference in pessimism and optimism, Harington suggests that once a Harry Tongue story has ended, it becomes something of a dead history, relegated to dusty bookshelves and the vaults of museums. In other words, the power of Harry's story dies when the story ends, which is quite unlike the stories of Lion Jude (Harington 87).

Lion Jude's stories in "Telling Time," which might be more fanciful than his rival's, center on everyday people and do not have tragic endings. In fact, we are told that "If a story had to end, people felt, perhaps knowing that Stay More itself was ending, it ought to end with a smile on its face" (Harington 85). A story ought to end, we are told, if not with some revelation that leaves you feeling good, it should leave you with at least some hope for yourself, for your town, and for the region in which you live. Lion Jude's stories do just that in Haring-ton's tale, and because they do, he begins to win over the audience and to win the contest between the two storytellers. The town grows to appreciate Lion Jude's success, not necessarily because they really want to choose one storyteller over another, but because the town of Stay More was dying, the townspeople beginning to disappear from the porches of both stores. People in that part of the Ozarks, we hear, were moving away to California, or at least to the larger towns surrounding the Ozarks, like Springfield or Little Rock. Both stores eventually close their doors for good, due to the fact that modern-ization has crept into the heart of the Ozarks in the form of the first "supermarket" just outside of little Stay More, Arkansas (Harington 86). As the stores close and the town dwindles, Harry Tongue disappears, too, with rumors of him spinning windys and holding forth on the steps of county courthouses in Harrison, in Little Rock, or in Memphis or New Orleans (Harington 86). Like the stories he used to tell, Harry becomes lost to history.

Lion Jude stays in Stay More, however, and in part because of his refusal to leave, the town itself survives, literally and in the all of the memories that Jude has treasured and kept. To say it another way, the town really survives because the stories about it survive, kept alive by Lion Jude in the world of the short story and by our narrator and Donald Harington himself. This layered effect of the storytelling comes to the forefront as the story itself winds down. In this regard, the last lines of "Telling Time" are remarkable and bear some attention: They transform the simple story about the competition between Harry Tongue and Lion Jude into a story that is really about the significance of storytelling. The narrator, upon last inquiring about Lion Jude, hears that Jude is often spotted telling stories along the banks of the local creek or in neighboring meadows, and that he always has some kind of an audience, even if that audience is occasionally in the form of birds, rabbits, squirrels, and sometimes insects (Harington 87). The narrator tells us in the story's last sentence, "Harry Tongue made Stay More into a mythical place that belongs in books on dusty shelves; Lion Jude Stapleton keeps the time of Stay More and tells the time to stay more, and be *one* time" (Harington 87). The significance of this line is that the story ends with the same two words with which it started, coming full circle and forming a story that does not end but, in effect, starts over again.

Lion Jude's stories, like the story Harington has just told about him, get their power from a sense of what might be termed the "continuous present," and this last line in "Telling Time" is that transformational moment. The continuous present of Jude's stories merges into a continuous present with Harington's own story. Those last words—one time—repeat the first words of the story, which begins "One time there was a man in our town" and thus become not an ending but a sense of starting again, a sense of the story's own continuous present (Harington 76). Harington says that "To really love a story, [for it to have any meaning] we sometimes have to lie to ourselves, and the biggest lie we tell is a telling of time: We have to believe that the one time of the story" we are hearing or reading "is our time," that we are in the moment of the story and that it is "*now*, for the life of the story, for the life of our listening to it" (87). The sense of a continuous present that arises from Harington's story allows for the past and the current moment to exist together, to mingle together, and this makes the story not a dead story on a bookshelf (like Harry Tongue's stories), but a living story that suggests a future is out there waiting for us. If we are able to make the story our story and our time, even if the survival of the people and towns in the stories isn't assured, we are left with a sense of hope.

There is one more detail that is important in the last view we get of Lion Jude, who is telling stories to any creature that will listen, and that is the fact that our storyteller, and the story he is telling, always depends on an audience. Recall the connection between storyteller and audience in stories of individual survival. If it's an oral story, then the person spinning the windy or stretching the blanket must have listeners to hear the tale, or it is already a dead tale. As the storytelling tradition evolves from an oral to a print form, which has been the case for Native American literature and the stories produced here in the Ozarks, then the poems, stories, and books being written in the Ozarks must have an audience/ readership to survive. They need an expanding readership to thrive, and recent developments indicate this is happening.

In the *Yonder Mountain* anthology from which Harington's short story is taken, we are presented with many poems, essays, and stories that convey the same sense of this continuous present in which we may experience the lives, the work, the loves, and even the deaths of typical, notable, and sometimes laudable Ozarkers living in a very real, yet wholly unique and still mesmerizing region: for example, Pattian Rogers's "Fury and Grace," Marideth Sisco's "Butterfield: An Introduction," or Michael Burns' "Sweet Potatoes," in which the poet's father teaches the son how to harvest vegetables in the garden they have been growing, and the poet realizes that he is, at the moment he is telling his story, the same age his father was when they bent together in the garden that day so many years ago (45).

The examples of storytelling's serious function, even in a single Ozarks anthology, are numerous, but I hope the point is clear. If a story—and the meanings contained therein—is to endure, then storytelling, as Harington shows us, as we have learned from the earliest survival stories, depends on both a storyteller and an audience. The Ozarks region and its people, like any culture so heavily steeped in the storytelling tradition, will not only survive but thrive as long as new stories are produced and as long as the audience for those stories continues to grow. This ensures a continuity in cultural and regional memory. In other words, through participating in storytelling, we inhabitants of the Ozarks are able to understand who we are, who we have been, and what the future might be like for this special place we call home. We in the Ozarks know that stories aren't just entertainment; we aren't fooled.

Works Cited

Burns, Michael. "Sweet Potatoes." *Yonder Mountain: An Ozarks Anthology*. Ed. Anthony Priest. Fayetteville: University of Arkansas Press, 2013. 45. Print.

Harington, Donald. "Telling Time." *Yonder Mountain: An Ozarks Anthology*. Ed. Anthony Priest. Fayetteville: University of Arkansas Press, 2013. 76-87. Print.

Silko, Leslie Marmon. *Ceremony*. New York: Viking Press, 1977. Print.

--------. *Storyteller: With A New Introduction and Photographs*. New York: Penguin, 2012. Print.

The Present Past: Loft Barns

We often fail to record the present past, extant things from earlier eras. Then they are gone. Old loft barns are a present past that will soon be the past. Several realities—the availability of custom-made metal buildings, changing farming practices, increased tax and insurance liability—have coalesced to increase their attrition rate. In the summer of 2005, I undertook to photograph all the loft barns in my home county, Dallas County, Missouri. I never finished the project, and many of the few dozen barns I photographed have collapsed or have been torn down.

Sucker Flats

Matt McGowan

Two days before Thanksgiving, Patsy and I were sitting in the office and arguing about stuffing. You have to cook it inside the cavity of the turkey, I told her, or you can't call it stuffing, but she just kept on about a fancy casserole she'd learned from her sister-in-law in Oklahoma City. It's not stuffing then, I countered. "Fine," said Patsy, "dressing's the better word, anyway."

"Y'all argued about this last year," said Katie, tossing a file on my desk.

This time she didn't walk away, so I obliged her by opening it. Right away I noticed one of the witnesses lived on Malugen, a gravel road way back in Sucker Flats, the old mining camp north of town.

"Ah hell," I said. "Can't say I'm surprised."

"You remember it?" said Katie.

"I do. It was all over the news. Ole boy got run over."

Katie tapped the file. "I'm sorry he died," she said, "but it looks like he wasn't much of a contribution."

"It don't matter, I guess." I finished reading the list of witnesses, while Katie thrummed her fingers on my desk.

"There's children involved," she said.

"I see that. What a damned mess."

She pointed to a name at the top. "That boy . . ."

"Yes?"

"He might know everything."

"How old is he?" I asked.

"Six."

"Kind of sensitive, ain't it?"

Katie crossed her arms. "You gotta talk to him."

"I will," I said.

She looked down at the list again and put her finger on a different name. It was the witness on Malugen Road. "And that one," she said. "She's the mom."

"Okay," I said. "I'll find her."

I read the police report. Sheriff's deputies had done a good job of putting the facts together. A thirty-two-year-old man had been struck by a car and killed. Two children, the six-year-old and a toddler, were in the vehicle driven by our defendant, a man named Jesse Sergeant, also thirty-two. But I found something odd in the report. It said as many as eight more people had been at the scene. According to Sergeant's statement, these people had "disappeared into the woods."

* * *

I met Sergeant at Chicken Mary's on the old highway south of Pittsburg. Not the one between Joplin and Webb City. That's Chicken Annie's. Annie and Mary are sisters. Everyone gets them confused. His mother came, and they brought the six-year-old boy. Terms of bail specified that Sergeant was not allowed to be alone with the children. Over the phone, I'd advised him not to violate that order.

I decided to talk to the boy first. That way he could go outside with the grandmother after. He was a cute kid with big ears, bright eyes and a shaggy mess of blond hair.

I turned on the recorder and slid it up onto the table behind the napkin dispenser. "Son," I said, "you mind if I ask you some questions?"

He looked at his grandmother. "It's okay," she said.

The boy told me what happened. He said dad came to get him and his brother at the house on Malugen. Mom was yelling at dad when they tried to leave.

"She was smokin' a cigarette," the boy said. "My teacher says they're bad for you."

"Well," I said, "she's right about that. Go on."

"Dad put Aaron in his seat. Mom was yelling. She came down to the car. We tried to leave, but the road was slippery. We went back and forth . . ." The boy had a Hot Wheels car. He put it on the table and moved it back and forth, showing me how it went in the mud. "My dad was trying to turn around," he said. "It took a while."

"But you got out?"

"We got stuck one time and had to use a witch."

"Winch," said the grandmother.

"What?" said the boy.

"Honey, it's called a winch."

"Then what happened?" I said.

The boy dropped his head and stared at his lap, where he'd put the Hot Wheels. He was playing with the toy and didn't want to talk.

"It's okay," said the grandmother. "Tell the man what happened next."

"They came out of the woods and banged the windows," said the boy. "Even dad was scared. He went back and forth like before . . ." The boy demonstrated again with the toy car.

"I understand," I said. "So then what happened?"

"They wouldn't get out of the way."

The boy stopped and played with the toy, spinning it, rolling it on the table, almost bumping into his grandmother's iced tea. Then he picked it up and dropped it in his lap again.

"It's okay, son," I said.

"Tell him what happened," said the grandmother.

The boy took a deep breath. "Dad was trying . . ." he said. "He got going, but then it bumped . . ."

"It bumped?" I said.

"I felt the bump again and we got out of there," said the boy. "Dad drove fast to the creek. That's where we stopped."

"Was that it?" I asked.

"My dad was breathing really hard," he said. "We got away from the people . . ."

"I'm glad," I said.

The boy was excited now and more animated. He squirmed for momentum and scooched forward on the seat. "My dad drank a whole beer right there," he said. "He was really nervous."

The grandmother took him outside, and Sergeant came in. He told me the same story that he'd had some words with the mother and a hard time getting out of there. "Then those zombies came out of the woods . . ." he said, looking away from me and shaking his head, ". . . and I just panicked."

I asked Sergeant who these people were as we headed outside to find the grandmother. Before we stepped outside, he grabbed my shirtsleeve. "You been around meth much?" he asked.

*   *   *

Folks round here don't like government. They make that pretty clear. It's why I don't drive a county car, especially to places like Sucker Flats or Zinc Town. They see me pulling up with a county decal on the car, I wouldn't even make it to the front porch. I drive my own car, a little Ford Escort. The salesman said it's purple. Patsy calls it eggplant. I didn't even know that was a color.

I started out to the Flats in the late afternoon, when folks would be drowsy or huddled around the wood stoves. The sun hadn't shown in almost a week, and that afternoon, a light gray cloud blanketed southwest Missouri. By the time I reached King Jack, around 4 p.m., the temperature had dropped below freezing and snow had started to fall. I noticed it first on the windshield and then later on the glassy surface of Turkey Creek.

I drove under the railroad trestle and farther into the woods until I reached the edge of the Flats. I knew where to go – to the end of the paved road and then some. I drove slow and kept my eyes open. It was quiet and lonesome back in there. A cat slinked across the road. I drove farther on, until I came to a cattle gate blocking the road. This was disturbing because I knew every road back in here was public.

Someone had twisted baling wire around both ends of the gate and tied it to a cluster of honeysuckle on one side and a hedge tree on the other. I had to step around rotten hedge apples to unwind the wire and open the gate.

I was on gravel road then and it was rough, divots everywhere and deep ruts carved out by runoff. The clay holding the gravel together was starting to loosen and getting slick because of the snow. The Escort's tires lapped against the wet clay as I bounced from hole to hole. At the top of a rise, the tree canopy thinned and the road flattened out, but it wasn't any smoother. The washboard surface shook and rattled the little Escort like M&Ms in a beer can. There was an old barbed-wire fencerow on my right, and I followed it to an opening.

I turned in, and the road in front of me now was a crude double track that would be hard to back out of. Here I saw a hand-made sign tacked to a walnut tree: "Warning: Angry Vet Ahead." I grabbed my binoculars out of the glove compartment and spied a house trailer and an old Ford pickup through the falling snow.

As I approached the trailer, I saw another one behind it, just inside woods. The first one was a broken shell, the roof caved in on the back side and saplings growing up inside it. Behind the truck were five badly rusted ten-gallon drums in a half-circle around a corner of the trailer. Sticks and trash spilled out of the drums, which had been used for burning, but not recently.

I heard dogs barking several seconds before I could see them. They came up the hill, crashing against each other as they sprinted toward me. They were a motley pack of shepherds and retrievers, collies and hounds and several ridiculously small dogs, including a dachshund. In all, there must have been a dozen.

A woman teetered among them. She was heavy and had long gray hair. She walked awkwardly, favoring a bad knee. Her hands were jammed into the pockets of a thermal jacket. A cigarette dangled from her lips, but somehow she still managed to cuss the dogs.

I cracked open the car door, and a few dogs backed off, but most sniffed around, ready to attack if I wasn't friendly. When I stepped out, they were all over me, pogoing on their hind legs and planting their paws on my chest and khakis.

"Git *down!*" yelled the woman, tilting and limping up the hill. "Git offa him!" She had that old-time twang, like my grandmother on my dad's side. "They won't hurtcha," she said. "They're just excited."

"And then some," I said. "What about him?"

One of the little ones, a coarse-haired terrier mix, had come up the hill behind the others carrying an object in his mouth. I thought it was a two-by-four, but it wasn't milled or symmetrical. It took considerable effort for the woman to bend over and pat the animal on its head. That's when I realized what I was looking at – a twelve-pound dog gnawing on a deer leg.

"Hell," said the woman, "he won't let go a that thing. It's his prize, I guess."

She again ordered the dogs to stand down, and she waded through three or four brave enough to defy her. The others, including the one with the deer leg, scurried off toward the trailer.

When I told her who I was looking for, she didn't act surprised. She nodded and gave her head a little jab to the left.

"I was kind of hopin' this was it," I said, meaning her trailer.

"Nope," she said, jabbing her head again. "Bit farther down."

I thanked her and turned back toward the car, and she said, "You might just walk it. It's awful wet down there."

I wasn't keen on leaving the Escort behind, but I didn't want to get stuck, so I followed the woman's advice and set out on foot. First I saw smoke from a stovepipe and then the greenish metallic sheen of a corrugated metal roof. The house wasn't that far down the hill, just inside the woods and out of view of the Escort.

As I walked, damned if I didn't hear flies – in late November and snowing! To my right, tucked away in tall grass about four feet off the double-track, was the deer carcass. Its eyes were open and the head was undisturbed, but those dogs and maybe other critters had torn hell out of that animal.

Farther down the hill, a young woman stepped out onto the porch. She was holding a can of Red Bull. I told her who I was, and I asked her if she was Carla Gibbons. She grunted. She was scrawny with sunken eyes and pasty skin. Her jeans had holes up and down the front, and she had a red scarf tied up around the back of her head. Her t-shirt said "SlipKnoT" in letters that looked like dripping blood.

Though I'd told her who I was and the reason for my visit, she asked if I was "the law."

"No," I said. "I work for the public defender."

She didn't say anything. She drank from the Red Bull and took a cigarette out of her jeans pocket and lit it.

"I'd like to ask you a few questions?" I said.

"'bout what?"

"Jesse Sergeant."

Gibbons huffed.

"Y'all have two kids together?" I said.

"I'll get'em back," said Gibbons.

I asked about the day Sergeant picked up their kids. Gibbons smoked her cigarette and slurped on the Red Bull. "I don't know nothin' about that," she said, over and over.

* * *

On my way out, it was snowing so hard that it was almost pretty in the Flats. I thought about the old woman over in Prosperity who told me stories about the miners, how they'd get off the streetcar after working twelve hours underground, their faces covered with gray soot from blasting limestone to find galena. They were rowdy as hell, she said, and ready to get drunk. I don't know what made me think of this, other than being close to the mine, which the Superfund project plugged a few years back. But in this quiet winter land, I could almost see them stepping off the platform elevator and trudging to the streetcar.

The icy mud was slick, but if I took it slow, the little Escort did just fine. I descended the hill down into the valley of Turkey Creek. Here, my eye caught the flash of something in the woods, just this side of the creek. I tapped the brakes and looked over there, but I saw nothing other than tree skeletons and falling crystals.

I passed through the narrow area where the gate had been, seeing it was exactly where I'd put it. As I approached the hill leading up to the box bridge, I saw movement on the right flank. The Escort's heater was running hot, and when I looked up after turning down the fan, the first one was at the passenger window. But he was gone as quickly as he appeared, and I wondered if I'd imagined it, until I felt a hard slap against the rear quarter panel.

The second one popped up here at my window, staring at me cross-eyed and spacey. He had dark eyes and scratches all over his cheeks. He flared his nostrils and then hissed, showing me his rotten teeth.

The third one climbed up onto the hood of the Escort. He moved slowly and mechanically, like an old man with rheumatism. He stood up and bounced, rocking the struts.

My mind conjured Jesse Sergeant's face when he told me about the "zombies" and "creepy-crawlies" coming out of the woods. It seemed melodramatic at the time, but now I felt foolish for not believing him.

Startled by another blow to the rear of the car, my foot slipped off the brake, causing the one on the hood to lose his balance and fall onto the windshield. He writhed there, slipping around on the slick surface and groping for a hold. He was right in front of me, but I couldn't see his face, because he was wearing a pullover cap with holes cut out for the eyes and mouth, like a bank robber or a Bald Knobber.

There was something pathetic about this one. He couldn't right himself, so he rolled off the hood and joined his partner at my window, where they commenced to thumping their fists against the glass and hooting like rednecks at a cockfight.

The one with rotten teeth hissed again and started bobbing his head like a rooster. I reached down under the seat and felt the butt of the .40-caliber Glock issued to me by the county and used only during mandatory training. Damn it, I thought, I don't want to shoot these boys in the face.

More of them came out from under the bridge and surrounded the Escort. Their frames seemed stunted, hunched over inside their hooded coats. As they formed a circle around the car, the two here at my window upped their game, jawing nonsense and shrieking like banshees.

The next blow to the rear of the Escort pissed me off. I took my foot off the brake again and started rolling forward. The hooded ones in front of me stumbled back and separated, now lining the ramp to the box bridge.

Through all the noise and commotion, not one of them had uttered a single word. Maybe they had no language, I thought, but this theory broke down when Rotten Teeth yanked on the door handle and shouted, "Open this *fuckin'* door!"

Again, I reached down under the seat. The pistol felt cold on my fingers. I took it out, but I did not point it at them. I palmed the side of it and pressed the other side against the window as my right foot tapped the accelerator.

I heard someone yell, and those lining the ramp scattered. Two ran this way, right by my window, recently vacated by Rotten Teeth and his rheumatic partner, and the other three took off in front of me, crossing the bridge.

I flicked on the high beams and saw these three scrambling to get away. Then they cut and dropped out of sight, disappearing alongside the embankment of the bridge ramp. I worried they might attack the Escort from the side as I moved through, but I was going faster now, and I neither heard nor felt a thing. At the bottom of the ramp, I gassed the accelerator and checked the mirrors, but there was nothing behind me except the flickering glint of snowflakes in the dim red glow of the Escort's tail lights.

*   *   *

At trial, Sergeant wore a dark blue suit that was two sizes too big. I've never seen anyone look so uncomfortable.

Katie marched him into Judge Reynolds' courtroom on the second floor of old courthouse, the one made with locally quarried marble. She carried half a dozen folders under one arm and a briefcase and a cup of coffee with the other. As always, she was smart and tough, but charming, and right away I could tell the judge and jury liked her. She even called me up to the witness chair, on account of what I'd experienced out at the Flats. In all my years of doing this job, it was only the second time I'd sat in that chair.

The judge didn't say a word the whole time I was on the stand. He was an old man, pushing eighty, a veteran of the Korean War. There was no way he could comprehend what was happening out at Sucker Flats. He knew the camp's reputation, had in fact decided the fates of more than a few of its inhabitants, but he underestimated the meth problem. Fifteen minutes later, when Katie grilled Gibbons, the young woman I'd talked to on the porch, Reynolds' face contorted like a man who's been told red means go and green means stop.

"Miss Fuhr," he said at the end of our testimony, "what's going on out there?"

Katie was standing at the library table next to the short wall separating the judge and attorneys from the galley. "Your honor," she said. "I don't really know." As the judge frowned and massaged the sides of his forehead, I looked over at Sergeant. He was already looking back at me, and his eyes said it all. He knew what was going on out there. So did I.

But none of it mattered because the case never should have gone to trial. Reynolds himself seemed confused by that alone, regardless of the facts. He showed little patience or courtesy for the prosecutor, a young man hell-bent on getting a murder conviction before running for state office. Twice, the judge said he disagreed with the charge. He wasn't saying Sergeant was guilty or innocent, just that he'd been brought up on the wrong charge. "This was accidental," Reynolds said. "This man was under duress." But the prosecutor charged forward anyway, and Reynolds just shook his head, almost mocking him. I guess you can do that when you're a seventy-eight-year-old circuit judge.

The jurors agreed. I saw them crack polite smiles during Katie's closing argument. Considering the facts of the case and the high burden of proof for a murder conviction, even second degree, they had no choice but to acquit. I looked at Sergeant again when the foreman declared him not guilty, but this time he wasn't looking back at me. He was up and out of his chair, shaking hands with Katie.

Behind them, on the other side of the short wall, I saw his boy. I nearly laughed at the memory of him tattling on his father for shot-gunning the beer. He was all dressed up, wearing a nice pair of pants and a clean white shirt. He'd combed his hair, and someone had let him slick it back with pomade. This made me smile. It was important to him to be a big boy. I watched him reach out to shake hands with his father, but Sergeant, instead of shaking, lifted the boy over the wall and gave him a big hug.

Featured Poet: Susan Powell

Susan Powell and her grey wolf, Idgie.

"I was born in Altus, Arkansas, during a snowstorm on January 31st, 1954, two weeks before my expected arrival that Valentine's Day. After the war and ten years of praying, my parents were finally credited with an off-beat child who did everything early, from walking at ten months to reading Sunday School stories 'for kids' at three." As if obsessed with making up for their lost time, Susan ran headlong into the truth of the only child syndrome: "You're always guilty, when you're the only one to blame." This philosophy gave her the right to do anything she wanted in her own time. Her very existence, these sixty-six years, has made a poet of her just "trying to clarify the imagery, squeeze the truth from the sublime . . . create a time zone that truly surpasses our time" (interview with Gerry Sloan, March 2020).

Powell attended high school in Danville, Arkansas, and started a music degree at Arkansas State University in Jonesboro, though her studies were interrupted by a serious auto accident, after which she continued her studies at Arkansas Tech University and changed her major to English, under the tutelage of B. C. (Clarence) Hall and especially Francis Irby Gwaltney, to whom she dedicated her poem "Southern Comfort" (published in *Nebo* and available online). She also formed a close relationship with the poet Miller Williams, who is included in the "Southern Comfort" dedication. Powell was student editor of the Tech literary magazine *5 Cent Cigar*, later rechristened *Nebo*.

Powell received her BA from Tech in 1976 and her MFA in poetry at the University of Arizona in 1981 where her primary mentors were Tess Gallagher and Richard Shelton. She subsequently taught at the University of Arizona, the University of Arkansas (Fayetteville, Little Rock, and Fort Smith campuses), Arkansas Tech University, and the University of Central Arkansas. She also taught at North Arkansas Community College (now NWACC) in Rogers and at Garland County Community College in Hot Springs, where she founded and directed creative writing and film programs. She was also a member of the Hot Springs Film Festival Committee, as well as the director of Serious Poets, Etc., a reading group that performed around the state.

In 1996, Powell was bestowed with what she considers a notable honor: she and her constant companion grey wolf, Idgie, were asked to serve as literary ambassadors when American grey wolves were reintroduced into Yellowstone National Park. It was a wonderful experience for both of them. Their cabin was located close to the wolf enclosure, so Idgie learned exactly what the wolf howl meant. In 2005 Susan started Talley-Ho Arts, conceived as an artist colony with its own printing press, which she inherited from her paternal uncle, Arkansas historian Norman "Bud" Powell. With the addition of an 1890s log pony-barn, also inherited from family, she sought her twin passions: fostering the verbal arts through workshops and printing, and the continual preservation of historic log structures. The Press at Talley-Ho is located in the Boston Mountains near Winslow, Arkansas.

"Powell is a recognized advocate of restoration vs. razing of historical log structures within her native state. Her quest to save these neglected and/or abandoned examples of original Arkansas architecture began in 1981 when she purchased the first of five log structures she would restore or rebuild over the next 25 years, proving the versatility of the antique log as a medium for Green construction. Powell effectively uses old and new methods, as well as materials, conducting all log restoration, new log construction, which includes peeling, chinking, wood finishing, and design. Each project is

Transcendental from conception to completion: the result is a union of traditional and artistic methods, antique and prepared materials, unexpected combinations of color and texture—a pure poetic vision that manifests off the page, a physical poem. The term NEW OBJECTIVISM takes the poet W. C. Williams' philosophy of poetic structure a step further by showing that a concrete object, such as a log barn, can be recreated in such a way as to become art, just as its process is an art form" (Talley-Ho Arts website).

Presently Powell is recovering from multiple aneurysms and strokes, with her new wolf companion, Kegan, by her side. She has re-envisioned Talley-Ho, and herself, like the logs she recovers and constructs anew. In this new vision of melding the past with the present she would like to include workshops for Traumatic Brain Injury survivors, which would help them address limitations through creative expression. Powell shares an Arkansas Tech background with fellow poet, Gerry Sloan. Three generations of Sloan's ancestors attended the Rudy (Arkansas) one-room schoolhouse, one of three log structures reconstructed at Talley-Ho.

Powell's publications include *Women Who Paint Tall Houses*, Goldentongue Press, 1995; *Any Act of Leaving*, The San Pedro Press, 1983; and *Sunshine and Shadows* (with Sandra Burns), Rose Publishing Co., 1976. Her poems appeared in little magazines like *Telescope*, *Ploughshares*, *Salmon Magazine*, *Nebo*, and *Rock Soup*. She can be reached at talleyholodge@gmail.com.

The Blue Moon Café

Susan Powell

It was three-story faded gray clapboard,
with petrified pine knots the color of rust.
Some of them had burst out of their shrinking
jackets and were missing,
vacant silver circles staring back
at those who remembered the heyday
of the Blue Moon Bar and Café.

When the county went dry in the early sixties
the law shut it down,
and bootleggers became a necessity
for those who couldn't travel
fifty miles to Paris
across Mount Magazine,
the highest point in the South.

No drinking meant no business,
which started to show on the building
that already looked older than it was,
abandoned for the price of a beer,
or a pint of 20/20.

The light didn't work anymore,
but the old ones still saw it,
a neon blue quarter moon
hanging above the door,
beckoning entry. The promise of loose women,
hot food, liquor, and dancing
could get anyone back in the mood.
Jazz and blues flowing from Ed Fountain's piano,
Chicago tunes meant to cure any depression,
had the power to ring hauntingly true
at the foot of the mountain,
most Saturday nights at the Blue Moon.

Awakening

Susan Powell

The one who wakes up and claims ownership
of the body may not be the same one
they counted down to sleep.
It's difficult to tell who she is from here
where mirrors aren't allowed, nothing subjunctive
for the brain-injured, especially those who lose
the bone shields around their temples, creating
Frankenstein foreheads, including the holes
where the bolts were, large sections of skull
missing, waiting for the swelling
to subside before anything can be replaced
with mesh wire.

Female patients don't handle the head-shaving
well at all, the longer their hair the harder
they take it, those garish bald spots,
full of staples like train tracks
along the borders of that new crevice
broken open between the bones.

Regardless of their sex, they all wake up changed,
some more than others, none without scars
and sorrows when they look
in the rear-view mirror, months later,
on the way to a place they won't recognize
called home.

What He Must Have Been Thinking

for Darrell

Susan Powell

Below the barn
where you practiced smoking cigarettes
for days 'til you could do it
in public like an old hand,
where at twelve
you lay in secret with your cousin
and couldn't kiss her
no matter how willing you both were,
you stood that day looking back,
the field perfect with snow behind you.

No one wondered when you walked out
from the dinner table
to set up your deer stand,
the shotgun thrown over your shoulder
like a fishing pole from another summer.
They never even guessed
when the gun went off
and the dog came back without you.
"Just like that boy to bag a deer
before the season opens,"
your father smiled into his steaming
coffee. "Like as not,
he'll want it skinned tonight."

Just that morning
you watched your face for signs
in the bathroom mirror,
as if at any moment it might turn
against you, showing everything at once
you couldn't tell them.

Snow blew up behind your footsteps
like powdered sugar
from too small a bowl. Nothing
resembling a trail they might find
you at the end of. Nothing
so physical as that.
For a long time,
you just stood there considering
the ways a body could fall
into that whiteness.

But we can only guess what you must
have been thinking when you trained the gun
like a light down your throat
and your shadow flew up to meet you
halfway in that cold, white awakening.

Words

Susan Powell

Sometimes it's not the grammar
but how the words roll out like ships
across your tongue. First, you must look
behind the facts, crawl backwards into
the smallest corners.
Second, you must have good hands, each word
shaped according to its color.
Some will walk or swim. Others will sing
incessantly. Some won't talk at all.
When I was in high school, I knew a man who could
twist balloons into any animal he chose.
This is analogy. A dog with a hat or a cat
holding its dish, which is red. The right words
are the ones that talk after themselves.
The rest fall down somewhere and never get up.
The bridge through the unconscious is a long one.
This is the beginning of all you will know.
The words will haunt you there, aiming
inflections like guns. After leaving and coming back
to the right occasion, the right amount of time
elapsing between visits, we give our whole bodies up.
To the air, we are indebted like birds,
each flight a syllable worth keeping.

Blue

Susan Powell

Your eyes will remember their blue,
not the green when you were sick
or the gray of your passion,
the *blue*. That particular shade
of blue when you had slept well
or had good sex or finished a poem
that needed no revision.

The West Plains Sewage Lagoon Drama, 1978:
A Lesson on Infrastructure Failure in a Karst Landscape

Denise Henderson Vaughn

Abstract

This paper chronicles the 1978 collapse of the sewage lagoon that served the city of West Plains, Missouri—a disaster that polluted local wells and sickened hundreds. The event reinforced lessons about building infrastructure in regions known to be vulnerable to sinkhole formation. The geologic term for the local terrain is "karst," which is characterized not only by sinkholes, but also by caves, springs, and losing streams. The ground in karst areas can be susceptible to collapse, and the groundwater below is vulnerable to contamination from the surface. In West Plains, a natural earth process was triggered by land development. As population and development increase, the potential for future similar disasters could increase.

Introduction

In the late afternoon on Friday, May 5, 1978, a city employee routinely checked the 37-acre sewage lagoon that served some 7,500 residents of West Plains, seat of Howell County in south central Missouri. He saw that a small sinkhole had developed. The water level in the lagoon had dropped about one foot, which translates to about 25 million gallons of sewage that had disappeared underground.[1] Due to the weekend and a state holiday on Monday, the situation was not reported to environmental authorities until Tuesday, and by the time a state geologist inspected on Wednesday, the lagoon appeared to have sealed itself.[2] Neither the city nor state officials involved issued any statements or warnings.

Also on Wednesday, the local health department found itself tracking a sudden epidemic whose victims suffered flu-like symptoms and intestinal disorders, but the health department was not aware of sewage in the groundwater. Not until Friday—a full week after the sewage loss—did the puzzle pieces fit together. The state director of health promptly issued a boil water order for a section of south-central

Missouri.[3] By then 50 people were reported sick, and finger-pointing began as to why the public had not been notified earlier.

By Tuesday of the following week, May 16, the illness tally was at 275.[4] Late that evening, two new sinkholes opened in the floor of the lagoon. Whirlpools formed, sucking down foul green liquid as if draining a bathtub. Most of the lagoon's remaining contents, an estimated 25-50 million gallons, disappeared by Wednesday evening.[5] During the following days, a host of government bureaucrats converged upon the city. The National Guard trucked in drinking water, the EPA ran water tests on hundreds of private wells, and reporters covered tense meetings that ensued between city, state, and federal officials. Media coverage thrust the city into a national spotlight.

City water remained safe; sick people had drunk from private rural wells, and those victims became angry with city officials. By the end of May, health authorities had collected reports of about 800 people ill with symptoms.[6] But within a few weeks, those who were ill had recovered, local wells cleared up and the publicity blew over. Several results endure. West Plains received emergency federal funding and by late 1979 completed a state-of-the-art sewage treatment plant to replace the faulty lagoon.[7] The Missouri Department of Natural Resources (DNR) evaluated other towns' sewage lagoons for collapse risk; several nearby towns subsequently also obtained federal funding to build new sewage treatment plants. Due to comprehensive site evaluations implemented by DNR, no sewage lagoons built in Missouri since 1978 have collapsed.[8]

This paper focuses on events in May and June, 1978, leading up to and during the media and agency flap that followed the collapse. Certain questions stand out. How was geology involved in the collapse? Why did the city build a sewage lagoon in a poor location? Why did word not get out to the public until a week after groundwater was contaminated? Did city officials cover up? A high percentage that became ill had eaten at the local Dairy Queen. Questions arose over whether that restaurant's private well was contaminated by the lagoon effluent or another source. Where did the lost sewage go? How did the public react?

These questions are addressed herein, but two threads run through. One thread addresses how relationships between government entities and the public played into the epidemic. The other discusses the relationship between geology—the land under West Plains residents' feet—and the structures that people had built there, such as wells and lagoons. This land's underside hasn't changed, and understanding its character is still important today as new structures are built upon it.

In 1978, the local daily newspaper extensively covered the collapse and resulting epidemic. Government agencies involved produced at least six day-by-day reports. These primary sources provide a thorough examination of events; they serve as foundation for this report, supplemented by personal interviews, maps, engineering reports, geological reports, and a survey of residents.

While a few recent publications briefly mention this dramatic 1978 event,[9] no comprehensive account of it has been published, thus the story herein fills a void in the historical record.

Karst Topography is Vulnerable in Two Ways

Land in karst areas—which is characterized by caves, springs, sinkholes and losing streams—is susceptible to catastrophic collapse and to groundwater pollution;[10] [11] the West Plains sewage disaster dramatically demonstrated both, but many more instances have been documented.

As populations grow and as land development spreads nationwide, the construction of buildings, roads, lakes, and lagoons is likely to take place on land at risk of sinkhole formation. Karst regions similar to those in south-central Missouri exist in Arkansas, Kentucky, Tennessee, Virginia, West Virginia, Florida, and many other places around the world (see Figure 1).

This topographic feature is common in areas once covered by seas, where sediment deposits were compressed into carbonate rock such as limestone or dolomite. After seas subsided, the exposed sedimentary rock was subjected to surface erosion and also to weathering beneath the surface. Rainwater found its way into cracks, dissolved the surrounding rock, and formed underground conduits. Some channels enlarged into massive caves that house vast underground water reservoirs; some are sources for springs.[12]

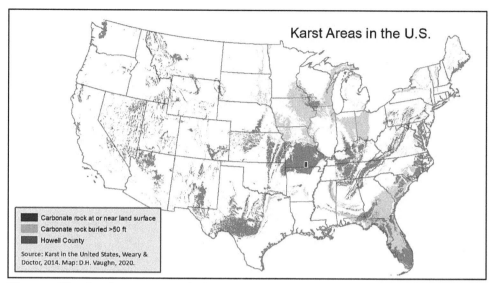

Karst Areas in the U.S.

Carbonate rock at or near land surface
Carbonate rock buried >50 ft
Howell County
Source: Karst in the United States, Weary & Doctor, 2014. Map: D.H. Vaughn, 2020.

Figure 1. The Ozarks are among the largest and most heavily concentrated karst areas in the U.S.

In well-developed karst areas, the ground beneath a surface stream can become so laced with conduits feeding into the subterranean system that the stream won't hold water at all except when flooding fills the underground voids. A number of dry losing streams such as this are in Howell and surrounding counties (see Figure 2).[13] Their water is drawn underground and channeled to Mammoth Spring, 28 miles to the southeast, which is the source of Arkansas' Spring River.[14]

In a karst area networked with underground tunnels large and small, matter from the surface inevitably washes downward into dark passageways, usually during storms. For rural residents who rely on this for their well water, murky water after storms is a fact of life. Normally this infrequent natural flush—typically soil, leaves and gravel—merely clouds groundwater temporarily, then settles, and water quality returns within a day or two. But when contaminants associated with development—like farm chemicals, sewage or other pollutants—enter from the surface, the defenseless condition of this open groundwater system becomes quickly apparent.[15]

Meandering through West Plains and then south past the city's wastewater treatment plant is Howell Creek, a classic losing stream. (Photo: D. H. Vaughn)

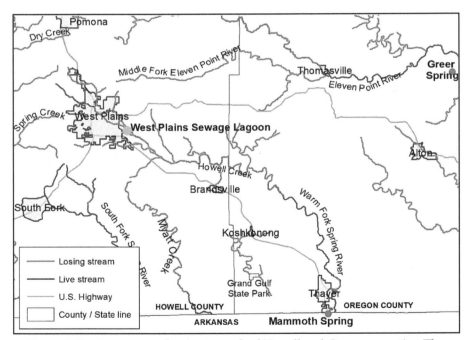

Figure 2. Losing streams dominate much of Howell and Oregon counties. The rainwater that disappears underground in these streams reappears in large springs, such as Mammoth Spring and Greer Spring. (Map: D. H. Vaughn)

Sinkhole Formation is Usually Slow and Subtle

As soil erodes and is deposited subsurface, the land surface lowers. Usually this occurs insidiously and can go almost unnoticed in sparsely populated forest land, or be a mere annoyance to a farmer trying to maintain pasture. But when human development intersects with a highly developed karst landscape, even small sinkholes become important. In a school district not far from West Plains, a small sinkhole opened under a school's foundation in 2007, leading to construction of a new school building.[16]

For the past half-century, the city of Farmington, about 70 miles southwest of St. Louis, has been plagued with some 48 sinkhole collapses, some seriously destructive to buildings and city infrastructure.[17] Forty miles east of Farmington, in Perryville, sinkholes also form frequently. That city actively manages some 300 sinkholes within city limits, many of which are close to houses.[18]

Catastrophic collapses, although rare, make news, especially when expensive construction is involved. A newly formed sinkhole—ultimately 75 feet deep—was caught on video in Nixa, Missouri, in 2006. TV viewers saw part of a suburban house collapsing into the hole. The garage fell in and the car inside was never recovered.[19][20]

Sinkhole Collapse Risk Increases when Impoundments Built

Dammed water can be particularly troublesome in karst areas because the weight of water bears down on the land that supports it. The West Plains sewage lagoon was neither the first nor the last Missouri impoundment built on karst to spill its contents into underground channels.

A number of sinkhole-induced lake failures were documented in counties near West Plains during the 1960s.[21] One spectacular collapse occurred in the early 1960s, only 15 miles north of West Plains, at the Dean W. Davis Reservoir. The lake's dam, built in a losing stream valley, held water for only a short period after construction. A sinkhole drained the lake overnight.[22]

In 2004, a 23-acre recreational lake—the centerpiece for an affluent residential development on the outskirts of St. Louis—drained suddenly via a sinkhole in a karst area. Homeowners paid about $650,000 for repairs to regain their waterfront properties.[23]

Band of Deeply Developed Karst Creates Unusual Conditions

While much of the Ozarks sits on karst terrain, one area stands out. The ill-fated Dean Davis Reservoir rests near the north end of "a band of intense karst development, several miles wide" that covers segments of Howell and Oregon counties. It begins a few miles south of Willow Springs and runs to Thayer. West Plains lies in the middle.[24]

This is a land of many sinkholes, home to sink basins up to several thousand acres in size (see Figure 3). In these basins, rainwater has no stream in which to flow. Consequently, storm water drops below the surface and flows southeast through deep conduits toward Mammoth Spring.[25] [26]

Geologists and hydrologists understood the vulnerability of this highly developed karst terrain prior to the lagoon collapse in 1978. Nearby lakes had collapsed in the 1960s. Then in the early 1970s, the pollution risk had been demonstrated through dye traces, which had proven a direct connection between sinkholes and discharge to area springs.[27]

During 1960s, Laws Less Stringent, Financing Less Available

But less of this was understood in 1964, when the West Plains sewage lagoon was built. Then, city wastewater systems were overseen by the Missouri Division of Health, and restrictions were less stringent than today.

The Federal Clean Water Act and environmental enforcement agencies did not exist. Geologists with the Missouri Geological Survey, Rolla, were available for consultation, but those receiving their expert advice were free to accept or reject it. Also at that time, federal and state financing for infrastructure, such as municipal wells or sewage treatment plants, was not readily available.[28] The Ozarks, with its generally limited natural resource base, has historically been sparsely populated and economically depressed, which has a negative impact on local tax bases.

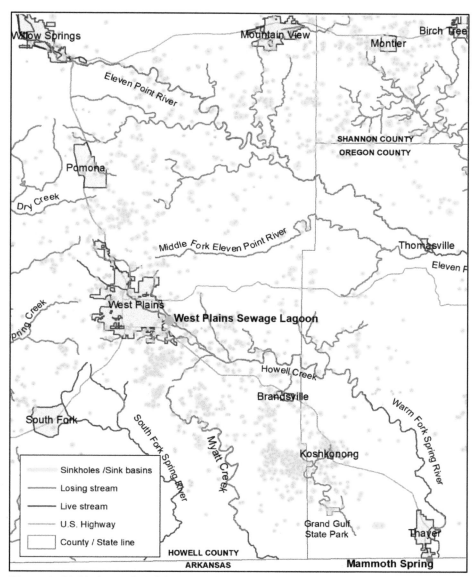

Figure 3. Sinkholes and sink basin are heavily concentrated in a band of intense karst development several miles wide that runs from Pomona to Thayer. Karst features are also concentrated in the upper Eleven Point River watershed. (Map: D. H. Vaughn)

City Leaders Examine Options

Against this backdrop, West Plains city officials were faced with a tough decision when the flow from the town's growing number of toilets outpaced capacity at their small sewage treatment plant on Bratton Avenue. Residents numbered just under 6,000 in 1960, but this number increased by almost 1000 by 1970.[29] [30]

They needed something better than the type of plant they had, which was an "old trickle filter system" consisting of merely "a big tank of rocks and filters, with some biological growth."[31] But the better system cost a lot more. It involved a central concrete basin, which allowed solids to settle, and expensive mechanical equipment and chlorinators.[32]

City leaders decided on a third option, a sewage lagoon, a common choice in the 1960s. These shallow artificial lakes were inexpensive in both construction and maintenance. Lagoons take advantage of gravity to settle solids and of sunlight to grow algae and micro-organisms that will kill bacteria and decompose organic matter.[33]

Finding a good site was more difficult than choosing the system. A state geologist looked at three potential sites. Apparently, the karst terrain was not a primary concern, because his report did not focus on such risks, although he mentioned that "cavernous bedrock" could contaminate groundwater. But collapse risk was not mentioned at all.[34]

Two of the sites were much too small. City leaders selected the largest site, about 60 acres in a broad, open plain next to Howell Creek, a classic losing stream. "The valley floor has been noticeably sculptured by sinks," wrote a geologist in 1972.[35]

Even though the site later led to a major drama, in the city's defense, options were limited. Both of the other choices were also in a losing stream valley. State geologist Jim Hadley Williams defended the city's 1964 decision, saying every nearby site was at risk of leaking or collapsing.[36]

A Lagoon is Built

West Plains voters passed a municipal bond issue, and the lagoon was built at a cost of $358,000.[37] During construction, earthen berms were built up above ground level to form a rectangular barrier around the lagoon's perimeter. The small lake was divided into two cells.

Untreated effluent entered the primary cell, 37 acres on the upstream side. Later the wastewater passed into the 12.5-acre polishing cell at the downstream end. The finished effluent was eventually discharged into Howell Creek.

The hidden treacheries of the subterranean karst topography caused problems from the start. The first collapse occurred in 1964 during construction, resulting in a hole in the polishing cell about 17 feet in diameter and 10-20 feet deep. Workers filled the hole with cement, clay and bentonite, a material that absorbs water and expands, commonly used to seal ponds.[38]

When a 34-foot sinkhole opened in the primary cell during 1966, it "created a vortex of such size" that a city worker "was unwilling to get close to it with a boat." The 37-acre cell drained in 52 hours. A peninsula was built into the lagoon to access the hole, which was repaired with clay and bentonite.[39] The peninsula remained in place, protecting the capped sinkhole.

The EPA reports "another minor collapse," believed to have occurred in the polishing lagoon in 1974.[40] None of these instances resulted in evidence of sewage downstream, or any reported illnesses. Nor was any agency, the media or the public notified; this set a precedent for 1978. [41]

New Laws Instigate Plan for New Sewage Plant

Increased environmental awareness nationally led to the creation of the EPA in 1970, the Federal Clean Water Act in 1972, and the formation of the Missouri Department of Natural Resources (DNR) in 1974. The Missouri Geological Survey merged with DNR. By 1975, the city had been told that the sewage lagoon's effluent being discharged into Howell Creek did not meet new water quality standards, especially since the receiving creek was a losing stream. Too much bacteria and suspended solids were descending into the groundwater.[42]

Thus, by 1978 when the lagoon floor gave out for the last time, the city had already hired engineers to design a new sewage treatment plant, and the city had applied for a federal construction grant. Karst terrain was still not being seriously considered; engineers produced a design that used a portion of the existing earthen lagoon as a wastewater holding area. As the new system was being designed, these engineers were warned by a state geologist who evaluated the site in 1975. His report predicted "a distinct likelihood of a catastrophic sinkhole collapse occurring beneath the proposed lagoon." The geologist recommended selecting a different type of sewage plant.[43] However, engineers proceeded with their original plan. A second geological report, issued in April 1978, only one month before the disaster, said "integrity of the existing lagoons is very questionable. Further collapses could occur at any time."[44]

DNR Tests a Problematic Private Well

One more separate scenario set the stage for the disaster. At that time, the Dairy Queen, located south of town on U.S. highway 63, was the only fast food restaurant along the highway, so many passers-by stopped there. Sitting just outside of city limits, the establishment was not served by city water; instead, a private well provided water for about a dozen businesses and residences in that area. DQ was a water customer and not the responsible party for this well.

This private well failed a water quality test in mid-April, 1978, and again in early May.[45] On May 3, a DNR staffer told well owner, Don Brown, that he would need to install disinfectant equipment. Brown said he would rather quit using the problematic well and hook onto nearby city water lines. Two days later he requested city water service for his water customers.[46]

Preludes to an Unfolding Disaster

On the evening of Friday, May 5, the same day that Brown requested city water hookup, Street Department Supervisor Jerry Lung conducted a routine inspection at the city sewage lagoon. The lake, normally four-foot deep, had dropped over a foot.[47] A small sinkhole had formed in the peninsula built in 1966 to cover the sinkhole that year.[48]

That day, Dairy Queen owner Lowell Shrable first noticed discolored water.[49]

The next day Lung told his boss, City Engineer Lowell Patterson, about the wastewater loss.[50] They opened pipes, allowing water from the primary cell to drain into the polishing cell, lowering the water level and easing the pressure on the new sinkhole.[51]

At DQ, water quality was worse. Schrable brought in tanks of city water; he used them until the city water lines were hooked up five days later. Saturday was the last day DQ used the private well.[52]

On Monday, Patterson tried to notify officials of the lagoon leak, but discovered that state offices were closed due to Truman Day, a state holiday. City Hall received two calls from people "concerned about water quality at Dairy Queen." They were referred to the health department.[53]

Both Patterson and another city employee on Tuesday called the DNR regional office in Poplar Bluff; their report of wastewater loss was relayed to supervisors in Jefferson City. The regional DNR director advised Patterson to get recommendations for repairs from DNR's geology division. Patterson told DNR that health authorities had also been notified.[54]

Wednesday morning, local health department director Eddie Wooldridge found two notes on his desk about people who claimed to be ill from eating at the Dairy Queen.[55] He notified the state epidemiologist in Jefferson City. "Investigate," directed Wooldridge's superiors. Later, a woman came into the office with several sick kids, saying they had all become ill after eating at DQ. She mentioned that some track meet competitors from out-of-town high schools were also ill.

Later on Wednesday, as Wooldridge was tracking down leads for the DQ illnesses, he and Patterson discussed the bad water samples from Brown's well. Patterson said the well owner wanted city hookup and was "trying to place blame (for their bad samples) on the lagoon." But at no time did Patterson "indicate a major leak," Wooldridge maintains.[56]

That day, the city council met with Don Brown and his attorney; the city agreed to provide temporary water service for his well users.[57]

Also on Wednesday, state geologist Jim Hadley Williams dropped by to inspect the city lagoon, detouring from other field work to West Plains. The sinkhole was no longer draining, Williams observed. Transferring effluent from the primary cell into the polishing cell apparently had proved effective, and the sinkhole had "sealed itself." No city workers were at the lagoon site, and Williams left town without contacting anyone.

On Thursday, city workers completed construction and disinfection of temporary water lines to Brown's well customers, including Dairy Queen.

Patterson learned of Williams' lagoon inspection conducted the previous day. He again asked for technical recommendations for lagoon repairs. The lagoon showed no signs of leaking.[58]

That day Wooldridge and a nurse traveled to Mountain Grove and Houston, investigating illnesses among female track team members. They began by assuming a food-borne illness, but "some of those made ill mentioned the bad taste of the water," and the trend of the interviews "tended to implicate water as the source of illness."[59]

Health Department Pieces the Puzzle Together

By Friday, May 12, a full week had passed since Lung first noticed water loss in the lagoon. That day, Wooldridge, while zeroing in on water as the probable cause of the DQ illnesses, remembered Patterson mentioning the city lagoon. He asked Patterson if there was "some major problem with the lagoon that should be considered." Patterson would only speak to him with the city clerk present. "To the best of my memory, that was when I learned that a major leak had occurred," Wooldridge later reported. He called his boss.[60]

The boss, Poplar Bluff sanitarian A. F. Crownover, had inadvertently just found out the same thing. Dairy Queen's water supply was under DNR jurisdiction, and Crownover had called DNR to say that the health department was considering closing the restaurant. The DNR regional director told Crownover that he "could understand the problem because the bottom had dropped out the West Plains sewage lagoon." Suddenly, the mysterious rash of illnesses made sense.

Like a lit fuse, the news sizzled up the chain of command. The health department chief in Jefferson City issued a boil water order within five minutes of hearing the news. Forces mobilized. The state epidemiologist was dispatched to the scene. A state geologist was consulted to delineate an area likely to be affected, and Arkansas health authorities were notified about possible effects on their water supplies. Press releases were hurriedly disseminated.[61]

The story finally broke into print news in the Friday issue of *The West Plains Daily Quill*, one full week after the sewage loss. The story said at least 50 people were suffering nausea, vomiting, and diarrhea, and it directed anyone not on a chlorinated water system to boil water to cook and drink.[62] But the news came too late for hundreds who were ultimately sickened.

In the foreground of this May 15, 1978, photo is the small sinkhole that formed in the peninsula within the city's lagoon. (Photo courtesy West Plains Daily Quill)

Reflections on the Public Notice Delay

Who-told-who-what-and-when was the subject of at least seven reports—written after the event—when staffers with nearly every government entity involved enumerated their day-by-day actions; apparently all were trying to diffuse blame for the delay in notifying the public.

Taken together, the reports resemble a string of dominos that just won't fall down.

Part of the delay was just unfortunate timing. Lung didn't tell Patterson until Saturday. State offices were closed Monday, so DNR wasn't notified until Tuesday.

Key clues in conversations were misinterpreted. During a discussion Wednesday, Wooldridge thought Patterson was referring to the "landfill" when he actually said "lagoon."[63]

Some reports are contradictory. The most significant inconsistency revolves around a claim about when or if the city notified the local health department about the lagoon loss. On Tuesday, Patterson told DNR that the wastewater plant operator had notified the division of health. The secretary in that office emphatically denies receiving any such phone call.[64] [65]

Some individuals may have underestimated the situation's urgency. Several days after geologist Williams dropped by to inspect the leaking lagoon, the city was still waiting for word on how to proceed with repairs. Williams, when prodded for a report, apparently misunderstood the request and sent background data, rather than repair recommendations.[66]

Contributing to the delay was the tendency for government officials to stick with their own agency. Staffers apparently did not feel responsible to notify anyone beyond their boss. Each agency has clear documentation of the word going up the chain of command, but crossover was minimal. DNR officials did not contact the health department or the EPA. That agency was not informed until even later, May 17; they found out when a reporter asked their role in the crisis.[67]

Clearly, intentional obfuscation also played a role. On Monday, a *Quill* editor thought city commissioner Joe Pyles must be joking when he heard Pyles tell a city employee not to make any statements to anyone about a leak in the city "reservoir."[68] When that same editor sent a reporter to question Pyles about the "reservoir," Pyles said "there was nothing to it."[69] When Wooldridge asked Patterson about complaints of bad water at the local Dairy Queen, Patterson replied that he "would answer questions but could not volunteer information by order of the city officials."[70]

Former *Quill* Publisher Frank L. Martin III has no doubt the city covered up. "We first heard about the leak when someone driving by on the highway noticed the water level was low," he said. That person called *The Quill* to ask why. A reporter checked and determined the lagoon was leaking. When asked about it, Patterson was evasive at first, but then came into the *Quill* office to explain. "He said he was supposed to have kept it quiet but filled us in since the cat was out of the bag," Martin said. "I think he feared for his job. Everyone did go to prodigious efforts to keep things quiet."[71]

Ultimately, illnesses resulted from the delay. In a May 16 *Quill* story, the state health director would not comment on the actions of "persons outside the Division of Health" other than to say the passage of time before the sewage loss was reported "speaks for itself."[72]

The Crisis Snowballs

Over the May 13-14 weekend, health authorities checked out more than 100 illness reports. The boil order was extended. School was cancelled in Alton for lack of chlorinated water. Several area meat-packing plants temporarily closed. DNR and health officials tried to rustle up temporary chlorination units for unprotected water supplies in rural schools and nearby towns.[73]

Meanwhile, Patterson again asked state geologists for lagoon repair recommendations.[74]

By late Monday, the health department reported 275 people sick.[75]

The Tuesday edition of the *Quill* described the illness as being "at epidemic levels." The state epidemiologist said that although the first illness reports came from people patronizing "a local restaurant," newly ill people had not eaten there, indicating contamination of other private wells. Since chlorinated city water remained safe, this poisoning of only rural residents' water source set the stage for antagonistic relations to develop between town officials and rural dwellers. Sales of distilled water and soft drinks were up. The local Coca-Cola bottling plant said the company uses only purified water.[76]

Lagoon Totally Drained

Late Tuesday afternoon, May 16, "signs of further deterioration" appeared at the lagoon in the form of "two swirls" about "75 feet north of the first sinkhole."[77]

On Wednesday, the serious situation suddenly worsened. "Millions more gallons of untreated or partially treated sewage were lost into the ground overnight" read *The Quill's* story. A reporter described "two distinct whirlpools" where "large quantities of green-colored effluent were rushing into the two holes."[78]

Above: State epidemiologist Pat Phillips photographed the two whirlpools that drained the West Plains sewage lagoon on May 17, 1978.

The EPA found out about the collapse, and a response team was dispatched that day.[79] West Plains residents were asked to "cut back on the volume of wastes going into city sewers."[80]

Mayor Glenn Roe "was anxious to initiate repair." He and the regional DNR director inspected the lagoon. State geologists were called, who cautioned that heavy equipment could cause more collapses, "engulfing operator and equipment in a swirl of rushing sewage."[81] A firm repair plan was still undecided, but Roe got on the phone and mobilized an army of dump trucks to haul limestone from a nearby quarry.[82] Construction of access roads capable of carrying heavy equipment began that day.[83]

Illnesses now totaled more than 400.[84]

Thursday, three members of the EPA team arrived; more were expected from Cincinnati, Louisiana, Denver, and Washington, D.C. The EPA agreed to help by testing private wells[85] "to reveal the extent and duration" of the spreading underground pollution.[86]

The lagoon's primary cell was virtually drained by Thursday afternoon, revealing two gaping holes plus a small one[87] and thick stinking sludge, littered with hundreds of condoms.[88] The former whirlpools, now exposed, appeared to be 15 and 20 feet in diameter.[89]

City wastewater continued to arrive in the supply pipe, only to go down these new holes. Thus, on Thursday, DNR agreed to allow the city to temporarily bypass the lagoon and release the sewage directly into the dry bed of Howell Creek, provided they treat it with chlorine.[90] This discharge disappeared into the ground 40 feet downstream."[91]

City officials were still waiting for instructions from state geologists. *Quill* Publisher Frank Martin remembers Mayor Glenn Roe as headstrong, who "was not going to let experts tell him what to do." Martin recalls that while out-of-town agency staffers were away, Roe ordered up gravel and "dumped truckload after truckload into the hole."[92] These truck drivers filled up the first sinkhole, formed May 5, because it could be safely accessed by way of the peninsula.[93] The various EPA and DNR reports do not substantiate any willful violation of their instructions, but a May 18 *Quill* article, "Mayor Starts His Own Repairs," says Roe "made the decision on his own . . . after growing tired of waiting for state authorities to issue specific recommendations."[94]

Later that day, DNR finally agreed to a repair plan for the two big sinkholes, and workers made rapid progress building a dike to isolate these recently formed craters. This approach was deemed safer than filling them. Former city wastewater supervisor Jim Woodworth was a dump truck driver in 1978. "We hauled for days and days," working for 10-12 hours a day, he said. "Everybody in driving distance was contracted. . . . The rock bill would have been tremendous."[95]

Above: Haulers dump rock to build a dike to isolate sinkholes on left.
(Photo courtesy West Plains Daily Quill)

Illness reports were at 425, but were tapering off. Few people had required hospitalization.[96]

Media Circus Descends on a Small Town

By Thursday, reporters from several broadcast and print news media had visited the empty lagoon.[97] A gas station owner said he gave "a lot of directions to out-of-staters" who wanted to see the lagoon.[98] The story went out on news wires and was featured on national network news.[99] News clippings in DNR files document publication of the story in at least 20 cities in Missouri alone.

On the day marking two weeks since the first sewage loss, Friday, May 19, a meeting at the Ramada Inn was attended by some 50 public officials—state, federal, and local—and was covered by reporters from "as far away as Chicago."[100]

The mayor was angry at the news media for suggesting that he and other city officials were "somehow to blame." Roe said, "It's just something that happened. It couldn't be helped." When the lagoon lost its contents in 1966, Roe said, no one was notified. "We just fixed it."[101]

Hiland Dairy and National Guard Deliver Drinking Water and Pamphlets

That day, Friday, illnesses tallied 520. Of those, 219 were directly associated with Dairy Queen.[102] National Guard troops added to the drama by traveling to West Plains with tanker trucks full of potable water for rural residents south and east of West Plains.[103] By May 30, the Guard had provided more than 10,000 gallons in 13 locations.[104] Hiland Dairy trucked in 4,000 gallons of fresh Springfield tap water in plastic jugs, which were distributed at cost to stores that sold that dairy's products.[105] Several thousand pamphlets printed by the state health department were flown by helicopter to West Plains and then hand-distributed by Guard members and also mailed to all postal boxes on rural routes. The flyers instructed well users how to sterilize drinking and cooking water.[106] [107]

During the following work week, between May 22 and 26, the crisis was winding down. Dike construction was far enough along that the mayor gave orders to divert incoming wastewater away from the creek bed and put it back into the unaffected part of the lagoon, now separated from the sinkholes. The EPA was uncomfortable with any interim plan that made use of the existing lagoon, fearing another collapse. But the decision was approved because chlorinating the raw sewage as it was being released into the creek had "proved ineffective."[108]

Next, the sinkholes themselves were filled with rock and clay. But before they were sealed, a geologist dumped in 10 pounds of fluorescent dye in an effort to trace the lost effluent's path.[109]

Preceding two photos: Heavy equipment operators fill the two holes that drained the lagoon. (Photos courtesy West Plains Daily Quill)

Money Issues Surface; Funding Friction Begins

Even as one element settled down, discussion on what to do next revved up. State and federal authorities were willing to help with funding. The regional administrator of the EPA went to Washington D.C. and hand-delivered a request for $600,000 in emergency funds for West Plains.[110] During a meeting between city, EPA and DNR officials, the EPA advised temporary use of a portable package mechanical treatment plant, and offered to pay 90 percent of its cost. However, the mayor objected to spending any city money on an interim solution.[111] Despite the EPA's displeasure, city leaders prevailed, refusing to invest in any kind of temporary fix, opting for the cheaper route—to take the risk of another lagoon collapse while a new sewage plant was under construction.[112] The gamble paid off, as the lagoon held up as long as it was needed.

Rural Residents Resentful

As the crisis unfolded, residents living south of town in the pollution's path were upset. The mayor of Thayer said "people out in eastern Oregon County are furious, scared, and mad."[113] When health officials held a public information meeting in Mammoth Spring, Arkansas, about 200 attended. Some "expressed dismay and hostility" toward government officials, primarily complaining about slow notification.[114]

Painfully obvious was the fact that city people caused the problem, but they weren't suffering the effects. When Mayor Roe said he didn't think he could get voter approval for a bond issue to pay for a new sewage plant when money was still owed on the present lagoon, Thayer's mayor pointedly reminded Roe that West Plains residents have a safe, chlorinated water supply, unlike the rural residents most affected by the spill.[115]

Tensions escalated between rural and city residents, particularly after Roe said "another collapse is the least of my worries" while arguing in a public meeting against spending money on a temporary sewage plant.[116] That attitude antagonized rural well users, many of whom had suffered gut-wrenching illness and incurred large medical bills. *Quill* letters to the editor were resentful. A Mammoth Spring business owner complained of lost business and of spending $500 for a private water treatment system.[117] A rural West Plains woman said she had been boiling water and caring for ill family members for weeks.[118] Both criticized the city council for resistance to spending money to protect those downstream.

Survey: Public Reaction Ranged from Anger to Indifference

"Why Flush," a newly-formed local environmental group, conducted a survey, randomly calling West Plains area residents. About 125 people filled out questionnaires or answered phone surveyors' questions. Some interviewees faulted the city for choosing such a vulnerable sewage treatment system. Many criticized the government for trying to cover up; they felt that "if the public had known about the collapse immediately, and the probability of widespread contamination, that much of the sickness, anxiety, and expense could have been avoided."[119]

Survey respondents said they learned of the collapse by news-paper, radio, and gossip. One person's water turned green. Nine reported they had become ill, and another 26 knew people who did. Eleven reported doctor bills. One person claimed to have heard over the scanner "city crews . . . checking [the] lagoon and they were avoiding the state inspectors." Some were angry and criticized the city. "[They] should have acted sooner," "The mayor made an ass of himself," "the experts screwed up again," "[I'm] disgusted at officials, mainly the mayor for not informing public."

About two-thirds surveyed were on city water, but some of them boiled water anyway. Of the 36 who tested their well water, 10 had polluted water. Two said it smelled bad.

Respondents' opinions were split on how officials handled the problem. Those satisfied thought the city hadn't been negligent and "were doing the best they can," and "it's just one of those things that happen." One person thought the situation was blown out of pro-portion. About one-third said they were satisfied with the proposed solution, which was to build a new mechanical treatment plant. Of those dissatisfied, one pointed to how city actions hurt rural people. "They weren't going to say anything until people got sick, so they had to [then]." Another said "the situation stinks worse than the lagoon." One was glad to be "up-wind of it, because folks downstream got a raw deal." Two said the people south of town should sue the city. "I think the city's cover-up was disgraceful, negligent, and that they are liable for everyone's sickness and expense." And finally, one person had "bad dreams of our house sinking into such a hole." [120]

Epidemic Numbers Finalized; CDC Proclaims Cause

In late May, even as local illness reports tapered off, the total tally continued to climb, in part because "travelers who were passing through . . . [had] later read about the epidemic" and reported in to the health department.[121] As of May 24, about 309 of 759 reported illnesses were directly related to DQ.[122] The last published daily tally was on May 26, at 780.[123] All subsequent reports put the final number at 800.

Not until June 5 was there an official proclamation that "con-firmed what health authorities [had] suspected all along." The Centers for Disease Control (CDC) in Atlanta said, "the gastroenteritis suffered by rural residents after May 5 could be blamed on raw sewage contaminating groundwater."[124]

Well Water Tests Inconclusive, But Show a Southeast Trend
Early on *The Quill* published a map provided by health authorities of a large "suspect area," which included areas north of West Plains and much of Oregon County.[125] Later, the suspect area was expanded even farther to the north and west (see below). Both maps were unrealistically large, and unnecessarily added to residents' fears.[126]

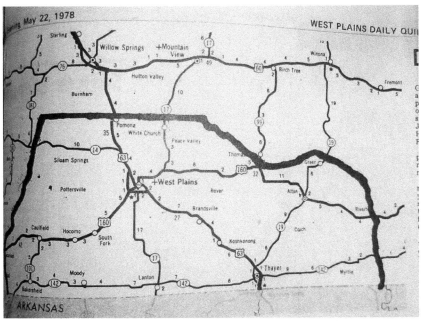

This map, published May 22, 1978, shows a large area of concern. Well testing and dye traces later determined that this map far exceeded the area where polluted water actually traveled.

The EPA tested about 1000 water samples from private and public wells in the affected areas south of town, plus a few wells farther away as a control group.[127] Tests showed 47 percent of private wells tested had unsafe bacteria levels.[128] The data were inconclusive, by EPA's own admission. "No simple interpretation . . . will make sense out of all the sickness and water sample reports" said health authorities.[129] Bad wells showed up all over, even in the control area. This percentage of polluted wells is not out of line with two other rural Missouri well studies, which were done during "normal" times.[130]

The EPA soon realized that so many variables affected well water quality that a proper scientific study was nearly impossible. Samples were collected on a voluntary basis, not randomly. Until 1974, Missouri had no well construction law for private wells.[131] [132] The EPA's Harry Gilmer said there was "no direct proof—other than the outbreak of illness following the sewage leak—that the high number of contaminated wells in the area resulted from the . . . lagoon." The problem was "too many of the wells in the area are improperly constructed, improperly maintained, and improperly located, resulting in high contamination from other sources."[133] Despite the "interferences and complex results," the EPA concluded that their data showed "a trend" indicating that "the sewage followed a very narrow path from the lagoon to Mammoth Spring." Around 71 percent of private wells in a triangle-shaped area southeast of West Plains (see Figure 4) were contaminated, as compared to only about 26 percent in a control area north of Pomona.[134] [135] Testing also showed that "bacteria were not remaining trapped underground and continuing to breed," which relieved people's minds.[136]

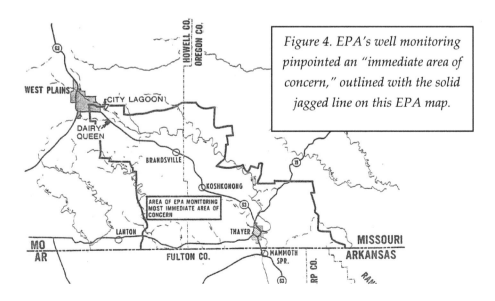

Figure 4. EPA's well monitoring pinpointed an "immediate area of concern," outlined with the solid jagged line on this EPA map.

Fate of the Vanished Sewage Suspected but Unproven

The foul contents of the West Plains lagoon were never con-
clusively located, but strong evidence gave clues to their whereabouts.
Charcoal filter packets had been strategically placed at several area
springs in hopes of intercepting the dye injected May 18 into the
lagoon sinkholes before they were capped. Dye was recovered on May
30 at Mammoth Spring (see Figure 5). No dye was found anywhere
else.[137] Fortunately, Mammoth Spring never appeared or smelled
polluted. Daily tests for fecal bacteria showed only a slight rise; spring
water stayed within the range considered safe for swimming during
the time frame when the lagoon failure was expected to affect the
spring.[138]

DNR investigators found another clue of the sewage's fate, a
"resurgence" at Culp Ford on Howell Creek, about 16 miles down-
stream from the lagoon. "Evidence in the stream bed suggests a flood
surge of short duration," with "a very odorous condition." The
streambed was dry both upstream and downstream from this area,
which suggests the surge came from underground and returned
there.[139]

Very likely much of the effluent merely mixed with groundwater
to the point that it became unidentifiable. Solids settle. They would
have drifted downward and lined the conduit cracks and cavern floors
as would any sediment washed into the system.

Reports are inconsistent as to the amount of sewage lost. The EPA
report says 28-30 million gallons of sewage went down the first hole,
and the second set of whirlpools upped the total to about 50 million
gallons.[140] Missouri Engineering puts the total at 25-37 million
gallons.[141] One DNR geologist used a 75 million gallon figure,[142]
another used 38 million.[143]

Whatever the total sewage loss, its impact on Mammoth Spring
would have been strung out over several days, thus pollution in any
one day would be a small percentage of the spring's 227 million gallon
per day flow. "Even though it's a serious environmental accident . . . in
terms of overall hydrology, it's not that a big of an event," said DNR
hydrologist Jim Vandike.[144]

Facets of Dairy Queen Contamination Source Still Mysterious

The Dairy Queen is only one-half mile from the city's sewage lagoon, close to due south, within range of the general southeast path of underground water's flow. It may seem obvious that the city's lost sewage caused DQ's water pollution, particularly because Don Brown's well—serving twelve homes and businesses—would have pulled a lot of water. This "drawdown" could easily have lowered groundwater levels, creating a low spot to which the sewage could have flowed in and filled, creating a pocket of polluted water in that area. Certain other facts implicate the sewage spill. Previously failed water tests suggest the well was poorly constructed or otherwise vulnerable to penetration by contaminates, either from the surface or from shallow groundwater. But even though bacteria had been previously detected in the well, no foul taste or smell was reported prior to May 5, nor were any illnesses associated with the bad tests.

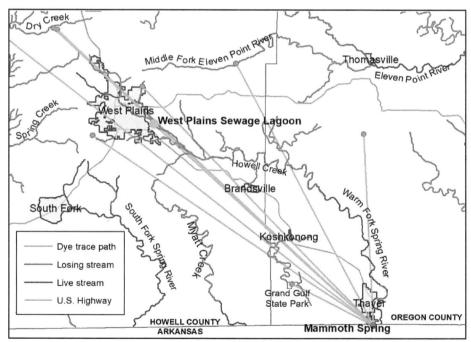

Figure 5. At least 11 dye traces in the West Plains area have been conducted between 1967 and 2016. Dye has consistently been traced to Mammoth Spring. (Map: D.H. Vaughn)

But this question is not totally resolved. Another factor tends to exonerate the city's sewage lagoon. DNR inspectors noticed a small private sewage lagoon behind the Dairy Queen; that lagoon received wastewater from DQ. It was quite close to Brown's multi-user well and it appeared to be leaking.[145] Further, the dye dumped into the craters in the city lagoon never showed up in Brown's well.[146] But months later, DNR ran a different dye trace, which established a clear connection between DQ's small lagoon and Brown's well.[147] DNR hydrologist Jim Vandike said the illnesses associated with DQ "could conceivably been from the West Plains lagoon but were probably from their own lagoon."[148]

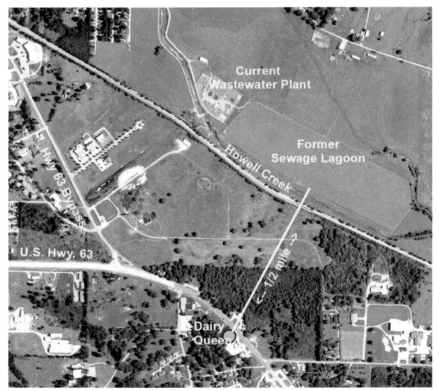

Figure 6. Aerial photo shows proximity of the sewage lagoon and Dairy Queen, which are approximately one-half mile apart as the crow flies. (Map: D. H. Vaughn)

But the lack of dye from the city lagoon entering Brown's well does not prove a corresponding lack of sewage.[149] If the DQ's own lagoon was the sole source of the illnesses, the symptoms should have shown up before May 5, because that small lagoon is believed to have leaked constantly. This writer concludes that the city's lost sewage sickened DQ customers.

Sewage Treatment Plant Built in 1979 in Use Today
The sewage treatment plant that now serves the city went online December 19, 1979. It had been built on time and "well within budget," at just under $3.5 million.[150]

Prior to the lagoon collapse, engineers Crane and Fleming of Hannibal had completed a design for a new sewage plant that would have used a section of the existing lagoon. But after the disaster, EPA staff tossed out four years' worth of design and permitting work; they firmly nixed any use of an earthen structure to hold sewage.[151] With the pressure on to quickly decommission the lagoon, engineers completely redesigned the new plant, selecting an "oxidation ditch" system in which all sewage is contained within concrete pools.[152]

Located on the north end of the old lagoon, the new concrete plant was designed with collapse risk in mind. The site was selected based on seismic tests conducted prior to construction to search for underground voids.[153] The structure is built on 460 steel H-beams, driven down to bedrock in a checkerboard pattern.[154] Despite the seismic tests, crews driving the pilings found karst-induced holes. "In one instance the piling broke through a void and dropped almost 25 feet" before reaching solid rock.[155]

After the new oxidation ditch plant was in full operation, the lagoon was drained, and the earthen berms were bulldozed inward to cover the remaining sludge on the lagoon surface. The area was seeded to grass. Today, cattle graze there, and the valley floor shows no obvious sign that it was once a lagoon site. City workers regularly spread sludge produced by the new treatment plant to fertilize this land; sludge is also trucked off site for land application elsewhere.

About two million gallons per day of clear, bacteria-free water exit the sewage treatment plant's effluent pipe and gush into Howell Creek, turning the dry watercourse into a flowing stream until it is lost underground some eight or nine miles downstream around the Oregon County line.[156]

These photos taken in 2011 show: (top) former Wastewater Supervisor Jim Woodworth looking over a cattle pasture, the site of the old sewage lagoon, and (above) discharge from the sewage treatment plant flowing into Howell Creek. (Photos: D. H. Vaughn)

Long-Term Effects: Improved Sewage Plants and Stricter Site Inspections

Shortly after the collapse, the EPA identified "49 additional municipal lagoons and 212 private lagoons" in karst areas of the Ozarks which were vulnerable to sinkhole formation.[157] The DNR's Geological Survey division visited and evaluated a number of them, and within a few years, the nearby towns of Alton, Mountain View, and Thayer received federal funding and replaced their earthen lagoons with concrete-bottomed treatment plants.[158]

In 2011, three long-time DNR geologists reflected on the long-term impact of the West Plains collapse. "Nothing about West Plains was new," said Jim Hadley Williams. He compared it to a 1968 sewage lagoon collapse at Republic. This earlier collapse, not West Plains, instigated the practice of conducting risk assessments. What made West Plains stand out, said Williams, is "it brought publicity. I think that helped move things along."[159]

Even so, said Jim Vandike, the West Plains collapse "had a big impact" and "shaped how we do things."[160] Peter Price called the event "a big turning point for a lot of our processes." DNR further developed its rating system used to evaluate any earthen wastewater storage in the state. The agency now insists on checking out all proposed lagoon sites that might be influenced by karst, looking for collapse potential. This approach appears to have avoided new problems. No lagoons built since 1978 have collapsed. "We learned from it," said Price. "As far as I know, Missouri is the only state that does this kind of evaluation."[161]

Conclusion

For an epidemic, the 1978 West Plains sewage disaster was relatively benign. No one died, few were hospitalized, and no cases of typhoid, cholera, polio, hepatitis, or other serious diseases emerged.[162] Rural residents' wells cleared up fairly quickly, and majestic Mammoth Spring barely blinked.

The drama played out in several stages. The first act occurred years ago when the city chose "the lesser of evils" in selecting their karst-susceptible location and lagoon-style sewage treatment. Even if city leaders did not understand the collapse risk in 1964, that risk had been revealed by 1978. But with finances tight, they gambled. The

second act opened when that gamble failed. The plot thickened when
city officials declined to tell the public or the press of that failure and
dragged their feet in cooperating with other government agencies.
They assumed such omissions were acceptable because the lagoon had
drained before without fanfare. But the city bosses probably were not
betting on the third act, staged at a very public venue: a Dairy Queen
served by a poorly sealed private well and perfectly positioned to
expose hundreds to gut-cramping sewage germs, which were
relatively traceable by epidemiologists. This exposed both the city's
gamble and cover-up, angering many, especially rural residents
downstream. Despite this questionable behavior, in the final act the
city was approved for federal funding; they built a new, better-
designed treatment plant.

Looking back, understanding among south-central Missourians
about karst topography and its vulnerability to collapse and to
groundwater pollution has greatly increased since the lagoon disaster,
due in part to lessons learned during the painfully public 1978 drama.

As population growth and land development continues, more
structures will be built. The likelihood of occasional karst collapse
remains. Whether those unavoidable collapses are merely geologic
spectacles or whether they are costly tragedies depends upon vigilant
evaluation of sites before construction begins.

A letter published in the May 30, 1978, *Quill* serves as summary.
"The lagoon disaster may be a blessing in disguise," wrote Kazie
Perkins of Willow Springs. "Tis a fact of life that no one pays attention
to any issue, any problem until it touches him personally. Perhaps, just
perhaps, thousands in Howell County and the south central Ozarks
will now open their eyes and minds to problems of growth, land use,
and the ecological fragility of the land they live on."[163]

Endnotes

[1] "Health warning issued: Sewage lagoon leak being investigated," (1978,
May 12) *West Plains Daily Quill*, 1.

[2] "Recap of the West Plains Incident, Howell County," attachment to letter,
James Hadley Williams to Lowell Patterson, May 18, 1978.

[3] Memo, William F. Raithel to Herbert R. Domke, 14 June, 1978, 3, Missouri Division of Health.

[4] "Illness at 'epidemic' levels," (1978, May 16), *West Plains Daily Quill*, 1.

[5] "Lagoon collapses again; Arkansas residents get warning," (1978, May 17) *West Plains Daily Quill*, 1.

[6] "Guard 'turning water off' Thursday," (1978, May 30) *West Plains Daily Quill*, 1.

[7] "The Solution: A New Wastewater Treatment Plant for West Plains" (1981, November) *Missouri Engineer,* 16.

[8] Peter Price, (2011, March 18) Personal interview. DNR Geology Section Chief.

[9] The sewage disaster was briefly described by Gillman, et. al. (2008) "Soil-cover karst collapses: A geologic hazard in Missouri," *Proceedings of the 18th National Cave and Karst Management Symposium* and in *Living on Karst, a reference guide for Ozark Landowners* (The Nature Conservancy, 2003).

[10] Thomas J. Aley, James H. Williams, and James W. Massello, *Groundwater contamination and sinkhole collapse induced by leaky impoundments in soluble rock terrain.* (Missouri Geological Survey and Water Resources, 1972).

[11] James Vandike and Donald Miller, *Groundwater Resources of Missouri*, (Mo. Department of Natural Resources, 1998), 62.

[12] *Living on Karst, a reference guide for Ozark Landowners* (The Nature Conservancy, 2003), 1.

[13] Vandike and Miller, *Groundwater Resources of Missouri*, 67.

[14] Vandike and Miller, *Groundwater Resources of Missouri*, 69.

[15] *Living on Karst, a reference guide for Ozark Landowners* (The Nature Conservancy, 2003), 16.

[16] In September 2007, in the Mountain View-Birch Tree RIII School District, some 35 miles northeast of West Plains, a six-foot wide by six-foot deep hole opened under the foundation of the middle school. School patrons became agitated; some kept their kids at home. Ultimately, the afflicted portion of the building was abandoned for student use, even though the foundation never moved. Voters passed bonds for construction of a new middle school.

[17] Joe Gillman, et al, "Soil-cover karst collapses: A geologic hazard in Missouri." *Proceedings of the 18th National Cave and Karst Management Symposium.* (NCKMS Steering Committee, 2008), p. 178. These 48 sinkholes "have damaged residential building foundations and collapsed sections of city streets resulting in broken municipal water, sewage, and gas lines." One was about 80 feet deep and 60 feet wide, it "sever[ed] utilities and swallow[ed] pavement and sidewalk."

[18] Denise Henderson Vaughn, *Karst in Perry County*, (Ozarks Resource Center, 2020).

[19] Joe Gillman, et al, "Soil-cover karst collapses: A geologic hazard in Missouri." *Proceedings of the 18th National Cave and Karst Management Symposium.* (NCKMS Steering Committee, 2008), p. 183.

[20] Underground Ozarks Blog, August 14, 2006.

[21] Aley, Williams, and Massello, *Groundwater contamination and sinkhole collapse induced by leaky impoundments in soluble rock terrain.*

[22] Aley, Williams, and Massello, *Groundwater contamination and sinkhole collapse induced by leaky impoundments in soluble rock terrain*, 16. According to local lore, the night that the doomed lake drained, the ground rumbled and shook in between the lake and the water's outlet, Greer Spring, more than 30 miles away.

[23] Joe Gillman, et al, "Soil-cover karst collapses: A geologic hazard in Missouri." *Proceedings of the 18th National Cave and Karst Management Symposium.* (NCKMS Steering Committee, 2008), p.180. When Lake Chesterfield developers built the impoundment in a known karst area in 1987, they were not required to seek or heed DNR advice, because lake water is not a pollutant. But a 1978 engineering report from DNR's Division of Geology and Land Survey was available; it "noted a severe collapse potential for earthen wastewater storage facilities and lake sites constructed in this general area." "Extensive drilling and grouting" was required to plug the sinkhole.

[24] Vandike and Miller, *Groundwater Resources of Missouri*, 65.

[25] Besides factoring into demise of a 1960s lake and the 1978 sewage lagoon collapse, this deeply weathered karst band has caused other trouble. During the rainy spring of 1998, West Plains' city wells produced water so turbid that it darkened white laundry and made orange ice cubes. Well-drilling records showed pockets of karst weathering in several of these wells at depths over 900 feet. The new sediment suddenly appearing in decades-old wells is believed (but not proven) to have originated from ground laid temporarily bare during highway construction, located in the "upstream" portion of the recharge area for the city's water wells. Along with DNR prodding, the turbidity prompted the city to build a million-dollar purification plant to filter out sediment, completed in 2001.

[26] Vandike and Miller, *Groundwater Resources of Missouri*, 65. The water level in a DNR-monitored well in downtown West Plains has been known to "rise as much as 200 feet within a few hours after a major rainfall."

[27] "Groundwater Series Reprinted," *West Plains Daily Quill* (Special Section, Fall 1998), 2. The town of Alton, some 30 miles to the east, closed its dump, located in a sinkhole, after water originating from the dump was traced in 1969 to Morgan Spring on the Eleven Point River. The use of a sinkhole dump

serving Dora, 20 miles west of West Plains, was discontinued after water from it was dye traced in 1972 to popular Hodgson Mill Spring.

[28] James Hadley Williams, (2011, March 27) Personal interview. Geologist with Missouri Department of Natural Resources, Division of Geology and Land Survey, retired.

[29] U.S. Census – 1960 Census of Population, Preliminary Reports.

[30] 1970 Census of Population, Characteristics of Population, Missouri.

[31] James Woodworth, (2011, March 21), Personal interview. West Plains Water and Sewer Department Supervisor.

[32] Stuart Liederman, "Report on Public Reaction to the West Plains Sewage Disaster, 1978" (Drury, Missouri, Why Flush, 1978), 6.

[33] Ibid, 6-7.

[34] James Martin, "Proposed Sewage Lagoon Sites for the City of West Plains" (Missouri Geological Survey, October 29, 1963)

[35] Aley, Williams, and Massello, *Groundwater contamination and sinkhole collapse induced by leaky impoundments in soluble rock terrain*, 14.

[36] "Recap of the West Plains Incident, Howell County," attachment to letter, James Hadley Williams to Lowell Patterson, May 18, 1978. To escape this threat, sewage would have to be piped under pressure five miles southwest, a prohibitively expensive option. Despite its dangers, Williams said the Howell Creek site was the "only possible location . . . given the economics." The other option, building the type of mechanical treatment plant common in the mid-1960s, would have released poorly-treated effluent at all hours. "The least of the evils" was to "risk occasional collapses with slugs of pollution rather than continual pollution," he said.

[37] *Report of the West Plains Lagoon Incident* (1978, June 30,). U.S. Environmental Protection Agency, 5.

[38] Aley, Williams, and Massello, *Groundwater contamination and sinkhole collapse induced by leaky impoundments in soluble rock terrain*, 14.

[39] Ibid.

[40] *Report of the West Plains Lagoon Incident*, 3.

[41] "Mayor starts his own repairs" (1978, May 18) *West Plains Daily Quill*, 1.

[42] *Report of the West Plains Lagoon Incident*, 5.

[43] Christopher J. Stohr, *Addendum: Preliminary Engineering Geologic Report on the West Plains Sewage Lagoon*. (1975, April 15, Missouri Geological Survey) attachment to letter, James Hadley Williams to Lowell Patterson, May 18, 1978.

[44] David Hoffman, "Liquid Waste Treatment Works – Engineering Geological Report." (1978, April 18, Missouri Geological Survey) attachment to letter, James Hadley Williams to Lowell Patterson, May 18, 1978. Hoffman

recommended building a foundation that could support a span 50 feet wide anywhere within the new treatment plant, to protect against effluent loss in the case of a collapse.

45 Memo from James A Burris to Jim Odendahl, (1978, June 5) "West Plains Incident," 1. The May water sample contained algae, of the type commonly found in farm ponds and lagoons.

46 Letter from Lowell B. Patterson to James Odendahl (1978, June 7), 1.

47 "Health warning issued: Sewage lagoon leak being investigated," (1978, May 12) *West Plains Daily Quill*, 1.

48 Memo from James A Burris to Jim Odendahl, (1978, June 5) "West Plains Incident," 1.

49 "Health warning issued: Sewage lagoon leak being investigated," (1978, May 12) *West Plains Daily Quill*, 1.

50 Ibid.

51 Letter from Lowell B. Patterson to James Odendahl (1978, June 7), 1.

52 "Health warning issued: Sewage lagoon leak being investigated," (1978, May 12) *West Plains Daily Quill*, 1.

53 Letter from Lowell B. Patterson to James Odendahl (1978, June 7), 2.

54 Memo from James A Burris to Jim Odendahl, (1978, June 5) "West Plains Incident," 2.

55 Letter and report, James P. Odendahl to Carolyn Ashford, "Report on the Sewage Lagoon Failure at West Plains, Missouri." (1978, July 5), 5.

56 Memo, William F. Raithel to Herbert R. Domke, "Events leading to the discovery of an epidemic of water-borne disease in West Plains, Missouri, 1978," (1978, June 14, The Division of Health of Missouri), 2.

57 Letter from Lowell B. Patterson to James Odendahl (1978, June 7), 2.

58 Ibid, 3.

59 Memo, William F. Raithel to Herbert R. Domke, "Events leading to the discovery of an epidemic of water-borne disease in West Plains, Missouri, 1978," (1978, June 14, The Division of Health of Missouri), 2.

60 Ibid, 3.

61 Ibid.

62 "Health warning issued: Sewage lagoon leak being investigated," (1978, May 12) *West Plains Daily Quill*, 1.

63 Memo, William F. Raithel to Herbert R. Domke, "Events leading to the discovery of an epidemic of water-borne disease in West Plains, Missouri, 1978," (1978, June 14, The Division of Health of Missouri), 2.

64 Memo from James A Burris to Jim Odendahl, (1978, June 5) "West Plains Incident," 2.

[65] Memo, William F. Raithel to Herbert R. Domke, "Events leading to the discovery of an epidemic of water-borne disease in West Plains, Missouri, 1978," (1978, June 14, The Division of Health of Missouri), 1. Also contradictory: *The Quill* said a city worker noticed missing wastewater on Friday. Patterson's report said the city discovered the loss on Saturday.

[66] "Recap of the West Plains Incident, Howell County," attachment to letter, James Hadley Williams to Lowell Patterson, May 18, 1978.

[67] Stuart Liederman, "Report on Public Reaction to the West Plains Sewage Disaster, 1978" (Drury, Missouri, Why Flush, 1978), 24.

[68] "Health warning issued: Sewage lagoon leak being investigated," (1978, May 12) *West Plains Daily Quill*, 1.

[69] Ibid.

[70] Memo, William F. Raithel to Herbert R. Domke, "Events leading to the discovery of an epidemic of water-borne disease in West Plains, Missouri, 1978," (1978, June 14, The Division of Health of Missouri), 2. Wooldridge said he "thought this was strange but decided this was some new policy."

[71] Frank L. Martin III (2020, March 30) Personal correspondence with author. Owner and publisher, *West Plains Daily Quill*.

[72] "State Health chief says passage of time before leak reported 'speaks for itself,'" (1978, May 16), *West Plains Daily Quill*, 1.

[73] "Health warnings expanded; massive testing underway as illness reports top 100," (1978, May 15), *West Plains Daily Quill*, 1.

[74] Letter from Lowell B. Patterson to James Odendahl (1978, June 7), 3.

[75] Memo from Harold L. Patrick to James P. Odendahl, "Sequence of Events Regarding Lagoon Failure at West Plains (1978, June 6), 2.

[76] "Illness at 'epidemic' levels," (1978, May 16), *West Plains Daily Quill*, 1.

[77] Letter from Lowell B. Patterson to James Odendahl (1978, June 7), 3. Discrepancies cloud this date. Seven reports offer similar details, but three place the second lagoon failure's start on Monday, while three others plus *The Quill* say it occurred on Tuesday.

[78] "Lagoon collapses again; Arkansas residents get warning," (1978, May 17), *West Plains Daily Quill*, 1.

[79] *Report of the West Plains Lagoon Incident*, 13.

[80] James P. Odendahl, "Report on Sewage Treatment Lagoon Failure at West Plains, Missouri," (1978, July 5), Missouri Department of Natural Resources, 11.

[81] Memo from James A. Burris to Jim Odendahl, (1978, June 5) "West Plains Incident," 3-4.

[82] James Woodworth, (2011, March 21), Personal interview. West Plains Water and Sewer Department Supervisor.

[83] Memo from James A Burris to Jim Odendahl, (1978, June 5) "West Plains Incident," 4.

[84] "Lagoon collapses again; Arkansas residents get warning," (1978, May 17), *West Plains Daily Quill*, 1.

[85] Memo from James A Burris to Jim Odendahl, (1978, June 5) "West Plains Incident," 4.

[86] Stuart Liederman, "Report on Public Reaction to the West Plains Sewage Disaster, 1978" (Drury, Missouri, Why Flush, 1978), 24.

[87] Letter from Lowell B. Patterson to James Odendahl (1978, June 7), 4.

[88] Dennis Crider, (2011, February 13) Personal interview. Photographer, *West Plains Daily Quill*.

[89] Memo from James A. Burris to Jim Odendahl, (1978, June 5) "West Plains Incident," 4. The EPA reports the holes as being 18 feet and 24 feet in diameter, and a four-foot hole. *Report of the West Plains Lagoon Incident*, 14.

[90] Ibid, 5.

[91] *Report of the West Plains Lagoon Incident*, 14.

[92] Frank L. Martin III (2011, March 18) Personal interview. Owner and publisher, *West Plains Daily Quill*. Martin remembers the cocky, Stetson-wearing mayor, Glenn Roe, who was "something else." During his tenure, he killed his neighbor's dogs, shot strays while he rode around with the police, and ran a union organizer out of town.

[93] "Mayor starts his own repairs," (1978, May 18) *West Plains Daily Quill*, 1.

[94] Ibid.

[95] Jim Woodworth, (2011, March 21), Personal interview.

[96] "Officials consider solutions," (1978, May 18), *West Plains Daily Quill*, 1.

[97] "Officials consider solutions," (1978, May 18), *West Plains Daily Quill*, 1.

[98] Stuart Liederman, "Report on Public Reaction to the West Plains Sewage Disaster, 1978" (Drury, Missouri, Why Flush, 1978), (no page number).

[99] "Officials consider solutions," (1978, May 18), *West Plains Daily Quill*, 1.

[100] "Local guard unit on duty: Governor dispatches water tanks," (1978, May 19), *West Plains Daily Quill*, 1.

[101] "Mayor starts his own repairs," (1978, May 18) *West Plains Daily Quill*, 1.

[102] Memo from Harold L. Patrick to James P. Odendahl, "Sequence of Events Regarding Lagoon Failure at West Plains (1978, June 6), 5. Unrelated cases were at 193 in Howell County, and 108 in Oregon County.

[103] "Local guard unit on duty: Governor dispatches water tanks," (1978, May 19), *West Plains Daily Quill*, 1.

[104] "Guard 'turning water off' Thursday," (1978, May 30), *West Plains Daily Quill*, 1.

[105] "Local guard unit on duty: Governor dispatches water tanks," (1978, May 19), *West Plains Daily Quill*, 1.

[106] Ibid.

[107] Memo from Odie Dickens to Jim Odendahl, (1978, May 26), "Informational pamphlet for West Plains area."

[108] "Emergency funding sought; lagoon put back in service," (1978, May 23), *West Plains Daily Quill*, 1.

[109] Thomas J. Dean, "Geologic Report of the West Plains Howell Valley Lagoon System," Missouri Geological Survey, (1978, July 11), 2.

[110] "Emergency funding sought; lagoon put back in service," (1978, May 23), *West Plains Daily Quill*, 1.

[111] "Present lagoon to be modified; plans call for new construction to begin soon," (1978, May 25), *West Plains Daily Quill*, 1.

[112] "Council balks at building interim treatment facility," (1978, May 25), *West Plains Daily Quill*, 1.

[113] "Local guard unit on duty: Governor dispatches water tanks," (1978, May 19), *West Plains Daily Quill*, 1.

[114] "No evidence yet of contamination in Arkansas," (1978, May 23), *West Plains Daily Quill*, 1.

[115] "Local guard unit on duty: Governor dispatches water tanks," (1978, May 19), *West Plains Daily Quill*, 1.

[116] "Council balks at building interim treatment facility," (1978, May 25), *West Plains Daily Quill*, 1.

[117] Woodrow Taylor, "Letter to the Editor," (1978, June 21), *West Plains Daily Quill*.

[118] Ruth Wade, "Letter to the Editor," (1978, June 22), *West Plains Daily Quill*.

[119] Stuart Liederman, "Report on Public Reaction to the West Plains Sewage Disaster, 1978," (Drury, Missouri, Why Flush, 1978), 36.

[120] Ibid, (no page numbers).

[121] "Warning area expanded; illness total up," (1978, May 22), *West Plains Daily Quill*, 1.

[122] *Report of the West Plains Lagoon Incident*, 16.

[123] "Lagoon investigation winding down, but don't stop boiling!" (1978, May 26), *West Plains Daily Quill*, 1.

[124] "Health Officials say 'keep boiling water,'" (1978, June 5), *West Plains Daily Quill*, 1.

[125] "Bold line shows extent of possible contamination," (1978, May 16), *West Plains Daily Quill*, 6. This map of Howell and Oregon counties shows the possible contamination area as extending northeast of West Plains to the Eleven Point River and including most of Oregon County.

[126] Jim Vandike, (2011, March 18) Personal interview. DNR Hydrology section chief.

[127] "Lagoon investigation winding down, but don't stop boiling!" (1978, May 26), *West Plains Daily Quill*, 1.

[128] "Guard 'turning water off' Thursday," (1978, May 30), *West Plains Daily Quill*, 1.

[129] "Lagoon investigation winding down, but don't stop boiling!" (1978, May 26), *West Plains Daily Quill*, 1.

[130] A study of Springfield area rural wells in 1962 yielded 60 percent with bacteria, and a 2006 Howell County study found bacteria in 42 percent of rural wells.

[131] *Report of the West Plains Lagoon Incident*, 8.

[132] "Regulations Governing the Construction of Water Supply Wells," (1974, June, revised), The Division of Health of Missouri.

[133] "Guard 'turning water off' Thursday," (1978, May 30), *West Plains Daily Quill*, 1.

[134] "Guard 'turning water off' Thursday," (1978, May 30), *West Plains Daily Quill*, 1.

[135] Thomas J. Dean, "Geologic Report of the West Plains Howell Valley Lagoon System," Missouri Geological Survey, (1978, July 11).

[136] *Report of the West Plains Lagoon Incident*, 9.

[137] Thomas J. Dean, "Geologic Report of the West Plains Howell Valley Lagoon System," Missouri Geological Survey, (1978, July 11), 3.

[138] "Bacteria count in Mammoth Spring rises sharply, falls" (1978, June 27), *West Plains Daily Quill*. Oddly, during late June, fecal coliform bacteria levels at Mammoth Spring rose sharply, to about double that allowed for safe swimming. But this time period was considered to be much too late to be associated with the batch of sewage from either May 5 or May 17. The source of this bacteria burp was never explained, but it moved quickly through and safe swimming levels returned within a few days.

[139] Thomas J. Dean, "Geologic Report of the West Plains Howell Valley Lagoon System," Missouri Geological Survey, (1978, July 11), 3. No dye was found at Culp Ford, but the surge surfaced at an unknown time prior to May 22, so it may have predated the May 18 dye injection.

[140] *Report of the West Plains Lagoon Incident*, 2.

[141] "The Solution: A New Wastewater Treatment Plant for West Plains" (1981, November) *Missouri Engineer*, 12.

[142] Joe Gillman, et al, "Soil-cover karst collapses: A geologic hazard in Missouri." *Proceedings of the 18th National Cave and Karst Management Symposium* (NCKMS Steering Committee, 2008), 175.

[143] Jim Vandike, (2011, March 18) Personal interview.

[144] Ibid.

[145] Thomas J. Dean, "Geologic Report of the West Plains Howell Valley Lagoon System," Missouri Geological Survey, (1978, July 11), 5. This small lagoon was built on the side slope of a 240-acre sink basin. An erosion gully had been plugged up to create the dam, and it was built in a manner that could collect "a considerable quantity of surface water." However, the spillway showed no sign that the water level had ever reached it; this lagoon did not hold much water and appeared to be leaking straight down through the bottom.

[146] Thomas J. Dean and Gary St. Ivany, "Summary of dye tracing results on Falcon Communications Well," (1978, October 23).

[147] Thomas J. Dean and Gary St. Ivany, "Summary of dye tracing results on Falcon Communications Well," (1978, October 23). After collecting several dye-negative water samples from Brown's well, which was no longer in use, the well pump was turned and allowed to run, creating a drawdown. Only then did DNR pull up dye-laden water, establishing "a strong positive connection" between the small lagoon and Brown's well.

[148] Jim Vandike, (2011, March 18) Personal interview.

[149] Brown's well was decommissioned May 11. Dye was poured into the city lagoon's sinkhole on May 18. If drawdown was a significant factor in originally pulling the sewage toward Brown's well, then that pull would have ceased before May 18, because the well was no longer in use. Therefore dye from the city lagoon would not have necessarily flowed in that direction.

[150] "The Solution: A New Wastewater Treatment Plant for West Plains" (1981, November), Missouri Engineer, 16.

[151] "Council balks at building interim treatment facility," (1978, May 30), West Plains Daily Quill, 1.

[152] "The Solution: A New Wastewater Treatment Plant for West Plains" (1981, November) Missouri Engineer, 12-16.

[153] "Council balks at building interim treatment facility," (1978, May 30), West Plains Daily Quill, 1.

[154] Jim Woodworth, (2011, March 21), Personal interview.

[155] "The Solution: A New Wastewater Treatment Plant for West Plains" (1981, November) Missouri Engineer, 15.

[156] Jim Woodworth, (2011, March 21), Personal interview.

[157] Report of the West Plains Lagoon Incident, 9-10.

[158] Jim Woodworth, (2011, March 21), Personal interview.

[159] Jim Hadley Williams, (2011, March 27), Personal interview.

[160] Jim Vandike, (2011, March 18), Personal interview.

[161] Peter Price, (2011, March 18), Personal interview.

[162] *Report of the West Plains Lagoon Incident,* 25.

[163] Kazie Perkins, "Letter to the Editor (1978, May 30), *West Plains Daily Quill,* 5.

The Lure of the Ozarks:
What's the Bait, and Who's the Fish?

2016 Ozarks Symposium Keynote

Steve Wiegenstein

In his 1867 book *Beyond the Mississippi,* Albert D. Richardson writes about traveling the Ozarks in the late 1850s. While in Springfield he recorded the following anecdote:

> I was told of eight North Carolinians bound for Arkansas, who stopped for a few hours on the public square, and were asked innumerable questions.
> One communicative fellow replied that they were going to found a town; the pursuit of each person was already marked out, and there were no drones among them.
> What was this man to do?
> He was to open a store.
> And that?
> Start a blacksmith's shop.
> And the other, standing behind him?
> Engage in sheep raising.
> So they were nearly all classified, when a decrepid [*sic*], white-haired octogenarian, venerable enough for old Time himself, was observed sitting in one of the wagons.
> 'Why, who is that?' asked the eager questioner.
> 'That's my grandfather.'
> 'What is *he* going to do? He can't be of any use to your settlement.'
> 'Oh yes,' replied the North Carolinian promptly, 'we are taking the old man along to start a graveyard with!' (208-209).

If this passage illustrates anything, which it might not, it is that people have been drawn to the Ozarks for many years, and with a wide variety of motivations both real and manufactured. Some come to stay permanently. Some come to extract something of value. Some come to hide. Some come just to look. The lure of the Ozarks is real and enduring. To speak of the lure of the Ozarks, appropriately enough, is to use the language of the fisherman, and prompts the metaphorical question of who is the fisher and who is the caught. Nowadays our talk about the lure of the Ozarks typically involves tourism, and rightly so, as it has become a mainstay of the Ozarks economy. Certainly tourism is a pretty benign sort of catchery. I suppose we could extend the metaphor and call tourism the "catch and release" version of the Ozarks' lure.

But from the earliest times, people have come to the Ozarks to take away something more tangible. From Pierre Renaud down to the Doe Run Lead Company, the Ozarks have been a source of minerals and ore. The Missouri Lumber and Mining Company and its fellow timber harvesting enterprises did the same thing from the 1880s through the early twentieth century. In a general way, I think one could describe the Ozarks as a kind of internal colony of the United States, a place from which to extract value at the lowest possible cost while returning as little as possible. As David Benac observes in his book *Conflict in the Ozarks,* a significant component of the Ozarks timber boom consisted of companies seeking to "tame" their workers, to bring them into compliance with the needs of an industrial-age enterprise concerning punctuality, sobriety, and adherence to the concept of "working hours" instead of living their lives by the clock of the seasons (6-11). What drew these entrepreneurs and companies to the Ozarks was what they could extract from it, and that's a facet of this landscape that will never go away. I recall during the years of my childhood that every town in the area had its factory—shoe factories, shirt factories, hat factories—each one staffed mainly by women paid on a piecework basis, overseen by men. It wasn't until the advent of the global marketplace that these companies discovered they could find workers elsewhere who were even more impoverished and who had even fewer options than the Ozarkers, and relocated their factories elsewhere. For an industry that needed unskilled workers to perform repetitive tasks, the Ozarks must have seemed like a little slice of heaven for a time.

And then there's escape, that time-honored lure of the Ozarks. Dad Howitt, the Shepherd of the Hills, came to the Ozarks to escape the noise of the city and the memories of his past, and ever since then one of the dominant themes of Ozarks culture has been that of the mountains as a place of refuge. Trappist monks came here, and the Harmonial Vegetarian Society, and so did Bonnie and Clyde. The hollows overflow with people who have come to the Ozarks for one sort of escape or another, whether it's from the traffic jams of the city or the long arm of the law. My own experience with these transplants has been overwhelmingly positive. People drawn to the Ozarks from elsewhere bring energy, new ideas, and often a fresh infusion of money to communities that need all three. Unfortunately, the Ozarks' mind-our-own-business reputation also draws the occasional Frazier Glenn Miller among the retired ad executives seeking a quiet place to meditate beside a stream.

Tourism is the most ephemeral of the forms of escape, confined to a short period of time and allowing the visitor to experience the imagined life of the Ozarker without having to engage with the challenges of the year-round inhabitant, such as distance and adequacy of medical care, minimal infrastructure, and a struggling and inadequately funded educational system. Tourism is also a sort of low-impact extractive industry, in which the tourist takes away memories and photographs, leaving the residents behind to pick up the trash and deposit the money. Natural beauty is the ultimate renewable resource. And it's a kind of extractive industry that requires us to guard and preserve rather than remove and deplete. The tourist, however, doesn't necessarily want to experience the Ozarks. The tourist wants to experience an imagined version of the Ozarks, the mythological Ozarks one might say, and the varieties of that mythology are many. The Ozarks of the touristic imagination, quiet, pristine, filled with adventures that are both thrilling and safe, and populated by friendly yet simple people whose rustic values hark back to an undetermined golden age in American history, is a familiar one, the myth of rural virtue with an added overlay of woodsiness. Foolish indeed would be the entrepreneur who did not do everything possible to promote it.

I remember the first time I saw a photograph of the Dogwood Canyon Nature Park near Branson. I thought to myself, "How on Earth could I have never visited this amazingly beautiful place? I thought I'd been everywhere in the Ozarks, the Missouri Ozarks at least, and here's a place with caves, waterfalls, Indian burials—how could I have missed it?" So I got down my copy of *Geologic Wonders and Curiosities of Missouri*, my indispensable back-of-the-car guide when I'm out and about, and none of those features were listed in it. Nor were they on the 1999-version USGS map. That's when I realized that Dogwood Canyon is one of those fascinating places that pops up from time to time, a place that tries to embody its own mythology in real life, constructing its own reality out of some choice real estate and plenty of development money. Like its companion projects Big Cedar Lodge and Bass Pro World Headquarters, and like its predecessors Silver Dollar City and Shepherd of the Hills Outdoor Theater, Dogwood Canyon is built to match the myth. On the topographical map, the hollow in which Dogwood Canyon was created looks like a great place, one of those deep, narrow Stone County hollows where the sun reaches the bottom only a couple of hours every day. But that's not enough, of course, so we add a waterfall, a wilderness chapel, a bear den cave, some log cabins, some trout, and so forth. This phenomenon is nothing new, of course. The power of a myth causes us to reshape our own lives in order to meet its psychic demands. It's interesting to observe the evolution of this Ozarks of the imagination through the years.

Any conversation about the imaginary Ozarks has to start with the hillbilly, that persistent and controversial figure whom anybody who comes from the Ozarks, writes about the Ozarks, or thinks about the Ozarks has to come to grips with. Anthony Harkins, in his study of the hillbilly, points out the dual nature of this figure. He writes, "'the hillbilly' served the dual and seemingly contradictory purposes of allowing the 'mainstream,' or generally nonrural, middle-class white, American audience to imagine a romanticized past, while simultaneously enabling that same audience to recommit itself to modernity by caricaturing the negative aspects of premodern, uncivilized society" (6). This, I think, sums up the problematic nature of the character. For most of its history, the hillbilly has been a comparatively benign figure, employed for easy comedy as a stereotypical bumpkin in ways familiar since Roman comedy and before. The undercurrent of lethal violence in the darker versions of the hillbilly is what distinguishes it from other stock rustic characters, but that capacity has not been deployed as often as one might imagine. Jed Clampett's long rifle is, alas, just a prop.

It seems to me that the classic hillbilly portrayal has become much rarer in the past decade or so, as cultural shifts have made it less appealing and thus less marketable. None of the big Branson attractions, like Silver Dollar City, Big Cedar Lodge, or Dogwood Canyon, use the word anywhere in their promotions anymore. Although the craftsmen at Silver Dollar City dress up in broadcloth and calico, their presentation emphasizes "the simpler life of days gone by" with no real Ozarks focus. A character like Herkimer in the Presley's Country Music Jubilee is as much cringe-inducing as amusing these days, with our heightened sensitivity to cultural stereotypes. The 2003 campaign by the Center for Rural Strategies to stop CBS's proposed reality series, "The Real Beverly Hillbillies," raised a lot of awareness about the demeaning qualities of the stereotypical hillbilly: backwardness, laziness, and ignorance. Unfortunately, it's a stereotype that is quick to resurface. It was disheartening recently to see, in the controversy over Kentucky county clerk Kim Davis' refusal to issue marriage licenses to gay couples, how quickly the cartoonists and comedians zeroed in on her eastern Kentucky accent, her Pentecostal hairdo, her multiple marriages and remarriages, and the uncertain legitimacy of her children to dismiss her as just another "hillbilly mama."

But as the old-fashioned hillbilly has faded, a new mythological inhabitant has emerged to take his place as the representative of the Ozarks, and I'm sorry to say that this creature is even less appealing. Here, for example, is the plot summary from a 2009 movie called *Albino Farm*: "College students, exploring the Ozark Mountains for a school assignment, stumble upon a group of scary, redneck cave-dwellers" ("Albino Farm"). People from the Springfield area may recognize the "albino farm" as a persistent Springfield tall tale, passed down through generations of credulous high schoolers, about a farm on the north side of the city, a tall tale that caused a great deal of unhappiness to the luckless family that owned the property. *Albino Farm*, filmed in Marionville and Willard with additional shooting in Warrensburg and other Missouri locations, heralds the arrival of the new Ozarks image—the Ozarker as inbred, bloodthirsty, supernaturally violent, and implacably hostile to outsiders. This figure has become so commonplace in our literary imagination that librarians and booksellers have come up with a new subgenre to describe it: "hillbilly noir."

The killer hillbilly appears in trashy movies like *Albino Farm* and well-regarded works like *Winter's Bone*. In place of the straw hat and bare feet, the killer hillbilly is marked by a hidden meth lab, a double-wide trailer, and an arsenal of weaponry. Here's a passage from *The Weight of Blood* by Laura McHugh, released earlier this year and perhaps the exemplar of the genre. Lucy Dane, the narrator, is reacting to the disappearance of her friend Cheri, whose body has been discovered some days after she vanished. "It was common knowledge that in the hills, with infinite hiding places, bodies disappeared. They were fed to hogs or buried in the woods or dropped into abandoned wells. They were not dismembered and set out on display. It just wasn't how things were done. It was that lack of adherence to custom that seemed to frighten people the most" (6).

It's impossible to miss the storytelling premise here, which is that everybody in the Ozarks knows how to properly dispose of a murder victim's corpse, and the failure to do so marks the murderer as either an outsider or an aberration. The old stereotypical hillbilly, at least, was a welcoming character, even if that welcome sometimes came out of craftiness. The killer hillbilly is predatory and vengeful. This motif has become prevalent enough in the public mind that actual incidents get recast into its framework; for example, retellings of the 2013 killing of a canoer on the Meramec River near Steelville frequently glide over the fact that both the canoer and the murderer were longtime residents of the St. Louis area, not Ozarkers at all. And the sad and horrific story of Dee Dee and Gypsy Blanchard, currently playing out in a Springfield courtroom, seems tailor-made for recasting as a hillbilly gothic, and the comments about the case on social media tell us that it's already gotten there.

I don't need to point out that this present-day mythical Ozarker, no longer a noble savage but just a savage, is no more representative of the "real" Ozarks than the hinge-tailed bingbuffer. But on the other hand, what are the real Ozarks? The question of authenticity dogs any discussion of Ozarks cultural representation. I try not to chase down a standard of authenticity, because every time I've attempted one, it comes up short. The Ozarks are as much a place of the mind as they are a geographical location, and trying to claim that *this* represents the real Ozarks while *that* does not is an exercise in rabbit-chasing. The benign artifice of a university-trained craftsperson at a folk festival making woven oak baskets, when in fact few if any of those baskets have ever been used for anything resembling the original purpose of oak baskets, is inauthentic, and yet it is also real, and meaningful.

To say that the Ozarks is a place of the mind is not to say that all representations of it are to be valued equally, however. As we have seen, some versions of the Ozarks are as dishonestly negative and destructive about the Ozarks as others are dishonestly idyllic. We should call attention to those versions we find disrespectful or destructive, while at the same time admitting that the "beautiful Ozarks" version is not always true or helpful as well. To this end, I want to point out some failings of the classic Ozarks picture of grist mills, sturdy homesteaders, and flowing springs, and like any author worth his or her salt I want to do it by recommending some books.

First, the mythological Ozarks of most people's imaginations is entirely white. Most Ozarkers, if pressed, will tell a questioner that there have always been a few black families in their town, the same names appearing from generation to generation, and usually a black district that consisted of a block or a few blocks. But inquire why so few, or why always there, and they'll probably not have a satisfactory answer. To counteract this blank place in our collective knowledge, I recommend Kimberly Harper's *White Man's Heaven: The Lynching and Expulsion of Blacks in the Southern Ozarks, 1894-1909*. It is unsettling reading, but it provides important context to our understanding of the African American experience in the Ozarks, an aspect of our story that is all too often neglected. The Ozarks is so overwhelmingly white, in part, because African Americans were driven from it. I fear that the great comprehensive history of African Americans in the Ozarks we all would love to have will never be written, now that time has taken most of the people who can give first-person accounts of events before the Second World War, and what we have left are documents and some oral histories. But Harper's book is surely a fine building block in that history.

Second, our mythological Ozarks doesn't always acknowledge the significant struggles that have divided it. My first two novels have dealt in one way or another with the Civil War in the Ozarks, but that's not the only cataclysm that has affected the region permanently. My current work-in-progress is set in the next era of great upheaval in the Ozarks, the timber boom of the 1880s and later. I've already mentioned David Benac's *Conflict in the Ozarks* in regard to this era, and I'd just like to mention it again. Like Harper's book, it is disturbing reading, but it introduces a history that needs to be explored.

And then on to another great struggle in the life of the Ozarks. One of my favorite possessions is a 1903 map of southern Missouri, which of course shows an Ozarks without lakes. It amazes me sometimes how many people think the lakes in the Ozarks are natural features, or that they've "always been there," when in fact they are comparatively recent developments. When I was a young newspaper reporter in the late 1970s, the elderly, semi-retired owner of the newspaper, Charles Ellinghouse, had once been the mayor of Greenville. And this was Old Greenville, founded in 1819 and depopulated in 1941 with the creation of Lake Wappapello. Like a typical young pipsqueak, I didn't even know there had *been* an Old Greenville until I heard him talk about it with such immense sadness. And now of course we know that there are drowned towns all over the Ozarks—Linn Creek, Oasis, Monte Ne, Custer, Elizabeth, Hand, Jordan—not to mention the many drowned individual homesteads.

Making this story more fraught is the fact that most Ozarkers whose land was not going to be inundated welcomed and worked on behalf of those lakes, pitting one set of long-time residents against another. Some did so with an idea of becoming personally rich, while others had the broader idea that the dams and lakes would bring overall prosperity to the region. If we look at assessed valuations as a sign of wealth, in Missouri at least, there seems to be some truth to that idea. Discounting counties, such as Jasper and Greene, which have urban centers, counties with lakes do seem to have a disproportionate amount of wealth compared to their population (Harrison). If we look at per capita income, though, the picture isn't as clear. Camden County clocks in at just over $25,000 a year, brag-worthy for the Ozarks if not for the rest of the United States, but other counties with significant lake country, such as Stone, Barry, and Miller, are no better than average ("Selected Economic Characteristics"). So if building the lakes brought prosperity, it was prosperity not widely shared.

So there's another angle to our portrait of the Ozarks that needs to be visited more—the complicated history, present, and future of development. It takes a crisis moment like the 2013 *E. coli* reporting scandal at the Lake of the Ozarks, the 2005 break of the Taum Sauk upper reservoir wall, or the periodic incidents of coliform bacteria in the Jacks Fork that are reported every few years, to remind us that the beautiful Ozarks we love, and which is ultimately the lure that draws us all, is sometimes beautiful despite us. A good read about Ozarks development is *Damming the Osage* by Leland and Crystal Payton. It's not an unbiased book—Leland Payton was one of the plaintiffs in the lawsuit that attempted to stop construction of Truman Dam—but it is copiously researched and richly illustrated.

Finally, a characteristic that the Ozarks of the imagination tends to overlook is just how hard the "good old days" were. When I go to a folk fair and see craftspeople weaving, making soap or candles, black-smithing, and the like, it all seems so picturesque and quaint. But imagine doing that work all the time, not out of an interest in pre-serving old folkways, but out of need. What we today memorialize in a hazy glow of reminiscence was once a necessity of existence, and I think we sometimes forget that. A great corrective to the nimbus of nostalgia that envelops days gone by is *Rocky Comfort* by Wayne Holmes. This book may become hard to find, as it was published by a small press that has since gone out of business, but it is worth the search. Wayne Holmes, longtime professor at Drury University, who died in 2014, grew up poor in the Ozarks, and his profane, profound, and searching memoir is like a splash of spring water to the face—shocking but cleansing as well.

So what is the bait, and who is the fish? We are both bait and fish. We create ourselves, we disguise ourselves, and we catch ourselves in the process. Let's just hope that we are a game fish worthy of the catch, and not some shad that is all flash and no flesh.

Works Cited

"Albino Farm." *The Internet Movie Database.* n.p., n.d.

Benac, David. *Conflict in the Ozarks: Hill Folk, Industrialists, and Government in Missouri's Courtois Hills.* Kirksville, MO: Truman State UP, 2010.

Beveridge, Thomas. *Geologic Wonders and Curiosities of Missouri.* 2nd ed. rev. by Jerry Vineyard. Rolla, MO: Missouri Department of Natural Resources, Division of Geology and Land Survey, 1990.

Harkins, Anthony. *Hillbilly: A Cultural History of an American Icon.* Oxford: Oxford UP, 2003.

Harper, Kimberly. *White Man's Heaven: The Lynching and Expulsion of Blacks in the Southern Ozarks, 1894-1909.* Fayetteville: U of Arkansas P, 2012.

Harrison, Charlie. "2015 Missouri County Assessed Valuations." Missouri Association of Counties Website.

Holmes, Wayne. *Rocky Comfort.* Bolivar, MO: Leonard Press, 2009.

McHugh, Laura. *The Weight of Blood.* New York: Spiegel & Grau, 2014.

Payton, Leland, and Crystal Payton. *Damming the Osage: The Conflicted Story of Lake of the Ozarks and Truman Reservoir.* Springfield, MO: Lens and Pen Press, 2012.

Richardson, Albert D. *Beyond the Mississippi: From the Great River to the Great Ocean.* Hartford, Conn.: American Publishing Company, 1867.

"Selected Economic Characteristics: 2009-2013 American Community Survey 5-Year Estimates." U.S. Census Bureau.

Cleaning Bluegill

Robert Lee Mahon

"Son," he said, "watch. First
The knife—freshly sharpened each time—point-first

Into the thick part of the head, hard, above and behind
The eyes, into whatever brain it has. And sever the spine.

Then slice down past the gills. One side, then
The other. Twist the head off. Now then:

Blade point inside the belly, off-hand fingers to pin
The backbone down. Slit the belly all the way to the anal fin.

Now dig in, next to the spine, and scoop all the way back
With the first two fingers. Next, clutch the guts and extract

With a firm pull. Don't be shy,
Boy, it'll all wash off—blood, entrails, shit, unborn fry.

To do it quick and clean you need to get your hands dirty.
It's this simple: only you are feeling anything."

The Altar

Robert Lee Mahon

He looks up from his work in mild surprise.
The lake is a mirror of the quiet sky,

And in it he can see
The first stars and the waxing

Moon. When he looks down to the picnic table,
The same moon shines in the luminous eye

Of one of the catfish heads, and then shimmers:
The head is still breathing. Or whatever

You call it when reflex is no longer attached to entrails.
The guts, in this light, are softened to hues

Of pearl, and the eyes are iridescent,
Glowing now like jewels against

The black velvet of redwood and dried blood. He holds up the knife.
The moon gleams and twinkles from the blade obediently,

As indifferently as in any other mirror.
The catfish mouth opens and closes. Silently as any oracle.

Fin Rot

Robert Lee Mahon

Peering into the clear water of Courdais Creek,
He had many chances over the years to muse
Upon the vagaries of a fish's life. How the meek
Rarely inherit the depths unless

They also have the speed and the moves, and how many dangers
Nature puts in the way of a creature with such an innocent eye,
Such a sporting, yet grave demeanor:
From the cunning turtles that lie

In pretence of rock, hunting the new fry, to the deception of hook
That bites the veteran (here too the discrepancy
Between experience and reality, which, lacking philosophers and
        books
The poor fish must discover through hard knocking experiences);

From the drought that shrinks the world
Toward slow suffocation in the alien air of an evaporating pool,
To the ice that lowers the sky till the furled fins
Slow and still completely, the spring's cool

Resurrection comes too late. But the worst
He watched one perfect spring: bass, perch, bluegill, healthy
Fish suddenly struck, apparently at random, with fin rot—
Spines dissolving as spring turned to summer, membranes fraying,

Movement faltering, swiftness to spasm. The lucky ones
Were eaten quickly. But it was a fruitful summer, with plenty
Of other prey, and after awhile even the cripples could not tempt . . . .
        So some
Ended, in fine irony, by drowning, trunks rolling and pitching
        aimlessly

In the swift current, unable even to bear upstream, to move
Enough water over their gills. Of course the epidemic
Eventually ran its course. He saw much new
Spawn the next spring, in the clear water of Courdais Creek.

The Closing

Robert Lee Mahon

The hands grasping the loan papers have long
Broad fingers, farmer-strong,
His father's gift to him, along

With the money that allowed the son
To escape the farm. The elder had worked hard, was one
Who had what is called luck. Why should the boy craft or husband

When he could do . . . something else? So he went
Dutifully to school, worked hard, was as lucky as his father. What he
      lent
Came back with interest. What he spent

Got him a wife from one of the town's old families, and
A reputation as a likeable fellow, an
Agreeable sort. Very few suspected his incompetence. The hands

That ached for the density of the tool's handle
Barely suspected it themselves. But now, in this latter
Evening when they turn to the paperwork, they only slowly shuffle
Through what solidity they can feel, loath to sign, to loose the none-
      existent hammer.

The Telling of the Dee Dee and Gypsy Blanchard Case: Reifying Negative Imaginings of Ozarks Mothers

Charity Gibson

For the Ozarks region, considering its depiction in national news coverage, no news is usually good news. Anytime an area is gazed upon by those who view the people and place as an Other, the likelihood of incorrect and sensationalized interpretations increases. Milton D. Rafferty notes, "The Ozarks evokes many images. . . . A popular image of the Ozarks is that of an idyllic, forested Arcadia, a place of. . . . small towns and farms nestled in picturesque valleys amid hills. . . .[or] as the last remaining region of pure cultural values" (4). However, Rafferty goes on to note an almost antithetical view of the same place: "It is the image of hardscrabble farmers, tough living conditions, isolation, poverty, and uneducated people with little ambition" (5). More often than not, when the Ozarks is discussed by outsiders, it is caricatured and oversimplified. Whether the region is being viewed nostalgically as the quaint and unindustrialized place the rest of the world has often speculated it to be, or whether it is being lampooned as a backward, dangerous place, media coverage tends to take a sensationalized view of the region.

The coverage and reception of the Dee Dee and Gypsy Blanchard murder case that occurred in 2015 in Springfield, Missouri, offers provocative commentary regarding ways that the Ozarks continues to be viewed. Furthermore, regarding this case, traditional views of Ozarks people coalesce with and reinforce typical interpretations of failed motherhood. The notoriety this case received and continues to receive illustrates how dominant cultural views of both the Ozarks and motherhood have colluded to turn Dee Dee Blanchard into a symbol. The public's obsession with Dee Dee's story was heightened by convenient stereotypes of place and gender that teach those outside the Ozarks that the place is one where crime and dysfunction can be expected to occur. This results in exaggeration of the bad as well as inattention to the good that occurs in the region, offering half-truths, at best, to the outside world and negative predictions for those within it.

Between 1991 and 2015, Claudine Blanchard, commonly referred to as Dee Dee, forced her daughter Gypsy to feign multiple serious illnesses, including epilepsy, asthma, muscular dystrophy, and waist-down paralysis, for which they received much public attention and monetary support. Dee Dee claimed Gypsy had leukemia, and she shaved her daughter's head bald, reassuring her privately that the hair would only grow in patches or fall out anyway. Gypsy had a feeding tube and ate very little food orally; she was forced to use a wheelchair although she could walk. She was heavily medicated for her falsified conditions and underwent multiple unneeded surgeries. She had severe dental problems due to the medications. Dee Dee and Gypsy lived alone, and Gypsy was allowed minimal interaction with the outside world, and when it did occur, it was only under her mother's surveillance. As Gypsy grew, she was not allowed to mature into a woman. Dee Dee lied about Gypsy's age, infantilizing her into an innocent little girl. Gypsy was physically abused and psychologically manipulated to accept and comply with her situation.

Around 2012, Gypsy began a secret life on the Internet, where she met Nicholas (Nick) Godejohn, who soon became her on-line boyfriend. In June 2015, Gypsy encouraged Nick to murder her mother, which he did, stabbing her in her sleep while Gypsy hid in the bathroom. They left Dee Dee in the house and fled to Nick's home in Wisconsin, planning to start a life together. Gypsy posted alarming posts on Facebook to notify the public of Dee Dee's death, and these posts were soon brought to the authorities' attention. Shortly afterward, Gypsy and Nick were arrested. Nick received a sentence of life in prison without parole for first degree murder. The prosecution did not seek the death penalty because Nick suffers from Asperger's Syndrome and has the mental capacity of a 15- or 16-year-old. Gypsy is currently serving a ten-year sentence for second degree murder, receiving such a light sentence because the jury recognized her victimized status. She will be eligible for parole in 2023, at which point she will be 32 years old.

Dee Dee and Gypsy's story has been highly publicized. As the case unfolded, online discussion groups formed in which people posed theories and swapped hearsay regarding details about Dee Dee and Gypsy. According to Michelle Dean, the *Buzzfeed* reporter who helped bring attention to the story, one group grew to having over 10,000 members. Gypsy's own Facebook page that she shared with her mother is still accessible as a memorialized account; while people can no longer respond, the page still contains her infamous post, which has been shared 80,000 times. Countless news stories have focused on the case. Dr. Phil hosted an episode entitled "Mother Knows Best: A Story of Munchausen by Proxy and Murder"; *Good Morning America* featured "Mother of All Murders"; *20/20* featured "The Story of Gypsy Blanchard"; *Investigation Discovery* featured "Gypsy's Revenge," and HBO featured the documentary *Mommy Dead and Dearest.* Gypsy was interviewed from prison in all these reports, and Nick was interviewed for some. The entertainment industry has also capitalized on the case. Lifetime produced the film *Love You to Death,* and Hulu created a television series entitled *The Act.* Another television show, entitled *By Proxy,* is reported to be in the production process.

Interest in true crime, specifically murder, in the Ozarks may be heightened because it contrasts the pastoral myth of the Ozarks as a peaceful place removed from of the sorrows of the modern world. Lynn Morrow notes that "a sentimentalized rurality called an Arcadian myth" has appealed to outsiders since the early 1900s (3). After becoming homeless during Hurricane Katrina, Dee Dee and Gypsy relocated first to Aurora and then to Springfield, Missouri, and early press coverage of their move to Springfield presented the region in an extremely positive light as the place allowing the Blanchards to start over and have the chance of a better life. In an interview, Dee Dee said, "It's so easy to live here, and it's so peaceful." Gyspy said, "It just proves that happy endings are not just in fairy tales; they are real and true in real life also" ("Youtube 'Authorities Investigate Possible [Finial] Scheme Involving'"). This interview took place in Springfield, with mother and daughter sitting in their new living room. The cheerful, clean, and modest home showcased the best side of "Ozark living." The idea of a destitute but kindhearted mother caring for her ill and invalid daughter within the safety of a quaint, rural community was a story the public yearned to be told.

The public attention given to the Blanchard's story during Dee Dee's life pales beside the attention given following her murder. The Blanchard case is not, of course, the first time the Ozarks has gained national attention due to murder. Brooks Blevins explores the alleged murder of Connie Franklin, which occurred in the late 1920s. Of the public's reaction to this story, Blevins says, "[R]eaders, and urban reporters, knew what to expect from rural Ozarkers. Stories about deviant rural upland southerners served two psychic, societal functions: they allowed modern readers to experience vicariously the lives of those on the geographical and social margins while simultaneously reaffirming faith in the superiority of the reader's modern world and its boundaries of appropriate behavior. To paraphrase Appalachian scholar J. W. Williamson, Americans wanted to be the hillbilly and they wanted to flee the hillbilly" (xx). Dee Dee's story, like Franklin's, allows those outside the Ozarks to watch and to comment upon the behaviors of others while maintaining an air of superiority.

The reception of Dee Dee and Gypsy's story as entertainment, through such vehicles as Hulu's television mini-series *The Act* and Lifetime's film *Love You to Death*, coincided with the public's exposure to other crime stories set in the Ozarks. Journalist Monica Potts notes that "[t]he Ozarks . . . are the setting for recent literary thrillers." Several current Ozarks authors, such as Daniel Woodrell and Laura McHugh, entertain the public with macabre stories of Ozarks people ensnared in cycles of abuse, betrayal, and bloodshed. Woodrell's *Winter's Bone* was published in 2006, and the subsequent film followed in 2010, highlighting Forsyth, Missouri. When Dee Dee was murdered five years later in Springfield, which is only about a half hour from Forsyth, coverage of her death may have reified to the public the rough and even dangerous persona of Ozarks people. Though McHugh's *The Weight of Blood* is set in a fictional town, she places that fictional town in the Missouri Ozarks. The release of *The Weight of Blood* in 2014, just one year before Dee Dee's death, may have prepped the public for a story of violence, missing persons, and murder. Other recent films and television series that focus upon the dark side of Missouri Ozarks culture include the movie *Gone Girl* (2014), an adaptation of Gillian Flynn's 2012 thriller novel; the movie *Sharp Objects* (2018), an adaptation of Flynn's 2006 novel; the mini-series *Three Billboards Outside Ebbing, Missouri* (2017); and the on-going television series *Ozark*. These depictions of southern Missouri revolve around murder and a dark set of regional elements, such as poverty, drug use, and limited education.

Although, as Libby Torres puts it, "Missouri is far more complex than most Hollywood representations would have you think," the fact that so much recent entertainment both preceding and following Dee Dee Blanchard's murder focuses on a depraved image of Ozarks life has only furthered the public's acceptance of Dee Dee and Gypsy's story as something that is common for the region. In his 2016 Ozarks Symposium keynote address, Steve Wiegenstein predicted the entertainment industry's capitalization on the case, saying, "And the sad and horrific story of Dee Dee and Gypsy Blanchard, currently playing out in a Springfield courtroom, seems tailor-made for recasting as a hillbilly gothic, and the comments about the case on social media tell us that it's already gotten there." Yet, Dee Dee's murder, while lining up with the tenants of gothic hillbilly fiction, may prove true the old adage that truth is stranger than fiction.

Following in line with current media trends, *The Act,* which is Hulu's eight-episode mini-series portrayal of the story which premiered on March 20, 2019, localizes this strange and macabre case as something specific to the Ozarks. From lines such as "There are no hurricanes in Missouri" to camera shots focusing on physical locations such as the Springfield mall or Springfield Emergency Center, to the camera zooming in on Gypsy's jump suit once she is incarcerated which reads, "Greene County," the backdrop of the Ozarks is highlighted as being important. Media reviews of *The Act* sometimes recognize the emphasis that place has on the story. However, beyond acknowledging the location, the reason why place is important is never explored. For example, an article from *The New Yorker* begins, "The central setting of *The Act,* now on Hulu, is a humble home in Springfield, Missouri" (Patterson). Such observations of setting without somehow tying the fact to significance within the plot may show an unrealized acceptance of viewing the Ozarks as a backward place.

It is rather ironic that so much of Gypsy and Dee Dee's infamy is linked to their association with the Ozarks when, in reality, they had lived in Missouri only ten years. Dee Dee had spent most of her life in Louisiana, and Gypsy had spent close to half of her life there. However, due to their Caucasian ethnicity and depressed socioeconomic conditions, they easily fit the well-established image of people living in the area. If the Blanchards had been people of color, this story would have received different treatment—perhaps better, perhaps worse—for it would have been less easily interpreted as indicative of Ozarks people, especially poor whites. The U.S Census Bureau confirms that in 2018, shortly after the murder and during the time it continued to gain notoriety, whites comprised 83% of the state population ("Quick Facts Missouri"). Because the Blanchards look like they are Missouri natives, place became a common focus in accounts of their story.

However, the Dee Dee and Gypsy case is complex because its infamy was colored by stereotyping of place *and* stereotyping of person. Dee Dee's positioning as an Ozarks resident, while significant, must share equal footing with the importance of her identity as framed through her role as a mother. In order to fully understand the public intrigue surrounding the case, we must acknowledge and unpack both implications of residing in the Ozarks and implications of failing as a mother. Within the study of Ozarks literature and culture, there is little research focusing on women's studies. However, as the field of maternal theory expands, there are important connections to be made to Ozarks culture. While Dee Dee's mistreatment of her daughter was not only illegal but also dehumanizing, the highly publicized nature of the case reflects ways in which Dee Dee serves as a symbol for fallen mothers, which is a trope that dominant culture is all too willing to embrace and nurture.

Western culture has a longstanding habit of blaming mothers. Adrienne Rich claims, "The institution of motherhood finds all mothers more or less guilty of having failed their children" (223). Susan J. Douglas and Meredith W. Michaels point out how the media and entertainment create fictionalized images of perfect mothers; to imitate them, women must be in competition with one another, essentially, to be super mom. Although no woman can live up to this benchmark, this "new momism," as Douglas and Meredith call it, cajoles women to find their identity in motherhood and perform maternity and domesticity flawlessly while simultaneously remaining beautiful and socially successful. Furthermore, the media juxtaposes this maternal ideal against stories of bad mothers, fueling the public's preconceived notions and continuing beliefs that mothers are either perfect or fail and are worthy of mother-blame. Douglas and Michaels point out, "Media imagery that seems so natural, that seems to embody some common sense, while blaming some mothers or all mothers, for children and a nation gone wrong, needs to have its veneer of supposed truth ripped away" (22). Furthermore, mothers tend to receive much harsher scrutiny than do fathers. Denyse Landry explains, "[M]others are held to a higher standard than fathers because of women's traditional association with, and relegation to, the so-called private sphere and the assumption that women are innately nurturing" (158). Also attesting to how gender affects expectations of parental conduct, the Pew Research Center divulges, "Mothers are seen as having the more difficult job, but they are also judged more harshly than are fathers" ("Motherhood Today").

Such a critique of a mother-blaming media agenda is needed regarding the case of Dee Dee and Gypsy. The mother-blaming is especially prevalent in portrayals of Ozarks women, who are commonly depicted as being backward and ignorant. Ruth I. Newman notes, "Women of the Ozarks traditionally have been described by a common and unflattering stereotype that they are ignorant, barefoot, and pregnant." This acknowledgement of Ozarks mothers as regressive seems to have easily turned into the slippery slope of accepting or even expecting their wrongdoing. While Dee Dee's actions were reprehensible, part of the fascination with her story exists because it is an example of a degenerative Ozarks woman who embodies the monstrous mother motif. Noting the heavy-handed mother-blame that the television series employs regarding Dee Dee, S. E. Smith writes, "In a culture where mothers are constantly subject to judgment and assessment, *The Act* invites the viewer to take a misogynistic load off: Go ahead and judge this mother." While Smith neglects implications of place, her comments regarding mother-blame are accurate.

Contrasting the current negative view, the initial media coverage of Dee Dee's life (before her murder and the subsequent findings of Gypsy's abuse) shows her as adeptly fulfilling her role of caregiver, which has traditionally been seminal in portrayals of good motherhood. Dee Dee appeared to successfully perform "intensive mothering," which is Sharon Hays' widely adopted term for a woman's identity largely centering on her role as an ever-nurturing and unselfish mother. Motherhood theorist Andrea O'Reilly explains that dominant Western culture today, despite its progressiveness in some areas, continues to have high and unrealistic expectations of mothers, including expectations such as "children can be properly cared for only by the biological mother . . . this mothering must be provided 24/7 . . . the mother must always put her children's needs before her own . . . the mother must be fully satisfied, fulfilled, completed, and composed in motherhood" (369). Dee Dee did not work outside the home or have any interests or hobbies, as she gave Gypsy the constant care she supposedly needed. Instead, she devoted all her time to her daughter. Thus, though she appeared as a quaint and simple Ozarks mother, she was viewed by the outside world positively.

While little attention has been given to women within Ozarks studies, one positive characteristic of traditional Ozarks women that has been noted is their connection to caregiving, which closely connects to how all mothers are expected to perform their good mother role. Sharon A. Sharp explains that "areas in the United States where folk medicine has flourished [such as the Ozarks] . . . provide valuable insights about the major roles women have played as midwives, herbalists and spiritual healers" (243). These roles require a woman to adeptly care for another, often exhibiting selflessness and compassion. Dee Dee appeared to do just this in taking care of Gypsy, to whom she actively served as a nurse in addition to a parent. Thus, despite the array of ways an Ozarker can be viewed negatively, an Ozarks mother's virtue, much like the virtue of mothers in general, lies in her ability to make life physically and emotionally better for another. Of course, once Dee Dee's failings as a mother and her fraudulent behavior as a caregiver were exposed after her death, her public perception was irrevocably sullied. This fall from grace not only moved her from a good mother to a bad one but also changed the image of their home in the Ozarks from Arcadia to backwoods. Gypsy and Dee Dee's story veers from what Anne Turner calls an "Ozarks tradition" regarding wholesome "strong kinship ties" (616). The story of Gypsy's abuse and

Dee Dee's murder prompts the public to view both the people (including those believed to be represented) and the place as suspect.

Dee Dee committed many injustices against her daughter, and, unfortunately, her public personas, first as a good mother and then as a bad mother, reinforced the cultural tendency to put mothers either on pedestals or deride them for their shortcomings. The angelic mother and the demonic one are extreme archetypes used to reduce women to symbolic objects while dehumanizing them. Sarah LaChance Adams acknowledges that mothers are perceived and portrayed dichotomously, saying, "The romanticization of maternity has divided mothers into the categories of either naturally good or pathologically bad" (12).[1] Dee Dee epitomizes both tropes. Interestingly, both Ozarks and maternal scholars have pointed out tendencies of polarizations within the fields. The public often views the Ozarks and its people as either pastoral noble savages or unsophisticated bumpkins, and it views mothers as either angelic caregivers or selfish and unfit parents. Of course, the reality is that most people are a multifaceted blend of numerous contending character traits rather than a simple extreme of good or evil. However, when the public learned of Dee Dee's story, many instinctively allowed stereotypes and cultural expectations to augment and color their negative views of her because she can so easily be characterized as a "bad Ozarks mother."

Part of the reason that mothers' stories have been so misunderstood is that mothers rarely share their own accounts. Mariann Hirsch claims that there is a longstanding tradition of mothers being written about rather than being active subjects or tellers of their own story. Hirsch argues that traditionally, "The woman as mother remains in the position of other" (136). Of course, due to Dee Dee's murder having already occurred when she and Gypsy's story gained notoriety, there is no way to access Dee Dee's defense. However, even a desire to understand what motivated her is missing in the accounts covering her story. Similar to the way mothers are written about by others, so too is the Ozarks typically written about by those outside the region. Its narrative is often told by those who do not understand it and who only view the region in ways that fit into their pre-ordained beliefs about the region. Phillip Howerton notes the way that the Ozarks is understood and misunderstood by those who gaze upon it: "[I]nterpretations of the region have ranged, depending upon the motives of the interpreters and the needs of larger culture, from a pastoral paradise maintained by pureblooded yeomen to a backwoods filled with deviant yokels " (xxii). Dee Dee and Gypsy's story has been reported at the national news level and produced for entertainment for a wide audience. The story is a multi-dimensional one of both the Ozarks and motherhood. But, it is neither objectively told nor objectively received.

Often, Ozarks literature, similar to the literature of dominant western culture, assigns mothers the role of a good or bad character. Harold Bell Wright's famous work *Shepherd of the Hills* idolizes the mother role, as the novel's namesake loses his wife, the mother of his children. Though she never appears in the story, she is valorized as the irreplaceable good wife and mother. Contrastingly, Daniel Woodrell typically presents failed mothers in his books. For example, in *Winter's Bone*, Ree sets out on a quest to find her father, or what has become of him. Her unresponsive and mentally ill mother serves only as a hindrance to Ree, functioning as an example of a flawed mother. Dee Dee's infamy as a negative Ozarks mother who "got what was coming to her" is not the first time such an Ozarks story received national bad press. In 1981, Ruie Ann Smith Park, a resident of Van Buren, Arkansas, was beaten to death. The case gained attention at the time, in part, due to outsider's voyeuristic interest in rough Ozarks life. Park appeared to be the pinnacle of a good mother and an upstanding member of the community. However, as the investigation unfolded and the murderer was found to be Park's adopted daughter, Linda, her image changed from that of a good mother to a bad one who had demoralized and emotionally abused Linda. Although this case did not become as popular as Dee Dee and Gypsy's, there are some important similarities which suggest the public's fascination in a good Ozarks scandal about mothers and daughters. Anita Paddock wrote the novel *Blind Rage* (2015) which chronicles Park's story. Paddock clearly employs mother-blame, saying she wrote the book to tell the daughter's side of the story, which is what most of the accounts of the Dee Dee Gypsy case do. This point of view relates to Hirsch's claim that mothers' perspectives are often obstructed: "It is the woman as daughter who occupies the center" (136). A television series called *Betrayed*, which focuses on a different true crime case each episode, covers Park's story in the episode entitled "Family Fatal" (2016). The making of this case into a television episode shortly after Dee Dee's death may not have been coincidental.

Both the Blanchard case and the Park case illustrate not only stereotypes about Ozarks people but also stereotypes about flawed mothers and tumultuous mother-daughter relationships. Rich claims that culture has largely bought into the idea that mothers and daughters are more likely than not to experience conflict and to have a fraught relationship. She points out that many mother-daughter relationships are negatively charged and strained, "This cathexis between mother and daughter—essential, distorted, misused—is the great unwritten story" (Rich 225). A woman inheriting her mother's characteristics is often considered as being undesirable, and a woman maintaining a close and positive relationship with her mother is considered unlikely or unwanted. Indeed, such beliefs may contribute to animosity between mothers and daughters in Western culture. Suzanna Walters argues that the belief that the mother-daughter relationship is "one constructed in conflict," may be "a phenomenon limited to white, bourgeois society" (173). Though far from bourgeois, the Ozarks is still predominantly white. Therefore, it is not surprising that conceptions of fraught mother-daughter relationships, most indicative of white culture, are associated with this area. Positive mother-daughter bonds most often occur in non-white communities which, according to Evelyn Nakano Glenn, "have constructed mothering in ways that diverge from the dominant model" (5). The fact that Dee Dee and Gypsy are white only adds to the likelihood of their story serving as fodder for mother-daughter failings.

Locating the angst of Dee Dee and Gypsy's issues within mother-daughter relationships in general, rather than identifying many elements of it as being specific to their situation, reinforces culture's already embedded beliefs about the negativity of mother-daughter relationships. Reporting on Hulu's *The Act*, *Glamour* magazine makes such a mistake saying, "*The Act* is about how complicated mother-daughter relationships are . . . . It's a female story, and I think it's a story that looks into the darkness and the humanity that can happen in female relationships and mother-daughter relationships" (Rosa). This view is based on the misperception that the Blanchards' relationship is flawed primarily because mother-daughter relationships are faulty. However, while Dee Dee and Gypsy are responsible for their choices, they did experience exceptional and challenging circumstances. For example, most now acknowledge that Dee Dee likely suffered from Munchausen Syndrome by Proxy, which, today, is referenced as Factitious Disorder. This is a psychological disorder in which a care-giver, usually a parent, typically the mother, exaggerates or falsifies her child's illness to receive attention as a good caregiver. Also, Dee Dee and Gypsy were victims of Hurricane Katrina and were homeless for a time before relocating. Mental illness and a natural disaster are extreme circumstances which impacted Dee Dee and Gypsy's rela-tionship, and these unusual elements should not be ignored. Their mother-daughter angst, while not uncommon as a theme, was undoubtedly exacerbated by these life-changing challenges. Yvonne Villarreal references Dee Dee and Gypsy's relationship as a typically complicated mother-daughter one, saying, "If you think your rela-tionship with your mom is complicated, Hulu's new series *The Act* will offer a dose of perspective." While this angle highlights that Dee Dee and Gypsy's relationship was worse than most, it also simultaneously relies on a negative association with the mother-daughter relationship, reinforcing this as acceptable and overlooking other circumstances within the Blanchards' story.

While bad mothers are a common trope, each woman's story has specificities influencing how her life is interpreted and the degree to which she is blamed for her child's shortcomings. In addition to acknowledging her physical and emotional abuse of Gypsy, stories of Dee Dee often additionally emphasize her status as a poor, single, and overweight mother. Though not overtly presented as negatives, these poorly perceived qualities work at the subconscious level to prompt the public view Dee Dee in derogatory ways. Interestingly, these elements coincide with typical and stereotypical beliefs about Ozarks residents. Society has long been skeptical of single mothers, largely because of the belief that they are likely to be poor and to be abusing social services. Dee Dee did not work, due to her alleged need to care for Gypsy. She not only received large gifts from organizations and individuals but, according to *ABC News*, also received childcare support from her ex-husband as well as regular governmental support, such as food stamps, disability, and social security (Diaz, et al.). Part of the public's outcry against Dee Dee stems from her stealing from charitable establishments, including Habitat for Humanity, which built a house for the Blanchards after Hurricane Katrina, and the Make a Wish Foundation, which funded a trip to Disney World. Thus, Dee Dee's exploitation of the system verifies the suspicion that many already hold about single mothers. Dianne Eyer says, "Unmarried mothers (at the moment, primarily just the poor ones) are perceived as a kind of social plague" (15). Although Eyer made this statement in 1996, Pew Research Center's 2011 report shows something similar, reporting, "Seven-in-ten Americans (69%) say the trend toward more single women having children is bad for society, and 61% say that a child needs both a mother and father to grow up happily" (Heimlich). While Dee Dee's fraudulent actions are an anomaly, she embodies society's worst fears about poor single mothers, which may have helped propel the fame and intrigue of the case.

Dee Dee's persona as an Ozarks woman only deepens her flawed ethos. As Ruth I. Newman reports, poverty has been a long-standing characteristic of Ozarks women, "In addition to being regarded as ignorant, Ozarks women were also usually very poor" (4). Poverty is an unfortunate reality for many living in the Ozarks. The 2018 Missouri Poverty Report shows the statistics regarding how Missouri compares to the national poverty level: "12.7% of Americans currently live at or below the federal poverty level. In Missouri the poverty rate is even higher at 14%. For a statewide population of 5,911,099, that's 826,358 Missourians" (3). Other portions of the Ozarks outside of Missouri also suffer from poverty. According to Emily Walkenhorst, state poverty rates for 2017 report Arkansas' to be 16.4% and Oklahoma's to be 15.8%. Thus, Dee Dee's positioning as a poor Ozarks woman may represent what is perceived by the outside world as a sinister reality of Ozarks people. Unfortunately, the fraud committed by Dee Dee reinforces stereotypes that people living in poverty are solely responsible for their economic situation and will abuse any relief program put in place to assist them. Potts says, "From the start, the Ozark spirit was passive, nagged by a vague feeling that life was beyond control: Sit down, and wait for the black sadness to settle in." Some may interpret this fatalistic mentality as one of apathy, resulting in self-inflicted poverty.

Dee Dee's obesity, which is less evident in televised reenactments but highlighted through real photos and video clips in news stories of the case, may have encouraged the public's negative perception of her. This physical state is a highly stereotyped one in which the public is more likely to negatively view the individual. This may have influenced Dee Dee's villainized status once her abusive behavior was revealed. According to Robert Carels et al., "Individuals with higher BMIs and women are more likely to be targets of prejudice and discrimination . . . [W]omen may not only fear but may also be targets of stereotyped evaluations more than men" (265-266). Dee Dee's being overweight may connect to her physical location, as "Missouri has the 17th highest adult obesity rate in the nation" ("The State of Obesity"). The Ozarks in general is known for having a high obesity rate, adult obesity being 30-34.9% in Missouri and 35%+ in Arkansas and Oklahoma (The State of Obesity). Thearis Osuji et al. conducted a study on the specific barriers to physical activity for women in the rural Midwest which can lead to obesity and specifically focused on Missouri women. This study suggests that it is not only aspects such as health condition and income which impact one's physical activity but that living in a rural as opposed to urban setting appears to negatively impact the likelihood of proper self-care for women (51). This data may be relevant regarding Dee Dee. While her extra weight, poverty, and singleness were overlooked when it was believed she was functioning as a good mother, once it became clear she was not behaving as a good mother, personal elements of her identity, which are not inherently connected to her actions, were viewed as evidence of her propensity toward failing in all areas of life. Furthermore, both poverty and obesity are proven struggles for those living in the Ozarks region, furthering a belief that Dee Dee is the product of a regressive place.

Though Dee Dee was not innocent, the elevation of her story to almost mythic proportions was spurred by the public's appetite for validation of Ozarks backwardness, monstrous mothers, and fraught mother-daughter relationships. Dee Dee's infamy was augmented by stereotypes of place and gender. In light of all the details surrounding this complicated account, the question then becomes, "How should one respond to the Dee Dee and Gypsy Blanchard case?" I would argue that although place can be important, regarding this story, it is not the most significant factor. The abuse and murder did not happen because the mother and daughter are stereotypical Ozarks people. They happened because the world is a fallen place, and bizarre stories happen everywhere. Howerton notes, "[A]lthough the Ozarks is a small corner of our world, it is, like most everywhere else, a crossroads of human experience" (xxix). When looking at the Ozarks, we should not only look for regional traits but also the universals. Deception and dysfunction are not unique to the Ozarks; they simply also happen here. Dee Dee was and Gypsy is a real person. They have been heavily associated with the Ozarks in the media, as if the place has served as some sort of self-fulfilling prophesy over their doomed relationship. Yet, as I have sought to show, their tumultuous mother-daughter relationship is indicative of all the burdens that dominant Western culture has unloaded upon women. Their notoriety is largely due to the public's desire to capitalize on the monstrous mother image becoming a reality, as well as preconceived notions of Ozarks people being fulfilled. We should look at Dee Dee and Gypsy's story with compassion. We can learn from them, but we should not view their story as indicative of mother-daughter relationships or those who live in the Ozarks.

Gypsy's life did not end with her incarceration. When she is released, she plans to move to Louisiana to be near her family. Since being in prison, she has become engaged to a man who initially contacted her to offer encouragement after learning about her story. According to Tierney Brickner, Gypsy now "just wants to live a normal existence with her fiancé and have a family and be happy." Some would argue that Gypsy's chances of being a good mother and having a healthy relationship with the future children she desires to have are slim. Journalist Gregory Holman reports that psychiatrist Marc Feldman has concern that Gyspy has learned from Dee Dee how to be manipulative and attention seeking. Holman poses the possibility of Gypsy inheriting her mother's shortcomings, saying, "A 2001 academic study in the journal *Attachment & Human Development* notes that 'a vicious circle' of attachment between parent and child may allow factitious illness to be passed from one generation to the next." However, the key to leaving behind the culture of mother blame is believing in individuals' ability to transcend their circumstances and faith in the possibility of strong and functional mother-daughter bonds.

Aurora Levins Morales quotes what a wise woman told her, and I repeat it now: "It takes three generations. If you resolve your relationship with your mother you'll both change, and your daughter will have it easier, but her daughter will be raised differently. In the third generation the daughters are free" (51-2). While Gypsy cannot resolve her own relationship with Dee Dee, she acknowledges both her mother's love for her (albeit dysfunctional) and her regard for her mother, despite the complicated situation; she acknowledges her mother's sickness and wrong doing, and she also takes responsibility for her own actions, saying, "What I did was wrong. I'll have to live with it" (Dean). Gypsy is seeking to move beyond the trauma to find healing and to extend it to others. This will have a positive impact on any future children and even grandchildren she may have. Fancy Macelli, a family friend of the Blanchards, reports on ways Gypsy seeks to use her story for restoration, "Gypsy has talked about being an advocate for children who are experiencing abuse, and possibly for people going through Munchausen by proxy" (Bricker). Although she will undoubtedly require ongoing counseling, I believe Gypsy's life will continue to improve, and it will be important for the media to report on this, to give evidence of the normalcy and simple happiness she will go on to experience rather than fixate only on the strange experiences she has had.

It may be inevitable that the bettering of Gypsy's life coinciding with her leaving the Ozarks will be interpreted as part of the solution. While in Gypsy's case, relocating is appropriate because her family lives elsewhere and locations related to her abuse and crime may cause her to relive the trauma, it is unfortunate that the public may perceive leaving the Ozarks as necessary for one to have a good, normal life. Thus, there is work to be done to resist stereotypes of regressive Ozarks people in general and Ozarks mothers in particular. The media must work to assist the struggling as well as to show the positive side of Ozarks life. It is unlikely that these stories will achieve the national attention that Gypsy's did, for bad news always travels faster and farther than good news, but stories of obstacles and their being overcome must be told all the same. Recognizing the challenges that poor, single mothers in the Ozarks face and working to do something to change their situation is pivotal. For example, KY3 News ran a story titled "A Group Offering Help and Support for Single Moms in the Ozarks is Expanding" which goes on to explore the ways mothers in challenging circumstances are flourishing due to the resources made available to them. We must also extend the image of Ozarks women from that of being uneducated and uninvolved in public life. While maternity is an important part of many women's identity, it is not the only part. The media portrayed Dee Dee solely as a mother; she was shown to have no identity beyond her role as a caregiver. Therefore, when her discretions came to light, they were attributed not just to Dee Dee as an individual but to Ozarks mothers as a collective.

A multifaceted conception of femininity is needed, and this work has already begun. For twenty years now, Springfield, Missouri, has hosted the "Most Influential Women" award which honors women in the community for their career and civic accomplishments. Christine Temple draws attention to this highlighting of women in the Ozarks, saying, "They're leading through action, and the next generation is watching and learning. Let's . . . toast with this well-known phrase: 'Here's to strong women. May we know them. May we be them. May we raise them.'" This is indeed what the Ozarks must champion to the rest of the world: the reality that is stronger than the misperception, the raising and rising up of real girls and women who, though not perfect, are too complex to be reduced by stereotypes.

1. For resources discussing the good and bad mother dichotomy, see the following: *Good Mums, Bad Mums* by Oluwakemi Ola-Ojo, *The Good Mother Myth: Redefining Motherhood to Fit Reality*, edited by Avital Norman Nathman, *So Glad They Told Me: Women Get Real About Motherhood*, edited by Stephanie Sprenger, *Don't Blame Mother* by Paula Caplan.

Works Cited

Adams, Sarah LaChance. *Mad Mothers, Bad Mothers, and What a "Good" Mother Would Do: The Ethics of Ambivalence.* Columbia University Press, 2014.

"A Group Offering Help and Support for Single Moms in the Ozarks is Expanding" *KY3 News.* 8 Oct 2019. www.ky3.com/content/news /Help--Support-for-single-moms-in-the-Ozarks-562517561.html. Accessed 23 May 2020.

Blevins, Brooks. *Ghost of the Ozarks: Murder and Memory in the Upland South.* University of Illinois Press, 2012.

Brickner, Tierney. "A Fiancé, Freedom and Fame: Inside Gypsy Rose Blanchard's Life in Prison." *E News.* 13 April. www.eonline. com/news/1032182/a-fiance-freedom-and-fame-inside-gypsy-rose-blanchard-s-life-in-prison. Accessed 23 May 2020.

Carels, Robert A. "Examining Perceived Stereotype Threat among Overweight/Obese Adults Using a Multi-Threat Framework." *The European Journal of Obesity.* 2013, pp. 258-268. DOI: 10.1159/000352029.

Carr, Erin Lee. *Mommy Dead and Dearest.* HBO, 2017.

Dean, Michelle. "Dee Dee Wanted Her Daughter to be Sick. Gypsy Wanted Her Mother to be Dead." *Buzzfeed.* 18 Aug. 2016. www.buzzfeednews.com/article/michelledean/dee-dee-wanted-her-daughter-to-be-sick-gypsy-wanted-her-mom. Accessed 5 Sept. 2019.

--- *The Act.* Hulu, 2019.

Diaz, Joseph, et al. "How a Young Woman Forced to Use[ ] a Wheel Chair, Treated for Several Illnesses Ended up in Prison for Her

Mother's Murder." *ABC News.* 4 Jan, 2018. abcnews.go.com/US/
young-wheelchair-bound-woman-treated-illnesses-ended-
prison/story?id=52138979. Accessed 4 Sept, 2019.

Douglas, Susan Jeanne and Meredith W. Michaels. *The Mommy Myth:
The Idealization of Motherhood and how it has Undermined Women.*
Simon and Schuster, Inc., 2005.

Duff, Chelsea. "Gypsy Rose Blanchard Plans to Wed Her Fiancé in
January — but Her Family Has Concerns." *In Touch.* 16 Jul, 2019.
www.intouchweekly.com/posts/gypsy-rose-blanchards-family-is-
concerned-about-her-wedding-plans/. Accessed 30 Sept, 2019.

Eyer, Diane. *Motherguilt: How Our Culture Blames Mothers for What's
Wrong with Society.* Crown, 1996.

"For Two Ozarks Communities, A Stark Contrast in Culture." *NPR.* 12
May, 2014. www.npr.org/2014/05/12/310998299/for-two-ozarks-
communities-a-stark-contrast-in-culture. Accessed 9 Sept, 2019.

Glenn, Evelyn Nakano. "Split Household, Small Producer and Dual
Wage Earner: An Analysis of Chinese-American Family
Strategies." *Journal of Marriage and Family*, vol. 45, no. 1, 1983,
pp. 35-46. *JSTOR*, doi: 10.2307/351293.

Heimlich, Russell. "Disapprove of Single Mothers." *Pew Research
Center.* 6 Jan, 2011. www.pewresearch.org/fact-tank/2011/01/06/
disapprove-of-single-mothers/. Accessed 4 Sept, 2019.

Hirsch, Marianne. *The Mother / Daughter Plot: Narrative, Psychoanalysis,
Feminism.* Indiana University Press, 1989.

Holman, Gregory J. "With all those interviews, is Gypsy Blanchard
just doing what her mother taught her?" *Springfield News-Leader.*
27 Jan 2019. www.news-leader.com/story /news/ local/ozarks/2018
/01/22/agreeing-all-those-interviews-gypsy-blanchard-just-doing-
what-her-mother-taught-her/1054059001/

Howerton, Phillip. "Introduction." *The Literature of the Ozarks*, pp. xix-xxix. The University of Arkansas Press, 2019.

Landry, Denys. "Maternal Blitz: Harriet Lovatt as Postpartum Sufferer in Doris Lessing's the Fifth Child." *Textual Mothers/Maternal Texts: Motherhood in Contemporary Women's Literatures*, edited by Elizabeth Podnieks and Andrea O'Reilly, Wilfrid Laurier University Press, 2011, pp. 157-68.

Morales, Aurora Levins. "...And Even Fidel Can't Change That!" *This Bridge Called My Back, Fourth Edition: Writings by Radical Women of Color*, edited by Cherrie Moraga and Gloria Anzaldua, State University of New York Press, 2015, pp. 48-52.

Morrow, Lynn. "Introduction." *The Ozarks in Missouri History: Discoveries in an American Region*, edited by Lynn Morrow, University of Missouri Press, 2013, pp. 1-18.

"Motherhood Today: Tougher Challenges, Less Success." *Pew Research Center*. 2 May, 2007. www.pewsocialtrends.org/2007/05/02/mother hood-today-tougher-challenges-less-success/. Accessed 9 Sept, 2019.

Newman, Ruth I. "Ozarks Women: Ignorant, Barefoot, and Pregnant?" *White River Valley Historical Quarterly*, vol 9, no 8, 1987. https://thelibrary.org/lochist/periodicals /wrv/V9/N8/s87c.htm. Accessed 12 June 2019.

O'Reilly, Andrea. "Across the Divide: Contemporary Anglo-American Feminist Theory on the Mother-Daughter Relationship." *Redefining Motherhood: Changing Identities and Patterns*, edited by Sharon Abbey and Andrea O'Reilly, Second Story Press, 1998, pp. 69-91.

Osuji, Thearis, et al. "Barriers to Physical Activity Among Women in the Rural Midwest." *Women Health*. vol. 44, no. 1, 2006. pp. 41-55. DOI: 10.1300/J013v44n01_03. Accessed 5 Sept, 2019.

Patterson, Troy. "*The Act*, Reviewed: A Juicy True-Crime Drama That Deconstructs Soapy Tropes." *The New Yorker.* 20 Mar, 2019. www.newyorker.com/culture/on-television/the-act-reviewed-a-juicy-true-crime-drama-that-deconstructs-soapy-tropes. Accessed 26 Nov, 2019.

Potts, Monica. "Sit and Wait for the Sadness." *The American Prospect.* 11 Mar, 2014. prospect.org/article/sit-and-wait-sadness. Accessed 4 Sept, 2019.

"Quick Facts: Missouri." United States Census Bureau. www.census. gov/quickfacts/MO. Accessed 30 Sept, 2019.

Raferty, Milton. *The Ozarks: Land and Life.* The University of Arkansas Press, 2001.

Rich, Adrienne. *Of Woman Born: Motherhood as Experience and Institution.* W. W. Norton & Company, Inc., 1995.

Rosa, Christopher. "Hulu's *The Act* Is Horrifying, Human, and Hard to Stop Watching." *Glamour.* 20 Mar, 2019. www.glamour.com/story/ hulu-the-act-review. Accessed 1 Oct, 2019.

Sharp, Sharon A. "Folk Medicine Practices: Women as Keepers and Carriers of Knowledge." *Women's Studies International Forum* vol. 9, no. 3, 1986, pp. 243-249.

Sikorski, C. "Perception of Overweight and Obesity from Different Angles: A Qualitative Study." *Scand J Public Health.* vol. 40, no. 3, 2012, pp. 271-7. DOI:10.1177/1403494812443604.

Slanchkin, Amy. "Local Woman Writes Book About 1981 Van Buren Murder." 5 News Online. 11 Apr. 2016. 5newsonline. com/2016/04/11/local-woman-writes-book-about-1981-van-buren-murder/. Accessed 7 Jan, 2020.

Smith, S. E. "Object Lessons "The Act" and the Ethics of Consuming True Crime." *Bitch Media.* 8 May, 2019. www.bitchmedia.org/

article /object-lessons-/the-act-true-crime-ethics-represention-disability/TV-3. Accessed 31 Dec. 2019.

Taylor, Ella. "A Director Ever in Search of Survivors." *New York Times.* 30 April, 2010. ww.nytimes.com/2010/05/02/movies/02granik.html. Accessed 4 Sept, 2019.

Temple, Christine. "2019 Most Influential Women." *Springfield Business Journal.* 7 Oct. 2019. sbj.net/stories/2019-most-influential-women, 65889. Accessed 23 May 2010.

"The State of Obesity in Missouri." https://www.stateofobesity.org/states/mo/. Accessed 5 Sept. 2019.

Torres, Libby. "Sharp Objects' and Hollywood's Warped Vision of Missouri." *Daily Beast.* 28 Jul. 2018. www.thedailybeast.com/sharp-objects-and-hollywoods-warped-vision-of-missouri?ref=scroll. Accessed 6 Jan. 2020.

Turner, Anne. "Ozarks Mountains." *The Companion to Southern Literature: Themes, Genres, Places, People*, edited by Joseph M. Flora, et al. LSU Press, 2001.

"2018 Missouri Poverty Report." www.caastlc.org/wpsite/wp-content/uploads/2018/03/MCAN-MEP-2018-MissouriPoverty Report-DigitalDownload.pdf. Accessed 8 Sept, 2019.

Villarreal, Yvonne. "*The Act* Shows a New Side to the Gypsy Rose Blanchard Case—And Its Two Stars." *Los Angeles Times.* 19 Mar, 2019. latimes.com/entertainment/tv/la-et-st-patricia-arquette-joey-king-the-act-20190319-story.html. Accessed 5 Sept. 2019.

Walters, Suzanna Danuta. *Lives Together/Worlds Apart: Mothers and Daughters in Popular Culture.* University of California Press, 1992.

Walken, Emily. "Census Figures Show Drop in State Poverty." *Arkansas Democrat Gazette.* 13 Sept. 2018. www.arkansasonline.

com/news/2018/sep/13/census-figures-show-drop-state-poverty/.
Accessed 7 Jan, 2020.

Watson, Ritchie D. "Gentleman." *The Companion to Southern Literature:
Themes, Genres, Places, People, Movements and Motifs,* edited by
Joseph M. Flora, Lucinda Hardwick MacKethan, pp. 293-294, LSU
Press, 2001.

Wiegenstein, Steve. 2016 Ozarks Symposium Keynote: "The Lure of
the Ozarks: What's the Bait, and Who's the Fish?" West Plains,
Missouri, September 2016.

"Youtube 'Authorities Investigate Possible [Finial] Scheme Involving."
17 Jun. 2015. www.youtube.com/watch?v=8i4JoQfvveA. Accessed
7 Jan, 2020.

When Hollywood Came to the Ozarks:
The Making of *Jesse James*

Kimberly D. Harper

Late in the summer of 1938, a pair of horsemen galloped across the fields of rural McDonald County, Missouri. The dust kicked up by their mounts drifted across the meandering country roads jammed with the cars of eager spectators hoping to catch a glimpse of Tyrone Power and Henry Fonda, the stars of Twentieth Century Fox's production, *Jesse James*. Hollywood had come to the Ozarks.

The residents of McDonald County were part of a rural, Ozark community that became caught up in the whirlwind of Hollywood filmmaking in the depths of the Great Depression. Locals pinned their hopes for economic growth on the film, but while the arrival of the cast and crew provided a brief respite from the financial misery of the time, it failed to bring sustained prosperity to the region. Instead, locals were left to wonder when Hollywood would return to their Ozark hills.[1]

Anticipation had been building for months for the residents of southwest Missouri, ever since the *Pineville Democrat* trumpeted, "*Jesse James* Picture Will Be Filmed Here," on July 28, 1938. Director Henry King, a pilot, reportedly flew 15,000 miles across the country looking for the perfect locale. After locating McDonald County, situated in the extreme southwest corner of the state, King and assistant director Bob Webb flew over the county a second time. Impressed, the men then embarked on a driving tour, and found the rugged picturesque countryside fit their needs. The hilly countryside interspersed with rivers, creeks, towering limestone bluffs, and caves was perfect for King's vision of the film.

In his address to the Pineville Chamber of Commerce, director Henry King declared, "It is our intention to want to use the city of

---

[1]The McDonald County Public Library in Pineville has a wonderful collection of candid photographs that were taken during filming. Unfortunately, no oral histories or other first-hand accounts written by local participants are known to exist.

Pineville as the original town of Liberty, because your courthouse stands in the center of the square as it did in Liberty at that time." He warned, however, that the appearance of the town square would have to be modified. The film crew would erect false store fronts, install hitching racks, and put dirt on Pineville's "beautiful concrete street." If locals were wary, King's promise to employ between 150 and 300 extras, 75 to 100 horses and riders, and to rent every wagon, hack, and surrey in the county must have assuaged any doubts. He even promised, "We can take care of the tourists, without hurting anybody's feelings."[2]

The editor of the *Pineville Democrat*, C. A. Poindexter, enthusiastically endorsed the film project. He asked, "What could ever happen that would give the Ozarks better publicity than the filming of a major movie production in this region? The Ozarks have long been seeking favorable publicity, and nothing could afford a better agency than an outstanding movie production." Poindexter added, "But the picture alone would not be the only publicity advantage. Thousands of people from places far and near will journey here to view the filming operations."[3]

By the next week, the *Democrat* reported, "Interest is running high among the people of the Ozarks and tourists here this summer over the expected filming of the picture '*Jesse James*.' Many inquiries are being received by mail and by visitors in person. Some merely want to know about the picture, while others want to be in the movie." Perhaps even more thrilling was the news that the movie would be shot entirely in Technicolor and would cost an estimated two million dollars to complete.[4]

Nearby towns took notice of the film's potential economic

---

[2] *Pineville Democrat*, 28 July 1938, p. 1. McDonald County was one of the least developed counties in the state of Missouri but was home to a thriving resort industry. Noel alone was home to ten summer resorts, while neighboring Anderson featured four resorts. For more, see the 1937 Official Guide Book of the Playgrounds of the Ozarks, published by the Ozark Playgrounds Association, Joplin, MO.

[3] *Pineville Democrat*, 28 July 1938, p. 2.

[4] *Ibid*, 4 August 1938, p. 1.

windfall. The *Neosho Daily Democrat* announced Twentieth Century Fox's decision to film in neighboring McDonald County. The newspaper highlighted the fact that Pineville merchant Lee Carnell was authorized by the studio to "issue a call for laborers, including 550 carpenters."[5] Those hoping to find employment were to register with Mayor F. T. Drumm at his office in Pineville and "await call." Although many in the Depression-stricken county eagerly awaited news of employment, their children may have been disappointed, as the McDonald County Fair was cancelled because of the film. An even bigger carnival was about to arrive.[6]

By mid-August, it was announced that the movie would star Tyrone Power as Jesse James, Nancy Kelly as Zerelda James, Henry Fonda as Frank James, and Randolph Scott as Marshal Will Wright.[7] The *Joplin Globe* cheekily remarked that just weeks earlier McDonald County residents had told summer resort tourists that the film was "just another promotion scheme" as they were, according to the *Globe*, "accustomed, through bitter experience not to put too much faith in 'city slicker' resort promoters." Now, however, the citizens of McDonald County "went around with their tongues in their cheeks."

The Pineville City Council held a special session to discuss problems with parking, the need for new outdoor eating places for tourists, and other necessary accommodations. Local resort operators found themselves inundated with new reservations as well as requests from tourists to extend their stay through the end of the summer. Marx Cheney, owner of the popular Shadow Lake resort in Noel, announced his resort would stay open an additional month to accommodate visitors. Lumber yards and hardware stores were doing "a land-office business." Pineville residents launched "one of the most intensive clean-up campaigns in the community's history, raking up and carrying away accumulated trash, mowing their lawns, and, in some instances, even installing modern plumbing equipment." Mrs. F.W. Baughman of Kansas City rented her air-conditioned summer cottage on a bluff overlooking Noel to the movie studio for use by

---

[5] *Neosho Daily News*, 11 August 1938, p. 1.
[6] *Pineville Democrat*, 11 August 1938, p. 1.
[7] *Joplin Globe*, 13 August 1938, p. 3.

Tyrone Power and his personal secretary.[8]

Power, the great-grandson of the famed Irish actor Tyrone Power, quietly arrived in Noel on August 18, 1938, after a bumpy flight from California. His arrival did not remain unnoticed for very long. Sharp-eyed locals spotted Power having a drink with director Henry King and financial unit manager Sidney Bowen in a downtown watering hole. Within minutes a swarm of tourists and locals gathered to watch the men. A bold few approached Power to ask for an autograph and the star politely obliged their requests.[9] But if locals were excited to play host to Hollywood's stars, they refused to be taken for rubes.

The *Springfield News-Leader* reported that some of the McDonald County residents hired as extras "refuse[d] to be chiseled on wages." One local told the *News-Leader*, "We hear those extras in Hollywood get $5 and $6 a day and so we don't intend to work for any $2." Henry King was expected to address the issue before he began filming. Undoubtedly, the opportunity to earn money was welcome in a time of economic hardship.

Residents of Pineville found their weekly Saturday ritual of coming to the town square to exchange and sell goods disrupted by tourists clamoring to look at the changes. Dirt now covered the streets, telephone lines had disappeared, and the roads into town were flooded with cars causing traffic jams for the first time in the history of McDonald County. Pineville barber Bill Martin was so busy he was thinking of hiring an assistant from Springfield.[10] Women walked the streets "in riding breeches and high-heeled boots, or, more sensitive to Hollywood styles, in slacks, shorts, swimming and play suits" hoping to be selected by a casting director.[11] Nearby Noel suffered a similar fate.

The *Joplin Globe* announced that, "Thousands thronged Noel tonight for the arrival early tomorrow of a special train bearing from Hollywood more than 150 members of the Twentieth Century-Fox studios' cast to be used in the filming of the production, '*Jesse James*.'"

---

[8] *Joplin Globe*, 14 August 1938, p. B5

[9] *Joplin Globe*, 19 August 1938, p. 1-2.

[10] *Joplin Globe*, 21 August 1938, p. 1.

[11] *St. Louis Post-Dispatch*, 22 August 1938, p. 4B.

Shadow Lake Resort, set on the banks of crystal clear Elk River, "took on a 'Fourth of July air,' with hundreds arriving there early, hoping that Tyrone Power" would appear. Marx Cheney, owner of Shadow Lake, remarked that he thought there were at least four to five thousand people in Noel, whose population was normally 431.[12] Everett Manning, president of the Noel Chamber of Commerce and a gas station owner, cheerfully observed, "It's worth three ordinary tourist seasons."[13]

Mordecai Schwartz, a reporter for the *Springfield Leader and Press*, described his visit to McDonald County, saying, "There was a closely packed, crawling line of automobiles, heading south on Highway 71, which leads to Pineville." When Schwartz passed through Anderson, a gas station attendant told him that the cars "have been a-comin' like that all night and all day. I never see the like of it. They must be 5000 cars at Noel now."[14] Traffic jams were the least of the star's worries.

Throngs of young girls and women clamored for a glimpse of Tyrone Power. According to Schwartz, Power and Henry Fonda were mobbed while trying to eat lunch in a small restaurant in Noel. He reported that although the "walls of the little restaurant didn't actually bulge, if one more woman had got inside, they would have." Unnerved by the growing number of women watching them outside the restaurant, the two men decided to escape, except that both the front door and rear entrance were blocked by enthusiastic girls. Co-star Brian Donleavy bravely ran interference for Fonda and Power as they burst out the door closest to their hotel. A group of girls followed in hot pursuit, but the two stars were too fast and disappeared into their hotel rooms. When a deputy sheriff threatened to clear out the crowds, reporter Schwartz snorted, "He was only talking, though. The crowd was too big for one deputy, or for 10, for that matter."

Power, despite giving up his air-conditioned cottage on a hilltop overlooking Noel due to the hordes of curious onlookers, refused to speak ill of his overeager fans. When asked what he thought of "this

[12] Larry Bradley, *Twentieth Century Fox's Production of Jesse James*, (Noel, MO: McDonald County Press, 1970), p. 3; *Joplin Globe* 21 August 1938, p. 1.
[13] *Neosho Daily Democrat*, August 22, 1938, p. 1.
[14] *Springfield Leader and Press*, 22 August 1938, p. 10.

mess," Power replied, "I don't think it's a mess at all. I like it. I'll admit I never saw a crowd as big as this at any place I've ever been on location." He diplomatically added, "And this part of the country is a perfect setting for the story. It couldn't be better."[15]

Still, Powers did not suffer the indignity that actress Jane Darwell endured on her first day in Noel. Although the film company had made arrangements for plumbing to be installed in the cottage where Darwell was staying, it was discovered that the installation had not taken place. Darwell was dismayed to find that the only bathroom available was a rustic outhouse. A young boy spied Darwell as she entered the outhouse and closed the door. He "ran to the outhouse, jerked open the door and then, to Miss Darwell's consternation, snapped her picture before he fled."[16]

While the overwhelming majority of cast members stayed in McDonald County, one did not. African American Ernest Whitman, who played the character "Pinkie," did not join the rest of the all-white cast in Noel. Instead, he stayed in Neosho with Andy Rich, a fellow African American. The arrangement was not explained by the local press, but it can be surmised that the local unspoken racial etiquette of the day required blacks to leave McDonald County after sundown.[17]

As filming got underway, there were fewer opportunities to catch a glimpse of the stars. The *Neosho Daily Democrat* reported that, "Spectators, heretofore encouraged, were barred today when the first of the outdoor scenes were filmed near here." Cars near Pineville "were stopped by state highway patrolmen during actual filming" and only those with passes were admitted to proceed. Weather, however, may have kept many away as the blazing heat of late August beat down mercilessly on anyone who ventured outside into the sun.[18]

Governor Lloyd C. Stark sent a telegram welcoming King and the

---

[15] *Springfield Leader and Press*, 22 August 1938, p. 10.
[16] Don Walker, "Fun & Games with Jesse James" (Pineville, MO: The McDonald County News-Gazette Printing and Publishing Co., 1976), p. 16-17. Walker's reminiscences about McDonald County residents are often derogatory and seemingly mean-spirited.
[17] *Neosho Miner and Mechanic*, August 26, 1938, p. 1.
[18] *Neosho Daily Democrat*, 23 August 1938, p. 1.

cast. King responded, "Our first weeks filming on *Jesse James* proves in color on celluloid that your Ozarks are as beautiful as we thought. The hospitality and cooperation of your people have been most grat-ifying."[19] In a subsequent letter to Stark, King apologized that he and the cast would be unable to visit the governor. He assured Stark that "Your beautiful Ozarks make an ideal setting, not only historically, but pictorially – effects we couldn't possibly attain on Technicolor film in Hollywood."[20]

Although Governor Stark welcomed the cast and crew, at least one Missourian protested their presence. Bernard Greensfelder, a St. Louis attorney, complained to Stark, "Since the scenes of this movie all lie within the state of Missouri, the good name of our state is going to be brought before the public, and it occurs to the writer that there should be a united effort on the part of all Missourians to prevent the production of this picture." According to Greensfelder, the movie "is going to place the state of Missouri in the limelight as a home for desperadoes and criminal characters." [21]

Despite the misgivings of some, others were eager to be associated with the film. N. C. Hardin of Louisiana, Missouri, wrote Governor Stark to ask if he would "remember Gloria and me to [Henry King]." Hardin and his wife Gloria had known King years earlier when the two men worked as actors in California. Hardin confided to Stark, "He has made a very big success as a director and has for some time been one of the very big directors." Citizens of at least one neighboring state also took notice.

Arkansas Governor Carl Bailey sent Stark a telegram to ask if he could intervene on behalf of a group of Little Rock businessmen who wished to obtain the assistance of Twentieth Century Fox in pro-moting a fall festival to "stimulate public confidence in business." Stark provided C. J. Dolan of the Arkansas State Department of Reve-nue with a letter of introduction to King that asked if King would "allow this gentleman and his wife to witness the method of pro-

[19] Lloyd C. Stark, Papers, 1886-1972 (C4), State Historical Society of Missouri Manuscript Collection.
[20] Ibid.
[21] Ibid.

duction in setting up the James motion picture."[22]

The editor of the nearby *Sulphur Springs (AR) Ozarkan* greeted the cast and crew:

"Howdee, Jesse James. The people of the Ozarks welcome you all people to the Ozarks for your picture of Jesse James' capers. You are right down in a country in which few changes have been made, except good roads, radio and mail order catalogues have been added. . . . The natives are never in a hurry, and from them you can learn patience and how futile is the mad rush for money. We still run after a 'possum, and work all night to cut down a 'possum tree. Talent is something we have so much of that it has become a nuisance. . . . Our men are just as crooked as elsewhere. In fact, we've got everything to be found anywhere else and then some thing elsewhere ain't got."[23]

Despite periodic rain showers during the first week, a reported 10,000 spectators flooded the area near the Crowder farm southwest of Pineville to try and catch a glimpse of the stars in action.[24] The *Pineville Democrat* reported, "Cars were parked along the road and even in fields as far away as two miles away and many persons reached the scene by way of ferry boats across Elk River." According to one account, a local farmer drove his horse and buggy into Pineville, only to find that he was surrounded by autograph seekers. Overwhelmed, the farmer beat a hasty retreat out of town. One of his friends called out, "Where you goin' in such a hurry, Wes?" The farmer yelled back, "Back to the farm. The whole town's gone plumb crazy."[25]

Among those who visited the set were Osage Chief Fred Lookout and Major Gordon C. Lillie, better known as "Pawnee Bill."[26] Surprisingly, Robert F. James, the son of Frank James, visited the movie set as

[22] Lloyd C. Stark, Papers, 1886-1972 (C4), State Historical Society of Missouri Manuscript Collection.
[23] Don Walker, "Fun & Games with Jesse James" (Pineville, MO: The McDonald County News-Gazette Printing and Publishing Co., 1976), p. 26.
[24] *Joplin Globe*, 30 August 1938, p. 7
[25] Don Walker, "Fun & Games with Jesse James" (Pineville, MO: The McDonald County News-Gazette Printing and Publishing Co., 1976), p. 31.
[26] *Joplin Globe*, 2 September 1938, p. 5A.

the guest of director King. He "appeared to relish watching the scenes, pointing out laughingly that a man had to be shot only once, but that in making a motion picture a man has to be shot several times before the director is satisfied he is dead."[27]

Perhaps jealous of its southern neighbor, the editor of the *Neosho Miner and Mechanic* chided the curious, "Of course nearly everybody in this section of the country will see the picture as soon as it is released, but just between us and no more, Mr. and Mrs. Churchmember, do you think we ought to be spending our money to encourage the making of such pictures?"[28] Within days, Neosho was inundated with onlookers who watched as the crew filmed a fictional St. Louis train station scene at the town depot.[29]

If anyone profited from the movie, however, it was the residents of McDonald County. An estimated 80,000 visitors to the county in four weeks had brought in an inestimable amount of revenue in addition to the $100,000 that Twentieth Century Fox was projected to spend during filming.[30] C. A. Poindexter, editor of the *Pineville Democrat* told his readers, "The future of the Ozarks region may depend greatly upon the success of the motion picture '*Jesse James*.' Should the Ozark scenery make good pictures and prove popular with moviegoers, then there is reason to believe that picture companies will make a great many pictures here." He noted the area's "favorable conditions" and "cheap labor," but warned, "The greatest test, however, will be box office receipts."[31]

Regrettably, the crowds were too much for Florence Crowder, owner of the farm where many of the movie's scenes were filmed. In poor health prior to the arrival of the film crew, she suffered "a nervous breakdown" caused by the crowds and died. It was at this time that filming began to conclude.

Director King issued a statement thanking the people of the Ozarks. He declared, "Reports from our studio of the filming we have

---

[27] *Joplin Globe* 10 September 1938, p. 3.
[28] *Neosho Miner & Mechanic*, 2 September 1938, p. 2.
[29] *Neosho Daily Democrat*, 3 September 1938, p. 1.
[30] *Pineville Democrat*, 8 September 1938, p. 1.
[31] *Pineville Democrat*, 15 September 1938, p. 2.

made in this section prove that you have one of the most beautiful regions of the world. Although we have been on motion picture locations in various parts of the country, never have we experienced a more pleasant time." He finished, "We want to comment particularly upon the fairness with which we have been treated. We have nothing but praise for the people and the scenic beauties of this section of the country."[32] But if King was pleased with the production, his chief was not.

In late September, Darryl Zanuck, the head of Twentieth Century Fox, sent Henry King a terse telegram that voiced his displeasure with the film. He growled, "After reviewing everything that has been shot to date, I am definitely convinced that the entire location trip [to Missouri] was, to a great extent, a financial mistake." Zanuck conceded, "I fully realize how you have been molested and hampered by crowds and other difficulties, but the fact remains we are now six days behind schedule with no prospects of improvement." The studio head, however, had little faith in King's film: "I always opposed the entire idea of extended location trips and now certainly realize that I was right."[33]

According to Zanuck, there was nothing unique about the Missouri Ozarks. He told King, "There is nothing in the way of scenery or backgrounds that we could not have photographed near here at far less expense and trouble." The studio head ordered the main film company back to Hollywood while Otto Brower, the second unit director, remained behind to do a few final background shots. Zanuck predicted, "At the rate we are going, this picture will never break even, no matter how successful it is, because of the expenditure."[34]

He could not have been more wrong. As one film historian noted, not only did *Jesse James* become "one of Fox's most successful films at

---

[32] *Pineville Democrat*, 29 September 1938, p. 1.

[33] Rudy Behlmer, "Memo from Darryl F. Zanuck: The Golden Years at Twentieth Century-Fox," (New York: Grove Press, 1993), p. 17. Despite Zanuck's status as one of the most influential studio heads of all time, his papers have not survived intact, and can be found scattered throughout various archives.

[34] *Ibid*, p. 17-18.

the time," but Zanuck, convinced by the film's success, went on to become "one of the leading advocates of location shooting all over the world."[35]

The citizens of McDonald County suffered at least one indignity after the film was completed. The *Pineville Democrat* remarked, "The picture *'Jesse James'* is soon to be released and theatre billings are carefully watched by practically the entire population of McDonald County. Especially anxious are the several hundred local extras and their families." The paper continued, "Many feel that the first showing should be at the local [Lyric] theatre at Anderson. Requests have been made by the Chambers of Commerce of both Pineville and Anderson that this be done." A select few of the county's residents attended "McDonald County Day" in Tulsa, Oklahoma, where an advance opening of the film was shown, but it was a luxury that few could afford.[36]

The film first appeared in neighboring Joplin, located over forty miles away, a distance that was too far for many residents to travel.[37] It was reported that 45,000 moviegoers watched the film during its nine day run in Joplin.[38] Curiously, the Ozark press failed to review the film, leaving the local response a mystery. Yet if it was unclear how the regional press and local residents may have interpreted the film, at least one local expressed his opinion as to its effect on the Ozarks.

C. A. Poindexter of the *Pineville Democrat* declared, "Through this moving picture, people all over the world will see our natural attractions and benefits will result for many years to come."[39] Poindexter was half right. Thousands of movie-goers and curious visitors saw the natural beauty of the Ozarks, but after 1938 the crowds faded away, leaving little more than memories. McDonald County was used for second unit scenes in 1941 for the Twentieth Century Fox film *Belle Starr*, but never became the Hollywood of the Ozarks that many had hoped for.

---

[35] *Ibid*, p. 18.

[36] *Pineville Democrat*, 26 January 1939, p. 1.

[37] *Pineville Democrat*, 12 January 1939, p. 2.

[38] *Pineville Democrat*, 9 February 1939, p. 1.

[39] *Pineville Democrat*, 18 August, 1938, p. 2.

The advent of World War Two had much to do with the failure of Hollywood's return to the region. Men, money, and material were thrown into an exhaustive war effort as the country focused on winning in Europe and the Pacific. After the conclusion of the war, Hollywood, not content to make every movie stateside, began filming on location around the world. But there may have been another reason that film studios failed to revisit the Ozarks.

Don Walker, a reporter with the *Joplin Globe* who was hired by Twentieth Century Fox to handle local publicity, later recalled, "the financial unit manager of the company hinted that a return to that section of the Ozarks would be extremely unlikely, despite the fact that the background greenery loomed up spectacularly in Technicolor." The reason, according to Walker, was because there were "a number of threats of lawsuits during the filming, resulting in out-of-court settlements because the film company did not want to face any holdup in production, was mostly responsible for 'killing the goose that laid the golden egg.'"[40]

By mid-October, movie sets were taken down, and workmen arrived to remove the dirt that had covered the pavement surrounding the county courthouse. The editor of the *Benton County (AR) Guide* wryly remarked:

> "Crops not tended;
> The still's run dry,
> Natives want a slice
> Of that Hollywood pie,
> Yet, my country,
> 'Tis of thee,
> But the Ozarks ain't
> What they used to be."[41]

After its brush with Tinseltown, the Ozarks clung to the hope that one day Hollywood would return to its hills and hollers, but all that remained were memories of movie stars and motion picture magic.

[40] Don Walker, "Fun & Games with Jesse James" (Pineville, MO: The McDonald County News-Gazette Printing and Publishing Co., 1976), p. 2.
[41] *Charleston Missouri Democrat*, 9 March, 1939, p. 3.

The Farm Youth's Companion

Douglas Stevens

Death was in the cemetery of strangely named ancestors;
in old farmers with abandoned cancer on their faces where cheek-
  bones angled skin always to sun;
in the family that slept through a flue fire on the first cold night of fall;
in the bloated circle of cows rounding a lightning-struck black oak;
in the ancient, shrunken uncle spitting tobacco juice and blood into a
  rusted coffee can in his wrought-iron bed;
in the little goats poisoned by spring grasses;
in the classmate who fell from a tractor and into his father's machine;
in the hound dreaming in a scent crossing a road;
in the remains of an old woman burning leaves alone in a long dress;
in the bullhead and bluegill minnows gulping at surface air in the last
  muddy puddle spared by drought;
in the blind boy who panicked while swimming and drowned his
  brother with him;
in the framed photographs of farm boys stiff in new uniforms;
in the lamb that could not nurse;
in every Sunday's soundings of vengeance and brimstone;
in young wrens and their mother swallowed into a blacksnake's
  darker night;
in the gutted deer hanging by hushed heels;
in the reclusive widow not missed for more than a month;
in the frantic, defiant cries of coyotes;
in the stillborn calf licked clean by its mother;
in prophecies of whippoorwills;
in the broken farmer hanging from a rafter.

It waited in the cottonmouth lying in the limbs overhanging the
  swimming hole;
in the undercurrents of the flooded stream;
in the falling of a log tree;
in the rock or stob pitched by the bush hog;

in the inviting silence of the thinly frozen pond;
in the rotted floorboards of the high hay loft;
in the nest of red wasps in the corner of the machine shed;
in the spinning whispers of the power shaft;
in the science of stagnant waters;
in the screaming jealous jaws of the mother sow;
in the hunger of the wood saw;
in the cracked rung of a ladder;
in the kick of a horse or mule;
in the hay dust stored for seasons in the lung;
in the proud bull in the pasture;
in the decayed rails of the tree house;
in the depths of the hand-dug well;
in the avalanche of hay bales;
in the poisoned rust of a nail;
in the airy and comforting whirl of the mill blade;
in the snap of tree limb.

Death was dealt to the bait in the bucket;
to the fish quivering under the blade;
to the pet steer called to slaughter by the rattle of his feed pail;
to the sack of unwanted kittens;
to an old dog led the last time to woods;
to young rabbits and mice in the freshly mown field;
to the possum in the trap;
to the water snake sunning in warm sand;
to the sinewy squirrel stripped of his skin;
to the 'coon in the tree;
to the frog impaled and gesticulating on the gig;
to the quail in their flush of rising;
to the chicken on the block blinking as the hatchet rose across the sun;
to the headless, croaking chickens tossed into tall grasses to bleed
    and settle;
to the gentle, worn-out milk cow sold to market;
to the fattened hog lifting his face to the rifle, smiling.

Casey Strong
An excerpt from *The Lakes of Southern Hollow: A Novel*

Steve Yates

Casey Strong steps to the mic and sweeps the neck of her bass at her two pals, Tyndall and Devon, drawing a heart around them. Casey has her mother's sandy, straight hair, piles of it, and she's neglected it, so it's looking like a golden retriever's fur, brassy, dry and rowdy. She has a round face, freckles that Tyndall can see even in the stage lighting. And she's tiny, shortest in their class and often mistaken for a grade school kid. For Tyndall, Casey Strong affirms that God made us all strangely and wonderfully—because there is nothing exceptional about Casey until she opens her mouth and sings. Once that happens, everyone agrees she's bound for something way bigger than Southern Hollow, way bigger than Springfield. Could be Casey, the next Ozark Mountain Daredevil-sized smash hit; or could be Casey, engineer of some legendary train wreck.

At their table right up front, Tyndall grips Devon as though he is the one about to escape the L5 of the Ozarks. She wants his solid arm pressed deeply into her chest. His denim shirt releases warm grease against her fingers. Casey, Tyndall, and Devon, all Southern Hollow kids, Glendale High School brats, have torn each other's hair and lied about each other's wounds since kindergarten. It's a Thursday night in September, their senior year. Anything, the worst or the best, seems possible. And Casey's band, The New Wave Vultures, packs the Cedar Shake, a teen club above a law firm right on the square.

Casey winks at some pierced chub dressed in black who's lowering the mic for her. The New Wave Vultures play no originals so far, only rearranged oldies—Squeeze, The Jam, Echo and the Bunnymen. Some of it is older even than their parent's music, yeah, but Casey, she changes everything. They launch into this Go-Gos song with synthesizers and drums. The rush comes the instant Casey starts her hook on the bass. Then she vaults the lyrics while still playing, really driving the whole train. It's girl power dialed to eleven seeing her perform this. That voice, its volume and depth, is better than the original. Devon swoons. Tyndall may as well be made of vape smoke. Here Tyndall is the one taking all the risks. She's the one who downed three Quietarol because it's the only pill she's ever found that allows her to tolerate all this commotion.

The New Wave Vultures have the Cedar Shake grooving. Tyndall leans into Devon. "Dance with me," she insists. "Right now." He doesn't budge.

"Wait," he shouts over the music. She jerks his hand so hard there's a pop. He glares at her. "After this next part. Okay?"

At the bridge, the stage lights drop to a circle around Casey, and her voice reaches way up, pleading. Even Tyndall feels hushed and consoled as if Casey really were some guardian angel. The groove resumes, and Devon surges to the dance floor but loses her hand. In a pause between songs, Tyndall swings his hand in hers. Then something moves in the crowd, such a stir that Devon tenses. Tyndall drops out of the moment and into emergency-room mode. How many times has she imagined this tension and then the gunfire erupting like Aurora or Parkland?

Patrick Turin strides from the back, and he's dressed like some cowboy vampire. He's applauding, eyes glazed.

Tyndall grabs Devon's face and dares to get eye to eye with him. "Don't you fight him. No one wins fighting Patrick Turin."

Casey and The New Wave Vultures, huddle around the drummer. The guitar player casts a vicious side-eye at Patrick Turin, once a bandmate. Turin is still applauding, but slowly. A wake opens around him.

"Why does he clap so slowly?" Tyndall asks loud enough for others to hear.

Devon brushes her ear with his lips and she swerves away. He holds up a finger, their signal for her to focus on what is said next. "He's an asshole," Devon says.

"Heaven," Casey announces, sticking her tongue out at Turin, who used to sing this song. She puts down the bass and straps on her Martin acoustic. She says into the mic: "We're gonna slow this down. So saddle up! It's a country song!"

What comes out of her next, someone should be recording this on something way better than a cellphone. It is hard to imagine. The whole place stills, and Casey is no longer any girl they ever knew. She's no longer the girl who jeered with them at numbing safety drills, who slept on Devon's shoulder in biology, who taught Tyndall piano scales. Even Turin is spellbound. If anyone is dancing, it's close, slow dancing, and it's only the truest of loves.

Tyndall mashes her forehead against Devon's collarbone, adrenaline flushing from her in a cold chill. She can't meltdown, not here, not now. No one is going to get shot. Breathe. No rain of automatic rifle fire. Breathe. The world will not end here tonight at the Cedar Shake. No death-plea video on the HexTerra app. Breathe. No one is going to die. She holds her finger up to Devon, and he's looking right at her. He is the best neurotypical she will ever meet, so adept, so adaptable. She whirls and wrenches his arms around her. "Dance," she commands. "Listen to Casey. Hold me way tighter."

Backstage after the Thursday show, Patrick Turin enters their narrow dressing room. Most of the equipment is up, and The New Wave Vultures are waiting on the manager of the Cedar Shake to come lie about the take at the door. A yeasty smell from the brewery in the adjoining building makes the dingy dressing room even closer and grosser. Who knows what this room used to be? In part of it, even Casey has to duck. There's hardly any privacy to the dressing space, which is back behind low pipes and amounts to just a ragged crimson and gold stage curtain hung on a folding partition.

Patrick Turin fingers Casey's Martin on its stand. Dwayne and Mitch step up to him and cross their arms on their chests. His first band, Three Bags Full, used Mitch on drums and Dwayne on guitar. The night after Three Bags Full headlined at a hipster brew pub downtown, Patrick Turin decked his father and ran away from home. That winter he turned up in Nashville, cut a solo album on vinyl, and was featured mainstage at the Telluride Festival. In a YouTube video, just him banging a strange acoustic guitar like from a Django Reinhart photograph, he sings his song about Sofia, Bulgaria, and a castle, and vampire rag dolls raining down from mountain clouds. Sixteen million views and counting. Mitch edges forward.

"As fucking if," Turin says. One of his teeth is gray.

"Who let you back here?" Mitch is way too small for this. He's a Cataldo, from the Northside, but he hunches, and looks like a squirt from Jersey Boys with his black hair, pale skin, brown eyes, and his cardigans.

Patrick Turin is looking only at Casey, who is chewing her thumbnail and returning his stare. This curly red hair of his, and his height and ginger skin—he looks more Irish than Italian. Why are the most handsome people sometimes the most reckless? But then to Casey it has never seemed fair how looks are doled out. Think of Tyndall, who has a gorgeous, strong body, perfect breasts, biceps and shit, and hair like honey, amazing when she washes and dries it. But she always looks like some kid from a church bus crash who's been found in the woods after a week, dazed, exhausted, no makeup. Jesus already burns her for a sunbeam.

"What do you want?" Casey asks, and spits skin on the slat floor.

"You," Turin answers.

"We're a band," Casey says. "And you're not in it." And talent. It's not fair how that's granted either. Dwayne told her that as soon as Patrick Turin figured out how to play guitar right handed, the thug taught himself how to play left handed to "challenge himself." And he did so while pedaling a bike around Jefferson Street in traffic. "You should leave."

"Your voice deserves a lot more than old cover songs."

"That's the longest complete sentence you've ever drooled," Mitch says. Dwayne drops his hands to his sides and stands like a hockey player ready to go.

Patrick Turin pays them no mind. "I write songs. Full of sorrow and waste and wind in abandoned places."

"Deep. Real deep," Mitch sneers.

"You'll never make it out of Springfield with these choades."

Maybe she shouldn't say this. But when your dad is a cop, and is murdered by tweakers, and you're thirteen, you've been thrown a grief hammer. Wield it and live, or get smashed. "Patrick Turin, you haven't seen sorrow until you seen a police widow dunk her head in the trough of a coffin and come up drenched." That usually shuts everyone right up.

"There's exactly why I want you. Authentic loss. My songs need your voice. Ditch these turds. You'll never make it coming out of Springfield with them."

Casey stops for a moment, and the narrow dressing room tilts, as if she's trapped in a chute going down. Recovering she looks at Dwayne, then nudges her chin at the door.

"Okay, Hot Shot." Dwayne bumps Turin's chest. Mitch takes up his wing. "Out."

Smiling, Patrick Turin backs away watching Casey until he reaches the door. Once he's gone, Dwayne shakes, and Mitch paces.

"I hate that guy," Mitch says, throwing his hands in the air. His neck and cheeks go red in bolts. "I wish I were fricking ten feet tall and three hundred pounds!"

Casey lets him fume as she strokes Dwayne's arm. "Settle down and write a song about it, Mitch. You did great. He's gone, right?"

There's a knock and the manager of the Cedar Shake comes in, cash in his hand. "Holy Hell! That was Patrick Turin, right? Y'all know him? Is he playing anywhere?"

Patrick Turin stays in a building that confuses Casey. Three stories tall and across from St. Agnes, the Catholic church downtown, it's called The Wiltmore. All brick, and tucked in across Jefferson. How could there be apartments here for anybody but priests or nuns? She pauses and watches the sidewalk and buildings. Behind her, the small cathedral glows like a new box cake. Is this right? Is this what she should do? She prayed about this, but whenever she prays she feels fake. Tyndall is so sure about the Lord, God may as well be an app on her phone. This is just jamming with someone to see what they've got and what I can learn. It doesn't mean anything.

She sees a blind raise up in a third story window, and a shadow. That's him. Casey lifts her guitar case, heavier with the Glock 43 in it. She's a fallen policeman's daughter, and at Midwest Tactical or Papaw's Gun Carnival, they never charge her for range time.

At the Wiltmore, in an arched entryway, there's a brass panel with black buttons, white numbers, and an intercom's speaker, as if this were an apartment building in some giant city. She pushes the button for 3D, and there's a hiss from the intercom, but no answer or greeting. Should she have announced herself? There's a thump and buzz at the door latch. When she pulls, the door opens. An anaesthetizing, natural C echoes inside the building.

A recorder song from childhood toots in her head. B# ¾ time.
Go to sleep before you see monsters.
Go to sleep before monsters see you.

Those lyrics terrified her, such an awful confirmation for a nine-year-old whose father fought real monsters. "Broke fingering!" Just a glimpse of her father's teasing face flashes in her memory. He refused to say Baroque, but he would skip any program on television, even a Blues game, to hear her play or sing. If she ever loses the ability to recall his face—the thought takes her breath away.

She tops the third flight of stairs, and the door to 3D opens with no light behind it.

"Close it behind you." Turin's voice.

"Lights on, Creep."

After a long pause, a light flicks on. Patrick Turin sits in a grand antique chair with its ornate wooden hood sheltering him, a chair like something from a Bollywood movie.

She shuts the door.

The apartment seems larger than the family room and kitchen at home combined, and the furniture all looks really old.

"Ever listen to Joni Mitchell?" His voice has a texture like shark-skin that makes you want its touch again.

"The paradise parking lot lady?"

With a remote he raises the lighting above a hulking dining room table. On it a laptop glows, and the gold, green, and red-topped bars of SoundBlaze dance like flames in a familiar fireplace on the computer screen. Headphones, mics, and cables coil at the ready.

He rises and begins drawing out and connecting patch cords and headphones. He's wearing a teal coat with tails, a bright yellow peasant shirt, tight black denim jeans and a pair of calf-length gray boots with fur bands at the top bound by a lattice of fluorescent laces.

"What are you trying to be?" She asks. "You look like someone from *Harry Potter* who got banished to Westworld."

"We are all trying to be. And yet we never become." He extends a mirror to her with lines of chunky blue-white powder. "Adderall?"

She shakes her head and tries not to make a face.

He leans over the mirror and pops a straw to one of the lines and vacuums it up his nose in one sharp snort. Wincing, he pushes the mirror away with great care. Then he places headphones on his ears and holds a pair out to her. They hang there rocking on his fingertips and make her think of handcuffs.

She lowers the guitar case to the floor and rubs the sweat off her palms onto her jeans. He could be smiling at her discomfort, but instead he's all slack-jawed and vacant. His eyes don't seem ever to blink. She approaches and tilts her head to him and lets him place the headphones over her ears. She's relieved how careful he is not to touch any part of her, and how his eyes stay on the headset and do not wander down her shirt.

He clicks the laptop and spins a finger over the mousepad and taps it. Then he watches her with his fingertips at his lips as if he is about to pray.

She rolls her eyes but stops. The woman on the headset sings about a child and a carousel, and she lifts round notes with an open clarity Casey has only heard in her dreams.

When the song finishes, they both remove their headsets. He shakes his head to get his hair from behind his ears. "At the Cedar Shake, I heard a vision. Your voice, like Joni's, but on my songs."

He drives a strange old sedan with a lion on the front and lots of leather inside. He calls the car "le Grande Routierre." He has to fold the back seat forward. Her bass and its case won't fit in the trunk. So now thieves can look in the windows and see choice musical gear.

"Don't sweat it," he says. "We're back in Southern Hollow. Nothing ever happens."

She checks the locks, which have to be pushed down by hand. "If these get stolen out of your Great Router, Buddy, I can have cops up in your business till Christmas."

He slings a backpack over his shoulder. "Whenever you think you need to be tough, you drag that casket out."

She hits him with a closed fist swinging as hard as she can at his stomach. But he sees it coming. He bends before she strikes, and his abdomen gives no more than hardened wax. Instantly he's got her wrist, but he's grinning.

She struggles.

"If you're gonna hit me, get something in your hands to hit me with."

She lets out a frustrated grunt. Working with him for two months has been a roller coaster. And here he insisted they lose valuable practice time and get to this party. "Is everything a lesson with you?" She jerks her wrist free.

"Let's go in here and have some fun and learn some shit. Cool?"

The party is at one of the biggest houses on Second Lake, dark, hulking in front with an aurora of orange light in the back. Casey recalls this is Andy Stone's house. Andy—several years ahead of her—took so many mushrooms and so much acid he suffered an aneurism or seizure or something (Tyndall would know). Now he lives permanently upstairs, unable to work and with a water bubble on his brain that could kill him any minute. Mindy Stone is a junior, so this must be Mindy's party. So Casey's walking into Andy Stone's house with Patrick Turin, the bridge troll of Southern Hollow. Maybe this isn't her ideal trajectory?

Turin leads them straight through the front door, through the house buzzing with Glendale kids and some she doesn't recognize—maybe from Parkview or Kickapoo. Out the back door, a patio glows from gaslight Tiki torches and a flickering gas fire pit with freaky blue crystals and dancing orange flames. All around the pit are lounging, hoodied kids in Adirondack chairs, each with a cellphone resting on one arm of the chair. One of the cellphones is playing a song so tinny she can't recognize it. Then just as that song quits, another kid in the circle holds a cell up and a new song starts. The sound is abysmal, like listening to a cricket trapped in a coffee can.

"There are speakers wired up out here," Casey whispers to Patrick. She has to stand on tiptoe, until he bends to her. A few of the kids around the fire pit give the two of them a look with raised eyebrows, a few wide eyes. She sticks her chin at one of the mounted outdoor speakers above them. "Those could rock the whole neighborhood."

Turin nods slowly. He's not watching the circle. He's watching her.

Someone in the circle blurts out a song title and the name of a band.

"Nope," says the kid whose cellphone is creaking out the noise. The one who guessed wrong rises and pulls the hood to his sweatshirt tight. He stalks off. A chic, also in a hoodie, takes his place.

Mindy Stone slinks up to Patrick Turin, and in her black dress, she's like an exotic python. She's adopted—mostly the Stones are pale white people—but Mindy is short for some unpronounceable Hindi name. Her flawless skin is a dark shade like walnut heartwood, but in the orange gaslight, her flesh seems dusty and shale gray. She removes a burning joint from her lips and places it on Patrick's. Then she coils more securely around him, her jet black hair flashing with orange highlights from the torches. Someone in the circle guesses a song correctly—there's applause, and the kid whose cell is squeaking silences it and leaves.

Mindy's lips part. Patrick exhales and she inhales, his smoke rolling up into her nostrils. In the firelight, they're like two dragons in a ritual. With Mindy wound around him and their exchange seeming so practiced, so natural, Casey finds herself turned on and at the same time disturbed and, to her surprise, jealous, possessively, even protectively jealous. Where's this coming from? She's played a couple months and written just one song with him and was mad as Hell at him minutes ago.

Mindy's voice is tight to retain the toxin from the pot down in her lungs. "The object is to remain in the circle. Continually introduce songs so new, they thrill and mystify." She has the joint now, and its coal flares orange against her face. Curling her bottom lip, striking in its deep brown which abruptly changes to a glistening pink, she pours out smoke, and Patrick vacuums this up his big nose.

"But the sound quality," Casey says. "It's so rotten."

Mindy uncoils herself from Patrick, then strokes Casey's left ear lobe. Mindy smiles. She has lovely but tiny teeth, and it's like she's inhaling Casey now. "Your talent. It can exile you from simple joys." Her Ls are delicious—Casey would love to hear Mindy pronounce a long sentence of nothing but L words. Since her eyes are so black, it's hard to tell how high Mindy really is. A girl Casey recognizes from gym class darts up and whispers in Mindy's ear. Mindy excuses herself, and they hurry off, leaving Patrick with the joint. He hands the roach to one of the hoodied kids in the circle.

He leans down to whisper. "Have some fun. Observe. I wanted you to see this game more than anything." He sticks his chin at the circle, where applause rises again. "That's your market. The newest sensation is all that matters."

Later she's desperately sleepy in the front seat of his car. Patrick puts the keys in the ignition. A football player, a bruiser named Ralph Samford, raps on the window. He and Patrick step well away from the Peugeot. Soon they are arguing. She can't see them through the cedar shrubs. But they're getting pretty heated.

Behind her, his backpack rests on top of the case to her Martin. She struggles, shoving the backpack aside, and manages to unsnap and part the guitar case and fetch the cloth sack. She pulls it open and draws out the Glock and its magazine. Glancing over her shoulder, she can still hear Ralph and Patrick fussing. Ralph thinks Turin has pain killers, but Ralph doesn't have money. She loads the clip into the Glock, and it responds with that reassuring Austrian click. She rests the pistol on the leather console. She turns to settle his pack and the Martin case, but there's the zipper on the backpack flashing in the streetlight. No lock. She glances over her shoulder—the argument is still going on behind the cedars. She tugs the zipper open.

In the salmon stripe of the streetlight, she sees rubber-banded rolls of twenties, tens, and fives, and a whole pharmacy of pill bottles and a box of snack-sized Ziploc baggies.

The argument is all Ralph now, and it's getting closer. Casey just gets the zipper shut and whirls around in the passenger seat. The dome light flashes, Patrick jumps in, but Ralph snags the top of the driver's side door. His big yelling face is in the cab. He shuts his yap when he sees Casey running a fingernail along the muzzle of the Glock.

"Ralphy, I'm so tired. I really want to go home and sleep, okay?"

"Sure," Ralph says. His beery breath floods the car. He raises his meaty hand from the doorframe. "Sure," he repeats, and backs away.

Patrick closes the door. He glances at the Glock and her, then grins as he starts the car. They roll away and head toward Third Lake and Lone Pine Road.

She lifts the pistol and points it between her knees then pushes the safety back on.

"That was great," Patrick says.

"So why does Ralph Samford think you have Mallies?"

Turin is quiet for a minute. They turn on Southern Hollow Boulevard and cruise down the big hill to the pool. Casey used to urge any parent driving her to rush down this hill and up the rise to the railroad tracks. The train tracks could launch even big Chevy Suburbans, all four wheels airborne, and as kids they would all scream with delight. Patrick takes the tracks at a crawl, as if he's driving a fiberglass Corvette.

"Music never pays."

At least he isn't a liar. "So this party wasn't at all about 'the music' or that game? This was a stinking sales call."

"Everything is more than one thing. See. You've learned a lot tonight."

He passes his parents' house at the corner of Southern Hollow Boulevard and Meadowview Drive without even a glance.

"You know how my Dad died."

"I don't sell meth. That's Dollar Store trash."

They turn onto La Monta, and he stops in her driveway. Mom flicks on the outside lights to the stairs, and then to Casey's bedroom— her sign that she's still awake and she knows how late Casey is.

"There's no 70/30 to this," he says. "Apartments, studios, guitars, what do you think is paying for all of this? I don't have some cop trust fund."

"Asshole! Open the trunk."

"Gonna search it?"

"My guitars are in it, Dip Shit."

He pops the trunk, opens the back door and shoulders his backpack. At the back of the car she lifts her cases, quietly, one by one. She's not going to be the emotional girl who slams stuff around and cries. He's beside her, and reaches to take the bass from her. She pulls it away. "What studios?"

"We'll be in one in the next two weeks or the week after." He reaches for her bass again, and this time she lets him carry it up the steps to the front door.

She's never been in a studio with any of her bands—just home studio stuff on Fostex and Marantz equipment and the arcane but wondrous reel-to-reel in the Cataldos' basement.

He sets her bass down on the stoop. "What we're doing, how we can sound, how different we can be from anything happening now . . . it's all worth it to me." He crams his hands down in the pockets of his Kiton jeans. You'd have to push a lot of pills to afford a pair like that. "What's it worth to you?"

The sound of their voices together singing—it's like a honeyed light on cracked leather. "I have a rule. No big decisions after midnight."

The look in his eyes is sad, but for the first time, she could convince herself that he cares. It's the look you give a seabird covered in oil. "Casey, all the big decisions in the music grind are made by warlocks and demons after midnight."

"Oh, fuck off with your vampire wisdom shit. Know it all."

"Is the music worth it to you?"

"You'll know if you hear me at your door." She gets her phone out only when he shuts his car door, and she doesn't disarm the security system until she sees the Peugeot's tail lights trickle away then vanish on Eureka.

The studio is way north on National Avenue past Silver Springs Park. In the streetlights, the building looks like a laundromat—one long rectangle of cinderblocks with a red roof and hardly any parking. It's small inside, just a black leather couch, a battered coffee table, a huge mixing and control board and monitor. A fit, older guy with close-shaved hair rises from a chair and hugs Patrick. His name is Jeff, and he's the owner and sound engineer. He bends to shake her hand and says he's eager to hear what she can do.

The mixing board and monitor almost block three floor-to-ceiling panes of glass. Beyond the glass are a drum set, a Baldwin upright piano, a KORG synthesizer, music stands and mics on stands and a few mics on adjustable booms suspended from the ceiling, and even some Fender amps, the reissue tube amps with taupe casing and silver lettering. Patch cords wait coiled on a tree of hooks. Casey tries to see this as a musical romper room for gifted children, but her heart is pounding. Everything is super clean and organized. The glowing monitor is SpaceX high tech, and it all looks like it's going to cost them piles of money. At home with SoundBlaze on her laptop she can goof around and make a weekend of mistakes and spend nothing but time. Not here.

Patrick and Jeff geek out about the gold velvet paneling in the adjacent sound room to the left of the control board and monitor. The sound room is thick carpeted and about as big as a walk-in closet. Sparkling gold acoustic foam with sharp ridges walls the room. There's not a speck of dust on any of the neatly packed blocks. On its black foam ceiling glow white starbursts of LED lights in black cans— Jeff pulls one down, bragging about them being his own design. He switches it on and off, then pops the black can back in the ceiling tiles in a new position.

Casey folds her thumbs against her palms and squeezes with her fingers until her thumbs ache. Is the clock ticking, is the meter running? When does this start costing them? But she can't bring herself to ask because Patrick and Jeff seem like boys with toys, and she does not want to show them how new this all is to her. She feels like a tiny child invited because she is so doll-like into the cockpit to meet the pilots.

Dominating the sound room is an enormous tube mic and the black circle of its pop screen attached with a curvy stalk. The mic, a big, gold canister, is mounted on a fearsome tripod of shining metal with wheels in its base. The tripod supports and extends the canister of the tube mic on a neck-like derrick that bows and swivels and rocks as Jeff demonstrates in slow, careful motions, one hand cradling and easing the sensitive mic. It's like the skeleton of a small, crouching dragon. The mic canister with one black eye socket is its golden skull surrounded by the gilled bones of a silver shock mount.

Patrick is quiet now, watching her, and she feels even more the amateur. He interrupts Jeff. "Hey, let's get your Martin out, Casey, and go in by the piano and warm up."

"Great idea!" Jeff says. He smiles a lot, which helps, but he's like someone who has had too much coffee, bouncy and too happy this late on a Sunday night. "Boots off!"

They enter the playroom, and when Jeff seals the glass door behind them it makes a kissing sound. The air pressure shifts in her ears. Patrick pulls out the piano bench, and sets down his leather binder of typed up lyrics. He swings one of the ceiling mounted mics in front of Casey, and hands her a headset. "So you can get used to hearing yourself and Jeff and me. He can take your volume up or down. He can do anything we need."

Walls of more sound foam bricks make cozy this part of the studio, and the piano and drum kit and music and mic stands are close, but not cluttered. From this side, those glass panes look out on Jeff's blue-lighted face floating above the mixing board. Beneath his console is a thicket of gray and black wires, backlit in blue, red, amber, and green.

"Anything tracking?" Jeff's voice comes over the headset super clarified, but his words feel separate from his floating face, as if they are delayed.

"Track this one," Patrick says, tapping the mic in front of Casey. "Just so you can get an idea of what we're working with."

The blue floating face nods. When Jeff sits down, he's just blue forehead, eyebrows, and eyeballs.

Patrick fetches lyric sheets from his leather binder and dithers till he finds what he wants. "Let's do that God, You're So Great thing you just taught me."

"'How Great Thou Art?'" Wouldn't Tyndall be thrilled? Casey taught this to Tyndall on piano after they heard it in church, and they played and sang it a lot as children. Then Casey taught it to Patrick because the song stretches your voice from pianissimo to fortissimo in less than eight bars. She watches him steadying the lyric sheets, home-made, with chord changes and tone and timbre notations: RISE—Am7, SOBER—F, JOY—C, BIG—G. He typed up something she taught him, and by choosing it now he's building her a calm space and bringing the familiar into this. A drug dealer, a thug, but his posture at the piano is super and his fingers are beautiful.

They start in softly and thoughtfully, and he's singing a baritone murmur that opens the front and center for her. Just before the chorus, she thinks of Tyndall praying, that golden hair falling forward and that smooth skin tightening along her neck. Casey closes her eyes and lets go, all out even backing away from the mic a bit. The headset is so crisp and clear, and she feels a fist full of redeeming light rising up from the bottom of her lungs, up through her throat and into the night.

They finish, and Patrick turns to look out at Jeff whose eyes are wide and eyebrows are raised. The instant they ended the song, with her eyes closed, Casey felt great. But now, trembling, she kneels and lowers the Martin to its case, while over the speakers Jeff goes on and on about some British missionary in the Ukraine and a German poem thing sung by repenting Russians. Geez! Decaf, Buddy. Even Patrick is bouncing and nodding.

Jeff apologizes and explains that just two hours ago he had six rappers in here, literally fighting, and he almost called the cops, and at lunch, the white Gospel group from Koshkonong wept and prayed over him, and here they were working on the Sabbath, and for breakfast there was a death metal band with a singer who bellowed like Cookie Monster.

As he talks he's leading Casey into the gold velvet closet. She feels like a child being led to a witch's oven. She's put this much together: that glass door will shut and she will be trapped in here with just her voice and this crouching metal dragon waiting to burn her alive if she does it wrong. She rubs her palms along the thighs of her jeans and frets over balancing Patrick's lyric sheets on the stand and where her water bottle should sit.

"It's the Ozarks," Jeff says smiling at her as he holds out a new headset. "Everyone forgets us, and yet we are the nexus. All this great music!"

Patrick, now in the control room, blurts a raspberry—loud as a grinding gearshift in the headset. "Nexus of no escape! Whoever made it out of here alive and beloved? Aside from Porter Wagoner."

"You did, Stupid," she says, her voice booming over the dragon mic.

Patrick scowls and says, "I've a feeling we're not in Aspen anymore, Toto."

She wrinkles her nose at this, and just then something softens in Jeff's face, and his shoulders slump. He's looking at her like her Dad used to, amazed and goofy, and Dad kept his hair buzzed like Jeff's, though Dad's never got the chance to show any gray.

"Hey, this is all going to be okay," Jeff whispers. He's adjusting the dragon's head and its black circle of a pop cover, moving it back from her. "Don't listen to us old guys about anything but the sound."

"Ain't that the fortune in my cookie!"

He shows her where he wants her to stand. "I know you may have seen people kissing the mic in movies and videos." He looks at her again with a smile. "But you have a crazy big set of pipes for someone your size. Like spinto soprano with a mezzo squatting the basement apartment. So . . . ."

"Got it," she says. "Don't smooch the dragon."

Jeff grins and looks over the tube mic and its boom. "It kind of does look like a dragon. He's your friend, though. You're going to love how you sound in him."

She massages her face with her fingertips and then palms. Jeff shuts the door on her and takes his seat at the console. Patrick wheels a chair over next to him. She runs through her tongue twisters but rather than just saying them she sings them in scales—Around the rough and rugged rock the ragged rascal ran. Quid pro quo quoth querulous crow.

"Okay," she says, but she doesn't feel it. "Wait. Can I play guitar while I sing?"

Jeff shakes his head. The mic is there to isolate her vocals. A guitar will clutter the track. He explains that all the instruments she and Patrick recorded at home are going to be in the headphones, and how he can make any instrumental track she needs louder or softer, and how she should just let everything fall away and be in the music. They can make as many takes as she needs.

"Ah, no we cannot," Patrick cuts in.

Jeff sits back and is quiet.

The room is freezing and soundless, like she's in an underwater nightmare looking out at them and their blue faces in the monitor's blast.

Patrick catches her eye. "'Lexus from Texas'," he says over the headset. "A little country, but all you."

She nods. Jeff raises his hand and counts her in as over the headset her Martin chips and rings. Step into it fun and then a big rise after the line about the Lord.

I clipped a Lexus from Texas
Just past the West Memphis Bridge.
The greyhound track was right at my back,
And I asked the Good Lord to give

Me some sense of his new direction,
A purpose between solid lines.
I clipped a Lexus from Texas,
Then sought your shoulder divine.

She feels that fist of light rising in her throat again and pours it all
out, digging her toes into the carpet. This song Patrick has written—
it's all new. It's funny. It's like an old Janis Joplin thing with Porsches
and Mercedes, and God is in it. Patrick says it all came into his writing
because of her. She has a power and a current. At last the song winds
down.

She opens her eyes. Jeff isn't looking at the monitor but at her, his
eyes blank and his mouth open. He glances at Patrick and sticks out
his bare arm.

Patrick brushes the chill bumps, whatever Jeff's deal is. Patrick
says, "I know. Right?"

Jeff turns back to her. "Casey, that was . . . I . . ." He swivels in his
chair and looks again at Patrick. "You hear anything we need to . . . ?"

Patrick shakes his head. "Sing, 'Spokane', please, Casey."

"Listen. Wait," Jeff says, waving his hands above his head. "If she
can deliver like that, you two need to bring all the instruments in here
and get the level and the mix the same. None of this homemade muddy-
buzz. I can only push and blur a rotten input so far, okay. If she can do
that? Patrick. Jesus!"

He and Patrick get into such a row that she pulls her headset off.
There's no crowd, no dancing, no happy recognition from listeners
hearing the first chords of a song they love. The carpet beneath her
toes gives like a sponge. Even though she can see Jeff and Patrick
through the glass door arguing she feels trapped and sinking. There's
a clock somewhere that's costing them money. She is costing them

money, and she could and maybe she just did do it all wrong. Where is this dream-come-true thing?

Jeff is red in the face, and he's pointing to his ears. She puts the headset back on. "I just want to say this to you." He stops for a long while. Patrick is hunched and equally red. "I've had a lot of talent in here. But I've never felt that. Nothing like what you just did. You two don't need to cheap out with half-at-home recording. That's not fair to what you are." He turns to Patrick. "That's not fair to what she can do."

Patrick keeps his arms crossed and his head down.

Her heart is going to fly out of her chest. More frightening than failure is that she cares what Patrick thinks of her now. When did that start? Why can't they record it all here if Jeff says that's better? She glances at the dragon crouching and waiting, and wishes she could throw a fit like Tyndall. "Can I at least hear it back?" she asks. "Just once." She puts her palm to the icy glass door. "I don't even know what I just did."

"Bank on the Old Blood Every Time": Native Inferiority in *The Shepherd of the Hills*

Phillip Howerton

Harold Bell Wright's *The Shepherd of the Hills*, although published more than 100 years ago, remains the most popular and influential novel set in the Ozarks. The novel was a record-setting bestseller, selling more than two million copies in the ten years following its release in 1907 (Blevins 61), and it was largely responsible for the commercial development of Missouri's White River Valley (Morrow and Myers-McPhinney). Readers generally agree that the novel, through its central characters, depicts the Ozark people in a positive manner, but many readers overlook how the novel reinforces the hegemonic depictions of the Ozarks people as inferior as it identifies two distinct groups of hill people: those who identify themselves as having a history and bloodline from outside the Ozarks and those who appear to be native Ozarkers without an outsider identity. After placing his characters into these two groups, Wright demonstrates that the characters who are native Ozarkers are intellectually and morally inferior to those with a heritage outside the region and prompts these native characters to be defeated or annihilated.

Wright, a pastor forced from the pulpit by poor health, was determined to carry on his ministry through writing, and his sermon of love and forgiveness is obvious in *The Shepherd of the Hills*. The protagonist, who has assumed the alias of Daniel Howitt, comes to the Ozark hills of Taney County, Missouri, to escape the degenerative effects of city life in Chicago and to regain his physical and moral health. On the evening of his arrival, he is forced by darkness to spend the night with Grant and Mollie Matthews, who immediately trust him and hire him to oversee their sheep herd. Years earlier, Mr. Howitt had coerced his son, an artist visiting the Ozarks hills, to end a love affair with a local mountain girl. Soon after his arrival, Mr. Howitt learns that the Matthews' daughter, who died of a broken heart, was the young woman whom his son had loved. In his former life, Mr. Howitt had served as the pastor of one of the largest churches in America, and he soon becomes the spiritual leader in his adopted hill community. In this new role, Mr. Howitt convinces the leading lady, Sammy Lane, a mountain girl of high character, to remain in the hills and not to marry Ollie Stewart, a local boy who has sought his fortune in the city. He also guides the central hero, Young Matt, to become a moral and self-controlled man. Perhaps most importantly, this shepherd reveals his true identity to the Matthews family, forgiving himself and leading them to forgive both him and his son.

In this admittedly melodramatic and didactic novel, Wright seems to depict the Ozark people as heroic and moral. Historians Lynn Morrow and Linda Myers-Phinney point out in *Shepherd of the Hills Country* that readers so admired the central characters of the book that shortly after it was published "tourists started coming to explore the book's setting" hoping "to see Old Matt and Young Matt, Uncle Ike, Sammy Lane, and other characters" (31, 32). Such admiration is well grounded. Mr. Matthews (Old Matt) is described as being "fully six feet four inches in height, with big bones, broad shoulders, and mighty muscles" and "no one had ever successfully contested his place as the strongest man in the hills" (24). In addition to being a physical giant, Old Matt is also a moral giant, for he has resisted the allure of becoming a vigilante, works hard to earn a living for his family, and is willing to forgive those he believed responsible for the death of his only daughter. Likewise, Old Matt's wife, Mollie, is described as a "sturdy figure" with a "patient, kindly face, across which time had plowed many a furrow, in which to plant the seeds of character and worth" (39-40).

Even more idealistic are Wright's portraits of the younger generation of Ozarkers, Young Matt and Sammy Lane. Wright describes Young Matt as being "made of the same metal and cast in the same mold as the father; a mighty frame, softened yet by young manhood's grace; powerful neck and well-poised head with wavy-red-brown hair; and blue eyes that had in them the calm of summer skies or the glint of battle steel" (24). Wright goes on to comment on the character of this young mountain lad, noting that Young Matt's "countenance [was] fearless and frank, but gentle and kind, and the eyes were honest eyes" (24). Near the end of the novel, Young Matt and Sammy Lane marry and begin raising children, and Wright, in his opening pages, points out that Sammy is equal to Young Matt in physical attractiveness and character:

> she was tall; beautifully tall, with the trimness of a young pine, deep bosomed, with limbs full-rounded, fairly tingling with the life and strength of perfect womanhood; and it may be said that her face was a face to go with one through the years, and to live still in one's dreams when the sap of life is gone, and, withered and old, one sits shaking before the fire; a generous, loving mouth, red-lipped, full-arched, with corners tucked in and perfect teeth between; a womanly chin and nose, with character enough to save them from being pretty; hair dark, showing a touch of gold with umber in the shadows; a brow, full broad, set over brown eyes that had never been taught to hide behind their fringed veils, but looked always square out at you with a healthy look of good comradeship, a gleam of mirth, or a sudden, wide, questioning gaze that revealed depth of soul within. (26)

These four hill people are perhaps summed up best by Dr. Coughlan, a visitor from the city who comes to the Ozarks to find his friend, Mr. Howitt: "Old man is a gentleman, a gentleman, sir, if God ever made one. His boy's like him. The mother, she's a real mother; made to be a mother; couldn't help it. And that young woman, with the boy's name, bless my soul, I never saw such a creature before, Daniel, never!" (259).

Although Wright heaps praise upon his hill protagonists, he repeatedly reminds readers that the admirable and heroic among his characters, the Matthews and the Lanes, are not native-born Ozarkers and that they are, in fact, transplants who are extremely self-aware and proud of their outsider heritage. For example, Wright is cautious to establish the non-native bloodline of these families. In his introductory chapter, Wright points out that Jim Lane came "from nobody knows where" and that "[t]hen came the giant Grant Matthews with Aunt Mollie and their little family" (15). Wright reminds readers of the Grants' status as outsiders several times; for example, during his first conversation with Aunt Mollie, the shepherd asks her if she ever considered returning to her old home (40), and when Old Matt tells the shepherd the story of the love affair and death of his daughter, Old Matt prefaces the story by stating, "Our folks all live back in Illinois.

And if I do say so, they are as good stock as you'll find anywhere" (51). Sammy Lane points out to her father that the Matthews have "got kin back in Illinois" (72), and the narrator observes, "The Matthews family were different in many ways from those born and raised in the hills" (59).

Wright also demonstrates that Jim Lane and his daughter, Sammy, are outsiders with a bloodline superior to the hill natives. Jim is introduced as "a tall man, well set up, with something in his face and bearing that told of good breeding; southern blood, one would say" (68). When Sammy questions her father about their family, he assures her that she has "got as good blood as the best of the thoroughbreds" (73). This "good blood" is mentioned each time Sammy makes a heroic decision or performs a heroic action. For example, when she asks the shepherd to provide her a cultural education, he believes she will succeed because he recognizes that she "has a quick mind, and a good heart; and, if I am not mistaken, good blood" (107). When Sammy rejects the advances of Wash Gibbs, her father observes, "She got mighty good blood in her veins, that girl has" (113). When Sammy refuses to marry Ollie Stewart, Jim joyously tells her, "I knowed it, girl. I knowed it. Bank on the old blood every time" (211). After she has made her father promise that he will quit riding with Wash Gibbs and the other outlaws, Jim tells his daughter, "I'm glad you're like the old folks" (226). Wright, in fact, is so intent on clarifying to readers that the Lanes are not native Ozark hill folk that he devotes an entire chapter, "Sammy Lane's Folks," to explaining where her "old blood" came from and how she is a representative of that heritage.

In addition to highlighting the outsider pedigrees and the moral and physical superiority of his protagonists, Wright also stresses the inferiority of several of the apparently native-born characters. By not giving Mandy Ford, Ollie Stewart, and Wash Gibbs histories outside of the region, Wright implies these characters are Ozark natives, and, as such, they are depicted as inferior, and each is defeated in some manner. Mandy Ford is Sammy Lane's best friend, and although Mandy is a minor character and is present in only one scene, the contrast between Mandy and the superior Sammy is striking. In this scene Mandy and Sammy are discussing the new arrival, Mr. Howitt. Although the girls have apparently been friends for most of their lives,

Mandy speaks with a much heavier dialect than Sammy. Sammy objects to Mandy's suggestion that Mr. Howitt might be a revenuer by saying, "Revenue! You ought to see him! Revenues don't come in no such clothes as them, and they don't talk like him either" (63). Mandy replies, "'can't tell 'bout revenues' [. . . .] 'Don't you mind how that'n fooled everybody over on th' bend last year? He was jest as common as common, and folks all 'lowed he was just one of 'em" (63). Mandy's dialect becomes even thicker when she is asked by Sammy to define love, and her answer implies her inferiority by simultaneously exhibiting her dialect, her shallow thinking, and her difficulty of talking while thinking: "Hit's a-goin' t' live with somebody an' a-lettin' him take care o' you, 'stead o' your folks.' [. . . .] 'An' hit's a-cookin' an' a-scrubbin' an' a-mendin' fer him, an' — an' — sometimes hit's a-splittin' wood, an' a-doin' chores, too; an' I reckon that's all" (64). Sammy, not satisfied with Mandy's answer, states that it might be all of those things but that it was something more: "Mandy; it's a-doin' all that, without ever once wishin' he was somebody else" (64). The narrator then intercedes to affirm Mandy's ignorance and her inferiority to Sammy by noting, "This was too much for Mandy" (64). The narrator reaffirms Mandy's inferiority again just a few paragraphs later after Sammy notes that Mr. Howitt is not different because his clothing is different but because *he* is different. The narrator observes, "This, too, was beyond Mandy" (65).

Ollie Stewart is also shown to be inferior to the pedigreed Sammy. Ollie and Sammy are childhood friends who promised several years before to marry one another. However, now that that they are young adults and Ollie has evolved into a weakling and is planning to take Sammy to live in the city, Sammy begins to recognize flaws in Ollie's character. When Ollie returns from the city to claim his bride, it is apparent that city life has only augmented Ollie's negative character traits. Ollie, as a representative of the backwoods culture, is used to demonstrate the innate inferiority of these natives. Ollie has always been a weakling, but now, due to his exposure to corruption of city life, he allows his flaws to make him a coward. His weakness and cowardliness are exposed when he refuses to try to protect Sammy when they are attacked by the drunken villain, Wash Gibbs. Young Matt is forced to step in and save both Ollie and Sammy from Wash's antics, and soon after being saved by Young Matt, Sammy tells Ollie, "I know now that I do not love you. I have been slow to find the truth, but I have found it. And this is the one thing that matters, that I found it in time" (216). Ollie realizes then that Sammy cannot be persuaded to marry him, and moments later Sammy "watche[s] him out of sight for the last time" as he follows the trail out of the backwoods to the city (216).

The other central native in the novel, Wash Gibbs, is also shown to be inferior to the bloodline of the Matthews and the Lanes. Although he was once a childhood friend of Sammy's and once had a legitimate hope of being loved by her, Wash, like Ollie, has become corrupted and is rejected by Sammy. In addition to losing Sammy's love, Wash also loses his honor of being the strongest man in the hills when he is defeated in his fight with Young Matt. Wash is the representative unreformed hillbilly who rides a mule, wears a black slouch hat, and always carries a gun, and, after being wounded in a gunfight at Jim Lane's cabin, he dies unseen and alone in the woods. In fact, no one is aware that Wash has been wounded or is dead until buzzards are noticed "flying low through the trees" (247). When the shepherd and Young Matt find Wash, nothing remains except "shreds of clothing," a "weapon lying near," and "the horrid thing, from which [. . .] carrion birds flapped their wings" (247). Here lies the body of the Ozark hillbilly who must be eradicated so that the hills can be made safe for the people of good bloodlines. Wright seems to be suggesting that the native Ozark male, due to an innate character flaw, will, like Ollie Stewart, be incapable of self-improvement when exposed to advancing civilization and will, like Wash Gibbs, be incapable of experiencing self-improvement when living in a frontier.

This novel implies the inferiority of its native characters in numerous other ways, several of which are exhibited in its first chapter, "The Stranger." This chapter contains the first moment of encounter between the outsider protagonist and a regional insider[1], and in this meeting the cultural and intellectual superiority of the protagonist is quickly established by the description of his clothing, body language, facial features, knowledge of the larger world, and speech patterns. It is a "dank and cold" evening shortly before nightfall when Mr. Howitt meets Jed Holland, a local lad returning from the Matthews' mill (17). Mr. Howitt is wearing "carefully tailored clothing," "carrie[s] himself with the unconscious air of one long used to a position of conspicuous power and influence," and has "the face of a scholar and poet" (17). When he speaks to Jed, his speech is so different "from the high keyed, slurring speech of the backwoods" that Jed senses that he is "in the presence of a superior being" (18). If Wright's description of Mr. Howitt's appearance and Jed's recognition of Mr. Howitt's superiority is not enough to convince readers that Jed is an inferior, Jed will soon do so. Jed is described as a stereotypical backwoods simpleton; he has thin legs and long arms (18) and wears a "tattered old hat" (19), voices a thick dialect comparable to that of Mandy Ford, and repeatedly displays his ignorance of the larger world by incessantly being surprised that Mr. Howitt has never "heard tell o'" such locals as Old Matt, Colonel Dewey, and Jim Lane (19).

More than 100 years after its publication, many people still find *The Shepherd of the Hills* to be an entertaining and inspirational novel, as is made evident by the continued popularity of Branson's play version of *The Shepherd of the Hills*, which "has entertained millions of Branson visitors" since the play opened in 1960 (*The Shepherd*), and by the fact that the novel has now sold approximately twenty million copies (Chudleigh). Unfortunately, this novel also serves as an example of the pervasive and hegemonic stereotypes used to define Ozark natives. Indeed, the novel does not merely suggest that the native Ozarkers are inferior; it suggests that they are not capable of moral and intellectual improvement, and it implies, through the disappearance of Mandy after one scene, the banishment of Ollie from the hills, and the mutilation of Wash's corpse in the woods, that the natives will prove incapable of surviving an influx of superior peoples.

Works Cited

Blevins, Brooks. *Arkansas/Arkansaw: How Bear Hunters, Hillbillies, and Good Ol' Boys Defined a State.* Fayetteville, AR: The University of Arkansas Press, 2009.

Chudleigh, Gerry. "The Shepherd of the Hills." Harold Bell Wright. Gerry Chudleigh, 26 May 2011. Web. 07 Jan. 2012.

Morrow, Lynn and Linda Myers-Phinney. *Shepherd of the Hills Country: Tourism Transforms the Ozarks, 1880s-1930s.* Fayetteville: The University of Arkansas Press, 1999.

The Shepherd of the Hills Outdoor Theatre. Home Page. n.d. Web. 08 Jan. 2012.

Wright, Harold Bell. *The Shepherd of the Hills.* Gretna, LA: Pelican, 2002.

Notes
Such moments of encounter are a common feature in the many novels in which an outsider protagonist enters the hills. For other examples, see Sidney Stanton in Grover Clay's *Hester of the Hills: A Romance of the Ozark Mountains* (1907), Boyd Westbrook in Clyde Edwin Tuck's *The Bald-Knobbers: A Novel of the Ozarks* (1910), and Jean Carroll in John Homer Case's *Jean Carroll: A Tale of the Ozark Hills* (1912).

Wampus Conundrum

Mark Spitzer

there's something creepy
about this bobcat bust
I bought in Missouri
for 65 bucks

it's a good size wildcat
head & shoulders & partial chest
stuck on a stick

it's definitely a sloppy job
its nose is missing
its stuffing is lumpy
which gives it a weird
smirky grin

maybe it sees
what's in my head:

> back in Missouri
> I had a student who
> trapped these cats
> to track their range

> I went out in the field with him
> learned about their mass migrations
> stealthing down to Louisiana
> sneaking up to Canada

> which got me thinking
> about their status
> of "Least Concern"
> while still holding out
> after two million years

nabbing rabbits
scoring squirrels

just like those opportunists
who tend to blast
the hell out of them
because they've got guns
and hey
        there's one
        over there!

which is why bobcat cadavers
can be found across the continent
in pawn shops and flea markets

in fact, there are several for sale
at this moment
in Van Buren Arkansas
forever mummified

so now I'm part
of that cycle too:

Shoot, Stuff, Sell, Repeat
Shoot, Stuff, Sell, Repeat . . .

and I'm staring at those tufty ears
and its green glass eyes
are staring back at mine
with the intensity of
        a super live
        super cool
        super alert
        lynxy thing

but beyond that tattered nose
        brisk whiskers
        and spotty

       tawny
          fluff of fur

I know there's nothing
in that shell
but cotton and
Styrofoam

      where there used to be real
        feline fire
           out there in the woods
              licking
              stalking
              rolling in the clover

but those eyes
those uncanny
unblinking eyes
I'm always staring
into those eyes

probably looking
to start a poem
about why I'd engage
in such a scurvy commerce

yep, that's what it's gotta be:
me using a crude
and ludicrous corpse
to activate
an activism.

So okay
now that that's
been established
we can all
move on.

Memories of the Old Cannon Trail:
A Civil War Battle in the Ozarks

Dr. Jim Vandergriff

Delivered at the Missouri Folklore Society Conference
October 11, 2019

One of the things I wonder about fairly often is how I have come to know or believe this and that. So, this article is mostly musings about the source of some of my memories and about how we gather information. But it is also about some Missouri Civil War history that most people probably don't know about. My central assertion is that we don't always know *where* our beliefs and knowledge come from, so the list of ways that knowledge—and folklore—is created and/or transmitted perhaps needs to be expanded. I just call this knowledge source "congealed from thin air." It is information or ideas learned indirectly, perhaps by way of unknown or unrecognized or unremembered sources.

When I was a child between the ages of nine and twelve, our farm in eastern Laclede County, Missouri, had a double fence all along its east side. The fences were roughly twenty feet apart and constructed of barbed wire and woven wire. This was unusual, and thus always something my brothers and I wondered about. I don't know if the double fencing extended beyond our property to the north. It never dawned on me to check. Sadly, the fence is gone now. I wish I'd had the insight 65 years ago to photograph it (though I didn't have a camera in the 1950s). I never knew, and still don't know, to whom the property between the fences belonged. I suspect it was ours, because now that the westernmost fence has been removed, and that piece of land that was between the two fences is now part of what was then our property. The westernmost fence was ours; the easternmost belonged to "Doc Oliver" (Dr. Francis Oliver), a medical doctor in nearby Richland, who owned the next property to the east, as well as the one to the south, of our farms.

About an eighth of a mile north of our house was a wet weather creek and just east of the fence on Doc Oliver's was the remnants of a small, clapboard house. There was a trash midden just a couple of paces to the northwest of the house. My brothers and I would dig in the midden once in a while, but seldom found anything of interest, except that once we found a ceramic dish with a reclining, semi-nude woman on one side of it. It was one of those very Victorian geegaws. Here's a photo of it:

Aside from that dish, all I remember finding in the midden was a few tin cans so rusted we couldn't tell what they had once held.

My brothers and I often played in that area during the three or four years we lived on that farm, though not often on Doc Oliver's side of the fence—except when we wanted to dig in the midden, to swim in his pond, or to hunt frogs at his pond. On our side of the double fence was a steep-banked valley with a little usually dry creek at the bottom. Up the creek bed to the west was a large, flat limestone slab, under which the water source had been—a wet weather spring, of which there were several in the area. Downstream a bit was a stand of ancient hickory trees strung with huge grapevines. My brothers and I had cut a number of the grapevines at ground level so we could swing on them Tarzan-like to the north bank of the stream, some 30 or 40 feet away.

Now, here is the central idea of my article. We believed at the time that somewhere in the vicinity I've just described was a buried Confederate treasure, which included gold and weaponry, so, occasionally, we dug awhile in spots we deemed "likely," such as in natural depressions in the soil, hoping to find swords and muskets, and maybe some gold! Of course, we never had any such luck; we were young, so we couldn't dig very effectively. We moved away in 1954, so I guess the loot is still there, if it ever was.

I have no idea why we believed in this treasure or where or from whom we got the idea that there had been Confederate military activity in the area. Keep in mind that the area I'm talking about was in a fairly dense forest that covered hundreds of acres to the north, east, and west. As I mull it over, I can't imagine who or what our source might have been. I suspect that the idea was "congealed from thin air," that is, learned indirectly, perhaps via unknown or unremembered sources.

The people we knew didn't talk about the Civil War—or any other kind of history—except occasionally to mention that so-and-so's family were Cherokees who had dropped off of the Trail of Tears, the northern branch of which ran just six or so miles south of our farm, pretty much where Interstate 44 now runs, or to mention the German POWs who had been interned at Ft. Leonard Wood during WWII, or to mention that Ed and Sarah, a black couple, who came to town in their buggy once a month or so, had been slaves.

We also knew that our maternal great, great grandfather, a couple of his brothers, and two of our maternal great, great, great grandfathers had fought in General Price's army during the Civil War. The only battle I remember hearing about, though, was the Battle of Helena, Arkansas, where great, great grandfather John Armstrong was wounded while charging a cannon emplacement on Graveyard Hill (he was one of the 687 wounded Confederates in that battle) on the same day Gettysburg was being fought. But, otherwise we didn't hear much about history.

I have no clue where we got our belief about the Confederate activity in our particular area. I learned some 45 or 50 years later that those parallel fences bordered an old Civil War era military road called the Cannon Trail. During that war, a military supply road ran from Linn Creek, Missouri, to the Union fort at Waynesville. Linn Creek was at that time a steamboat port on the Osage River, though that town is now at the bottom of the Lake of the Ozarks. Because of stories about the road during the California Gold Rush, I believe that the Linn Creek Road was there considerably before the war, as was the Cannon Trail, as there had been at least two houses along the Cannon Trail, one just across the double fences to the east, and one some 100 yards to the north and west of it, and a small town, Henrytown, some five or six miles north of our farm.

During the war, just a few miles west-northwest in Camden County where Richland now sits, a road cut off from the Linn Creek Road to the southwest along Murphy Creek, through Monday Hollow, then due south for a few miles, and then meandered to Lebanon. That road—called The Cannon Trail—went along the eastern edge of our farm, crossed Bear Creek about a half mile southwest, and then turned still more southwesterly toward Lebanon. Here's a map of the area:

The red line near the center of the map is the Cannon Trail, in part. The green circle is where our house, which we called the Jennings house, sat. The yellow line is the old Linn Creek Road; and the blue circle is my birthplace. The Trail of Tears ran about where the red line is at the bottom of the image.

The next picture is a Google image of the current tree line by our house.

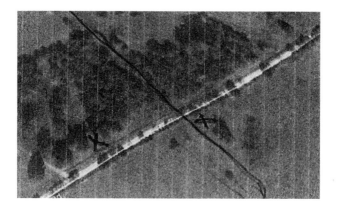

The house sat where you see the red X on the left. The tree line is the red marking to the right. The red X to the right is where the remnants of the old Burhans house sat.

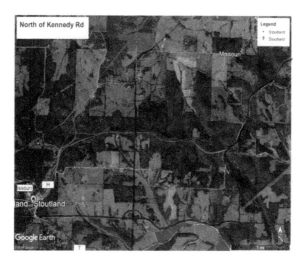

The image above is a map of the area north of our house. The red line follows the tree line where the road used to be. Where the red line curves is where the current Missouri highway H uses an eighth of a mile or so of the Old Cannon Trail. The red half circle and the red X in the center near the bottom show where our house was. The blue line is Kennedy Road as it runs from Stoutland to Richland.

On October 13, 1861, Confederate troops set up an ambush near the intersection of the Cannon Trail and the Linn Creek Road, the first of several battles along the Linn Creek Road during the next few days. Below is a picture of part of the battlefield, taken about 1985:

Union scouts had spotted the ambush prior to the engagement, which put the Rebels at a serious, and costly, disadvantage. The battle was fierce and, according to official reports, cost the Confederates at least 27 dead. (The numbers vary greatly in the reports. One says 66 dead Rebels.) The Confederate dead were buried by the Union Army in a mass grave near a small town then called Henrytown. Here's an image of the grave:

The town no longer exists, though a few foundations remain. The following is a photograph of one of the last remnants of Henrytown:

The map below shows the general vicinity of the town:

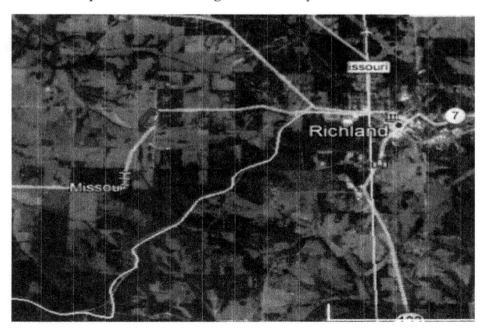

The larger red circle on the upper left is the approximate location of Henrytown; the smaller circle center left is the location of the Henry graveyard.

The remainder of the Rebel troops reportedly retreated along the Cannon Trail toward Lebanon, and thus would have passed within just a few feet of where our house later stood.

In the official reports, the battle was variously called the Battle of Wet Glaize, the Battle of Henrytown, the Battle of Dutch Hollow, the Battle of Monday Hollow, the First Battle of Linn Creek, and the Battle of Shanghai. Though the first five names for the battle reflect local places, I have no idea where "Shanghai" comes from.

I knew nothing about the roads or the fight until sometime in the mid-1980s, though I have since acquired and read all of the surviving official reports about it and visited the site a couple of times. The site is on private property and pretty difficult to get to; one has to walk about a mile through various fields. A mile or so south of the site of Henrytown is an old graveyard called the Henry Graveyard. Below is a photograph of this small cemetery:

I used to ask people why it was called the Henry graveyard, but I gave up asking because nobody I asked had an answer. There are some Henry families in and around Richland, but they deny any connection to the graveyard or to Henrytown. My assumption is that the cemetery was the graveyard for Henrytown. I've never been inside the graveyard, but I've been told that there are only three gravestones, one of which I have recently learned is perhaps a relative of Doc Oliver, whom I mentioned earlier—one Corporal S. B. Oliver, probably Shadrack Oliver. No date of death is given. My guess (because the gravestone seems to suggest it) is that he was a Union soldier in the Cannon Trail fight. If I ever get to where I can walk again, I will go into the cemetery and read the stones for myself.

According to James King in *The Tilley Treasure*, there were additional battles in the Linn Creek area on the three days following the initial battle on October 14-16, 1861, but I have not attempted to find out more about them. There are remnants of an old corral a bit to the west on the Linn Creek Road, ostensibly a Union Army site.

But is it mere coincidence that my brothers and I associated the road with Confederates? I remember having, at that time, only two pieces of information about the road: one, it had gone past the old Burhans house, which was across the gravel road in front of our house, and, two, the road then angled south-southwest to where an old home place still existed (but no house) on the south side of Bear Creek. The old road bed was still visible south of Bear Creek in the 1950s. I vaguely remember being told that it had been an old stagecoach road. As the following map shows, the road crossed Missouri Highway T and then ambled toward Lebanon:

We used to go to the old house place to pick tame blackberries – both black ones and white ones. At the time, we had no idea the road remnant that ran by there was part of the old Cannon Trail.

Not that it really has much of anything to do with this article, I was born about one-fourth of a mile west of the Cannon Trail.

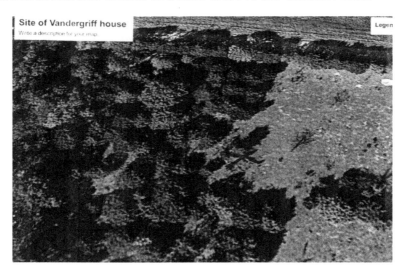

The house sat approximately where you can see the big red X. It is completely gone now; here's how it looked in the 1990s:

The road in front of my birthplace and the Jennings house is now called Kennedy Road, though it had no name when I lived there. Such naming of the road is a result of the 911 service expansion some years ago. The Vandergriff house was approximately 50 feet south of Kennedy Road.

As I said, I can't think of anyone who might have told us the double fence had been a military road or that it had been used by Confederate troops. My great-grandmother, from whom I heard so many of the stories I've shared with the Missouri Folklore Society in person and in print, never mentioned the fight, to my recollection – even though it occurred very near her husband's uncle's farm, which was on the Linn Creek Road. Right across from that farm was a site where a notorious Rebel officer named Laughlin was captured and killed while visiting his own home, and she told me about that. (He is mentioned in the report of Col. John B. Wyman, Thirteenth Illinois Infantry as having been captured). There is a Laughlin Cemetery there where he is buried but I couldn't find it with on Findagrave.com or on Google (a challenge exacerbated by the fact that there is another cemetery with the same name and also in Camden County some 15 or so miles west near where the Osage River ran prior to the Lake of the Ozarks being created). So, Grandma would surely have known of the Cannon Trail Road itself, though perhaps by a different name, since the road continued northwest to where the Ozarks Fishery now stands. And, according to my mother, the family used it to get to Richland when she was a child living with her grandparents in the 1930s, though I don't recall her ever naming the road, nor the creek that ran by it and by Henrytown. I'm sure my parents and aunts and uncles didn't know about the battle. And I'm sure it wasn't mentioned in school. Maybe it was just coincidence that we imagined it. I just don't know what put the idea of Confederate activity in our heads.

I believe there is a larger point to be made, though. That is, as I mentioned earlier, perhaps our definition of the knowledge transmission process is a bit too limited. Folklore theorists, such as Jan Brunvand, suggest that the process is fairly direct, that one learns from another—a parent, a sibling, a friend, a co-worker, and so on. In fact, he said, in the 1958 edition of his book, *The Study of American Folklore,* that "Folklore is oral; that is, it is passed by word of mouth from one person to another and from one generation to the next" (4). In the fourth edition of *The Study of American Folklore*, he says that "Folklore is the material that is handed on by tradition, either by word of mouth or by custom and practice" (5). Again, essentially person to person. He later elaborates a bit, writing that "Folklore is the traditional, unofficial, uninstitutional part of culture. It encompasses all knowledge, understandings, values, attitudes, assumptions, feelings, and beliefs transmitted in traditional forms by word of mouth or by customary examples" (8-9). Still essentially person to person. He goes on to say that "Folklore is never transmitted entirely in a formal manner through printed books, phonograph records, school classes, church sermons, or by any other learned, sophisticated, and commercial means" (12). He adds, "A story, proverb, or other text is living folklore only as long as it continues to circulate *orally* [my italics] in different traditional variations" (16). Much of what I know and think about folklore comes from Brunvand's books, but I am not in complete agreement with his definition. I'm more inclined to Toelken's view, which is that "the materials of folklore" are "tradition-based communicative units informally exchanged in dynamic variation through space and time" (Quoted in Brunvand, 16). I particularly like the idea of "informal" exchange. In my view that also encompasses something like my "congealed from thin air."

For instance, the lyrics of the song I wrote about that my mother sang to my daughter was modified by my mother (See my article in the *Missouri Folklore Society Journal*). She didn't want to say "pickaninny" or "colored girl" within my daughter's hearing, and the song was modified in other ways by other musicians. For example, Jack Armstrong and Peg Jennings of the Northumbrian Pipers in the UK moved it from a fiddle song to a small pipes song. Such modification is part and parcel of folklore transmission. The truth is that the song they were modifying and handing down orally seems to have had a commercial origin. I say "seems" because I think there is some pretty good evidence the commercial versions of the song began as a folk song. However, I have been unable to get a copy of the evidence, which is in a library in Long Island. I don't go there very often. Like never! So, I think its life was folk, then commercial, then folk again.

I think something similar applies to other kinds of knowledge, and that how we learn other things is much the same as how we learn folklore. We are not always aware of from whom or from what we have learned something. Perhaps we remember a specific book or person, but sometimes it's just "I read it somewhere" or "I heard it somewhere." We don't always recall our sources, sometimes just because our memories fail us, or sometimes because we just weren't paying attention to the source. My doctoral dissertation was a study of how English teachers learn how to teach English. What I found was that, for most of them, they did not learn teaching techniques from their teacher education courses so much as from watching, and imitating, their teachers in high school and college. Some, though, said that they have no idea where they learned some of the things or that they just thought them up themselves. I think I learned how to teach from reading journal articles. I wasn't paying enough attention in high school to notice how my teachers taught, and when I started teaching college classes, I mimicked my professors as much as I could, but I depended, to a very large extent, on articles in professional journals. That alternative learning is pretty much the same as the "congealed from thin air" category I've been talking about: it just came, we don't know from where or from whom!

What I've been trying to describe in this article is a much less direct process such as that. My brothers and I didn't learn about the Confederate activity directly from anyone, nor did we learn it from schoolbooks. I'm convinced that our initial beliefs about the Cannon Trail buried treasure were, at best, constructed out of snippets of information picked almost out of the thin air and that we expanded that into something else. I will concede that there are numerous stories about Confederate treasure in that part of Missouri, though I don't have any memory of hearing about them when I was a child; I have subsequently learned about them from books.

When my great grandmother told me the story of herself, as a 17-year-old, sitting up all night with a shotgun in her lap guarding a prisoner (whom she always called Black Pete) while her deputy U.S. marshal husband slept, in my mind's-eye the linoleum in that room was the same color and pattern as that in the house she lived in when she told me the story some 50 years later. Why had I even noticed her linoleum when I was nine or ten? It had to have been a completely unconscious noticing. But, when my mental picture of that little house in "The Nations," as she always called Oklahoma, required linoleum, the design from her house in the 1950s came into my mental picture. Even now, some 65 years later, when I visualize that incident, that linoleum is on the floor! So perhaps I, or one of my brothers, heard someone talk about the war and mentally and unconsciously switched it over to the Cannon Trail.

There was, during my youth, the discovery of some stolen money near Waynesville. It was purportedly hidden by a fleeing Rebel (Wilson Tilley) and plowed up in 1962 by a contractor who was delivering topsoil to Fort Leonard Wood to create lawns for an officers' housing development. The event is the subject of the first chapter of James King's 1984 book, *The Tilley Treasure*. In any event, that could not have been the source of our belief. That discovery happened several years after our playing on the Cannon Trail. We were playing there in the early- to mid-1950s. The money was found in 1962.

Since my older brother would have been in upper-elementary by the time we were playing on the Cannon Trail and may have perhaps been studying a bit of Missouri history, we might have had some smattering of Civil War knowledge for all this to congeal around. I reiterate, though, that we had no factual knowledge about the military road at that time, or even an understanding that it had been a road. Our entire belief was simply made up, very likely cobbled together from random snippets of information from unknown sources. Perhaps, as with Grandma's Oklahoma linoleum, data from one place was transferred to another place.

I must stress at this point that I don't consider our fantasy to be folklore. My point is about how knowledge and beliefs (folklore included) may be created and transmitted—that is, via overheard or even misunderstood information reinterpreted to meet one's own perceptions, and even misconceptions. My brothers and I were in a place that had some real mysteries associated with it—the double fence, the foundation remnant to the north, and the abandoned house to the east—and we perhaps had some pieces of overheard information that we kneaded into what was for us a rational explanation for how those things fit together.

I didn't continue to believe the whole thing about buried treasure in my adult years, but when I finally learned about the battle and the Cannon Trail, and realized exactly where the Cannon Trail ran, I was astonished. So *that's* why there was a double fence and *that's* what the road was that ran past the other old house place where we picked blackberries! It made me really want to go travel that road again, which I did not do because I had no clue to whom either of the properties then belonged. However, on November 5, 2014, with the permission of a caretaker who lives nearby, I went into the woods where the old house sat. No sign is left of the house and no remnant of the double fence remains on what was once our property. However, on Google Earth, one can see the tree line where the road used to be.

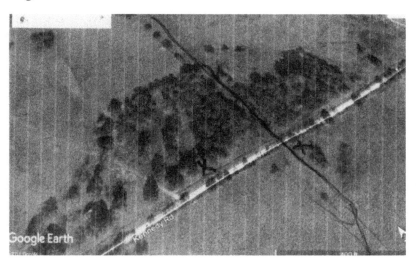

Our house sat about where you can see the red X on the left; the old Burhans house sat across the road and just to the right of the red line.

Perhaps it's just coincidence, also, that the "California House" near Buckhorn, some six or seven miles west of Waynesville, was also on the old Linn Creek Road and had stories of hidden gold from the California Gold Rush associated with it. Perhaps we appropriated some of those stories into our Cannon Trail story. Of course, I don't know if we had heard those tales when we were that young. I remember learning the stories when I was much older. I went to high school with a boy who was raised in the California House, so I may have heard some of them from him, but that, too, would have been much later than when we were playing in the woods. I'm sure I learned some of the tales from the *Old Settlers Gazette* in the 1980s or 90s, a paper printed once a year commemorating the history of the Waynesville area.

The California House, which was some six or seven miles west of Waynesville, began its existence as a private home in 1840 and later became a roadhouse along the trail used by those going to and from the California gold fields, thus its name. It was a private residence in later years.

This photo is not of the original California House, which was torn down after the Civil War. This new house, though, built on the same site, was supposedly built to look like the original house. The one in the photo burned a few years ago and was not rebuilt.

That trail, that is, the Linn Creek Road, later became the military road during the Civil War. In fact, across the road from the California house is the remnants of a Union Army cemetery, shown in the following photograph.

By the time I saw the cemetery in the 1980s, it had essentially been destroyed, but it was still fenced off and some of the military head-stones were still stacked along a fence. The Union Army had a fort, called Camp Waynesville, at Waynesville during the Civil War, located just a block from the city square. Many of the union soldiers in the battle of Henrytown came from Camp Waynesville.

So, let me restate my primary point: knowledge and/or belief doesn't always have a definitive and knowable direct source, so let's widen our definition of the knowledge transmission process to include this "congealed from thin air" source. Sometimes we know where our ideas and beliefs come from, and sometimes we pull them out of thin air. For instance, I remember hearing about razor blades in Halloween candy, but I don't remember where or from whom I heard it. But I *do* remember from whom I learned about Joe's Cave and about the hog-headed snake. The sources of some ideas I know, some I don't.

Life and Loss on the Eleven Point

Henry Hughes

I normally don't think about death in the morning, about crying women and well-dressed men in hexagonal pine caskets loaded into a black wagon. Driving down foggy Highway 19 from West Plains, Missouri, the morning after attending the 2016 Ozarks Studies Symposium and Abby Burnett's presentation on traditional burial practices, my mind floats over more old photos of the dead, then out the car window through an opening in the mist to rolling pasture, stands of oak, sagging barns, and a wiry old man carrying a pail down a hill. "Wonder how long he'll live?" I ask my friend at the wheel, Mark Morgan. "Odd question," he tilts his head, and we motor along at a cautious fifty miles per hour, watching for daybreak deer and talking about fishing.

"They's ketchin' a few," says the overalled man at the counter of Huffsteader's Canoes in Riverton. He calls to his assistant, Shorty, lounging on a heavy sofa and glued to a screen where a walleye splashes into a net. "They cain't ever show you them doin' nothin' for six hours," Shorty scoffs at the instant and endless success on fishing shows. I'm a northerner, an outsider, and I enjoy listening to the men speak—their vowels seem widened and "iron" has its old hard "r." Shorty rises slowly and spits tobacco juice into a plastic bottle, while the boss at the counter goes over distance and float times with Mark. "Fourteen miles'll take you 'bout six hours, if you don't stop much," he says. I study a government posting about the size and ages of smallmouth bass. A keepable fifteen-inch smallmouth can be eight years old. I wonder how many survive that long.

Out in the parking lot, Shorty walks around a rickety canoe trailer hitched to a dented maroon van. He opens the back door of the van, letting out a stench from a pile of moldy life vests, and Mark and I load our cooler, tackle and rods. I try not to touch the squishy vests and Mark chides me for being a Yankee wuss.

Mark has lived and worked all over the South, and he has great interest in the Ozarks. With Shorty driving us west along a wooded road, Mark tells me about the local economy, the collapse of the timber industry, and the rise of tourism. Shorty looks up and says he worked in a mill, but he's been with Huffsteader's for 13 years. When the canoe season ends, Shorty tells us, raising his voice over the rattling van and trailer, "I'm deer hunting." I inquire about small game, rabbit and squirrel, and he squints at me through the rear-view mirror almost smiling, "Sure, if I gets time."

The rig grinds north down a rough unpaved road and the clatter intensifies. "Anything you don't like about this job?" I ask Shorty. Maybe he's enjoying my questions and accent—I was born and raised in New York and now live in Oregon. This is my first time in the Ozarks. Shorty looks in the mirror a moment longer before answering. "The party crowd in summer," he says. "The drunks."

At Turner Mill South, our launch site, there's a few crushed beer cans and a pale condom pressed into the rocks. I help Shorty lift the red canoe from the trailer rack, and Mark runs his hand along a large bubbly patch where the hull has been repaired. "Any dangerous spots we should watch for?" Mark asks.

"Nah," Shorty says, "You been canoein' before, right?"

Mark nods.

"You want life jackets?" Shorty raises his chin. I'm surprised they're optional.

"We'll take a couple," Mark reaches out a hand.

"Just snap 'em to the seat there if you ain't wearin' them. So you don't lose 'em."

The only way we could lose them, I'm thinking to myself, *is if we flip over.*

I remember another of Abby Burnett's old photos of two boys who drowned in the nearby White River in 1901. Seeing them laid out in their caskets made me ache for all the things they missed in life. So much burning energy and expectation doused in a few thrashing moments.

I am not an experienced canoeist, but with Mark in the stern, I soon grow comfortable paddling over the blue-green water. Named by the French voyageurs for the eleven points marking sharp bends along a favored stretch of its 138 miles, the Eleven Point River retains much of its wildness, and it's easy to see why a 44-mile section was designated a National Wild and Scenic River in 1968. Numerous springs and the lush protection of the Mark Twain National Forest keep water flowing cool and clear over the pebbly chert. Huge sycamores bend off the banks, and above them oak, hickory, dogwood and short-leaf pine tingle with morning vapor and the calls of songbirds. When the light breaks and the rising mist undresses a quiet pool dimpled by a rising fish, I just hold my paddle and stare. "Oh my God. Now I know what heaven looks like."

"You remind me of my brother-in-law," Mark smiles and shakes his head. "He was always so high on life."

A year ago, Mark tells me, his energetic brother-in-law died in his sleep at the age of 62 from a heart attack. His wife lying in bed with him didn't even know what happened until morning. Mark mourned, but as a Christian he takes comfort in the promises of salvation and eternal life. My views align more with another Missourian, our forest's namesake, Mark Twain, and his skepticism over faith and miracles. "I am not able to believe one's religion can affect his hereafter one way or the other," Twain wrote in the late 1880s. "But it may easily be a great comfort to him in this life."

Mark Morgan knows I'm not a Christian, and before my visit is over, he'll challenge me to think about the condition of my soul. I'm moved that Mark cares so much about me, considering we met only a few days ago. And I respect his views on religion, but I'm also content with this earthly heaven and living in the moment. I lift my rod, unhook the crayfish crankbait, and start casting.

We glide into a cool cove walled high in mossy brown dolomite and dripping ferns. Mark tells me that we're in Oregon County — named in 1845 when the Oregon territory boundary dispute was national news — and this spot does feel like it could be on one of my home rivers in the moist mountains of Cascadia.

Mark casts his minnow-shaped plug into the quiet water, retrieves a few feet of line and sounds off, "Hey, here we go," hooking a slender emerald fish I recognize as a pickerel. "Great," I cheer, telling him I would never catch one of those back home. The pickerel shakes loose at the boat, and I cast intensely around the same area, only snagging a bit of weed. As we leave the dark pool, I switch over to a night-crawler, bouncing it along a seam where the river sweeps the stiller water and immediately feel a sharp strike. A nine-inch smallmouth bass rockets into the air, splashes down, and runs wildly around our canoe. I bring it alongside, admire its golden-green complexion and bright red eyes, and let it go. It's probably four years old. We paddle on, and Mark hooks, lands, and releases a pretty twelve-inch rainbow trout. Native to the Pacific Northwest, rainbow trout were introduced into lakes and streams all over the country, including the Ozarks. Most of these trout are raised in hatcheries where they grow quickly, and this fish is probably only a year old, but its ancestors draw another connection between Oregon and the Ozarks.

Time affects us all differently. Mark and I are in our fifties and we feel wonderful on this warm September day—the leaves just beginning to turn. Watching the river rush over the rusty red gravel, I can't help thinking of Thoreau: "Time is but the stream I go a-fishing in . . . I see the sandy bottom and detect how shallow it is." For Thoreau, "Nature" guaranteed "eternity," and that's a salvation I trust, but I still wonder how this river will look a hundred or thousand years from now. How long will Mark and I live? Will I ever return to the Ozarks or see Mark again? We spot a mature bald eagle diving over a riffle and plucking out a foot-long sucker fish. It's always life and loss on the river.

"The gods do not deduct from man's allotted span the hours spent fishing" claims a Babylonian proverb. I hope it's true, because time swims fast when you're catching fish or really want to. There's anticipation, faith even, that it will happen again, that the next cast will hook a fish, so you just keep going. Checking the time on the water, I'm often astounded by the late hour. But today on the Eleven Point, when the sun burns over the hilltop, raising the temperature and making the water nearly transparent to angler and eagle, the bites disappear, and we are left with the easy current and our conversation.

Mark's recent work at the University of Missouri has examined what parks and recreation people call "the non-catch factors of angling." In addition to bringing home supper, people often go fishing to escape into nature, develop hands-on skills, relax, and bond with family and friends. I enjoyed Mark's articles and emailed him only a few months beforehand. He read my work and invited me to Missouri and the Ozarks. Now we are fishing together, opening up about our lives, families and careers. His kids are grown, mine are still in school. We need a new kitchen, he's considering some property. We both love to travel and want to do more. We talk about teaching and writing, and I suddenly remember a deadline for a book review, overcasting my lure and tangling in a root wad.

Above us are high rugged cliffs capped in sandstone that 400 million years ago was the floor of a shallow warm sea teeming with trilobites and armored fish. Upriver, a scrawny kingfisher, surely born this spring, plunges into a turquoise pool and comes up with a weeks-old shiner. A mayfly that will live only a few hours as an adult lands on my finger. The vast time, space and wonder woven into this Ozark landscape make my preoccupations with a new kitchen or a writing deadline seem trivial. And yet, the impulse to make, repair or redo also feels absurdly urgent at times like this. Paradoxes abound. The oldest questions never get old—How should we use our brief time on this earth? What's the best way to live? What is our role in the world? Who the heck are we?

"Who the heck is this?" I say, as a jet-driven jon boat roars upriver. Ducks fly out of the way, a bale of nervous turtles slip off a log, and I'm about to cover my ears when the driver, a man in a Chief's cap and white t-shirt stretched over his belly, courteously slows down and shuts off his engine. "You-all ketchin' anythin'?" he asks. He hasn't caught a thing, but says he's "gonna go giggin' tonight." His boat is equipped with bow rail and lights for the spearman to lean over and skewer unsuspecting suckers that will fry up nicely. "We'll kill some fish tonight," he grins. Mark later explains that sucker gigging dates back to the mid-1800s in the Ozarks. Fly fishing purists back in Oregon and Montana might be disgusted by these methods, the explicit vow to "kill some fish," and the prospect of eating a sucker. I appreciate the tradition and the honesty, and I would gladly join in.

I also appreciate the singing and laughing from a flotilla of drunken men speaking rapidly in Slavic sounding consonants— probably Russian—sprinkled with the familiar "Fucking" and "Yeah, baby." They also claim to have caught nothing, "but an obvious buzz," Mark chuckles. They're certainly part of another long tradition— drinking and fishing. I'm reminded of Shorty's frustration with river drunks, but these guys seem harmless. Although I enjoy tipping a couple beers on the water, today's goal of paddling this precarious craft is to stay dry. A large green Old Town canoe zips past. The man and woman, their daughter, and even their little dog all wear stylish life jackets. "There's a ledge ahead," the man warns, perhaps noticing we are jacketless and drifting askew.

For an experienced paddler like Mark, the ledge is minor, but the approach is still important, keeping the canoe straight and pointed down-river. How we position ourselves before we enter a relationship, job, project or any new adventure can make all the difference. The sound of the water rushing over rocks gets me excited, the visible drop in the river horizon raises my pulse, and the surge and bounce as we slice through the whitewater thrills me. Mark is a good guide. I trust him. We talk some more in the last quiet stretch of water and he catches another trout, releasing it with a smile. "You know how to live, Mark," I say as a thank you and a compliment. It's late afternoon, the takeout is just ahead. Shorty will pick up the canoe and wretched life vests. Mark and I will drive back to Columbia in the dark, talking about our day, finding common water and some forks that dead end or run under the brush, eventually merging back into the living flow of our friendship on the river.

An Interview with Missouri State Poet Laureate, Karen Craigo

Molly Bess Rector

The following interview was conducted via Slack on May 26, 2020.

MBR: Hi Karen! How are you today?

KC: I'm great! How are you?

MBR: I'm doing well. It's gorgeous weather here—one of those porch-sitting days.

KC: It's nice, here, too, in a cloudy way. Perfect temps!

MBR: I know people say talking about the weather is boring, but I'm honestly always really taken by beautiful weather. I think it's worth commenting on!

KC: It's something we all have in common—so I agree!

MBR: Well, thank you for agreeing to chat with me. I've never conducted an interview on this platform before, so I'll be curious to see how it goes. Mind if I ask you a first question?

KC: Jump right on in! My first time, too!

MBR: We'll be patient with ourselves, then.

KC: Always!

MBR: So, let me ask you about civil service/community and the role of the Poet Laureate. It may be strange for people outside (or inside!) the literary world to think about how poetry can be seen as service. How do you approach this idea?

KC: Poetry seems like such an extra thing to most people, but from the inside, I see it as a powerful tool for personal growth, as well as one for change in the world. Every poem is sort of a little argument for a better way to think and be, isn't it? Maybe I'm just writing about myself, but I'm writing about my best self with my clearest vision, and the value of that is so evident to me. My chief job as poet laureate is to promote poetry in the State of Missouri, and I'm given a lot of free rein as to how I do that. With everything I do, I'm trying to share with people the clarity and understanding that poetry provides. It's so healthy to write it, and it's absolutely eye-opening and illuminating to read it.

MBR: I couldn't agree more. Every so often, someone will ask me whether it's possible for a poem to be "bad" and I like to say that poetry is just like any other art form in that way—some are better than others, but even if no one else would want to read the poem, it's still valuable to write it, precisely because of that clarity.

That reminds me of something that seems to come up a lot in your discussions of your work: that writing is unpleasant but having written feels wonderful. Aarick Danielsen in the *Columbia Tribune* quotes you saying, "Every act of writing is an act of clarity."

KC: I actually had a professor who said something like that, and it was a saying he had heard from one of his own professors: "There are two kinds of poetry: Good poetry and great poetry." There are no bad poems, since the act of writing a poem is, itself, ennobling. Now, that's not to say that you and I wouldn't be able to sit down right now and collaborate to write history's worst poem, and that would be a lot of fun, but a sincere attempt at poetic expression? That's always good, in my opinion.

It's true that writing is clarifying. I like to meditate, and I have a daily habit that I'm pretty proud of keeping up with, but writing gives me some of the same lucidity and relief that meditation does. The difference is that meditating is pretty relaxing and enjoyable, and writing poetry is frequently awful. Shh! That's not something a poet laureate should probably say . . .

MBR: Hah! I can't say I feel exactly the same way — in fact I may feel the inverse regarding meditation and writing poems — but I think I understand the feeling. You're sort of hovering there around the idea of catharsis, of breaking through the painful, uncomfortable thing to reach the clarity and relief on the other side. And I guess that bad/good/great idea sort of hints at the line (is there a line?) between what's catharsis and what's art.

KC: Yes! That's exactly right. You're probably right about the catharsis/art line, too — I've never thought of it in quite that way! I would note, though, that I think we've made a problem for ourselves in poetry by depersonalizing it so much. Most of my poems are about me, and though I consider myself an artist, I find writing to be cathartic and healing, too, no matter how much eye-rolling some workshop might do about that idea.

MBR: Yes. The critical workshop has a tendency to be prescriptive in what subjects poets are allowed to take, and those subjects tend to be viewed as smaller or less universal when they focus on the personal, or the domestic — both themes in your work. I think *domestic* (like *confessional*) tends to be a bit of a marginalized term in poetry; the realm of women and therefore not "universal," but I can't think of anything more universal than, say, cooking dinner.

KC: That's true! And some people may sneeringly deride the hired help as "domestics," I guess — that's not something I encounter a lot in my social group — but the word just means that the material is related to home life, and I don't know why that seems ridiculous to the same workshoppers who tell you to "write what you know." I'm not an astronaut, for heaven's sake.

MBR: Hah! Imagine if NASA sent a poet to the moon!

KC: Maybe the Space Force will beat them to it.

MBR: So, speaking of home life, I'm curious to know what this pandemic has been like for you. How has it impacted your poem-collecting project? And your writing itself?

KC: Oh, goodness, writing is so hard during a stay-at-home order, and even in the period afterwards. We're all on top of each other in my house—that's me, my husband, and my two sons, who are 13 and 7. Poetry requires a little head space, not to mention space-space, and I can't seem to get away from anyone. Even the cats want a little piece of me! I will say this: I have loved getting closer to my family during the stay-at-home order, and that is going to reap poetic benefits in the future. The myriad worries a pandemic brings make writing extra challenging. As for the poem-collecting project, I'm really just starting with that. Maybe people will welcome the diversion. I hope so!

MBR: I hadn't thought of it that way, but I think you're so right to think about how what's happening now is laying framework for new poems later. I'm a poet who goes long periods without writing, and I think it's really useful for me to remember that I don't have to be writing all the time in order to be a poet. Though, after fallow periods, I do think the writing becomes more uncomfortable for a while.

KC: It can be awfully hard to return to writing after a long absence from it, and I know—I have had years-long absences from writing in the past, usually following some sort of trauma. But writing will always take you back, and it really is as simple as sitting down and moving your hands to see what emerges. You're not guaranteed that this writing will be GOOD, but it will happen, and if it stinks, you can fix it. Having taught composition for a couple of decades, I have put a lot of thought into the writing process, and prewriting—a key part of the process—can include thinking about the topic. These times when we can't lift a pen or tap a key with a non-work-related thought are really just gathering times. If we want to come back to poetry, its arms are open.

MBR: I love that way of thinking about it. That reminds me of something you said in an interview with Karen George for *Poetry Matters*: you called poems "imperfect artifacts of the spirit."

KC: It's true. It's probably true that we can offer only imperfect artifacts of the spirit, which, in my view, is perfect. And it's possible that writing poetry consistently is a way to try to reach a little closer to that original perfection. We probably won't get there, but the closer we get, the more amazing it feels.

I love hearing myself quoted, like I'm Rilke or something. This poet laureate business has a lot to recommend it!

Thanks, too, for your obvious preparation for our conversation. I'm touched by the care.

MBR: It was honestly a delight to prepare for. Your voice so clearly translates from your poems to your interviews—your humor and your candor and that personal quality. It's fun to read interviews that make you feel the poet is authentically present with you. And to conduct them.

KC: Thank you so much!

MBR: On that note, would it be okay for me to ask you one more question?

KC: Of course! You may ask as many as you'd like. This is fun.

MBR: I'm curious what you have to say about frankness, candor, authenticity. I think there's a tendency to see these things as in opposition to generosity, but to me your work reads as both candid and generous. There's something there about the generosity of allowing ourselves to be honest, and how that extends to the reader. What do you think about the value of candor in poetry—both in your work and in poetry more broadly?

KC: That's a really complicated poetic issue, I think. Poems are artifacts, as I called them earlier—and that suggests that they are artificial. I specifically called them artifacts of the spirit, and the spirit is our authentic self; the best we can do is make a flawed artifact of that. Can an artifact—artificial by its nature—be authentic? That's probably the really hard thing about writing a poem, negotiating this inherent and unavoidable tension. Candor strikes me as the route to authenticity, although my cynical self sees it as a rhetorical tool in service to the artifact. You can see a politician in an apparent moment of candor on a TV news show, but that person has an angle, an end game. With every utterance, there's always something unsaid, since we can't possibly say it all. We're always editing, always sifting, even if only because of the limitations of language itself (Ferdinand de Saussure warned us about the huge chasm between sign and signified). I've resigned myself to the understanding that the most important thing I can do is strive to be my best self (not poet: self). I want to be honest and generous and transparent, and I try to bring that self to the page. But I often fail in the attempt to be this kind of human, and I even more often fail at bringing this effort to the page. There's an inevitable gap between spirit and artifact, and closing the gap is my lifelong project as a poet. I'll never succeed fully, so I'm generous first with myself. When I'm trying—when I'm doing the poetic work—I am at my very best.

MBR: A wise project for all of us, I think. And I think a good place to wrap up. I really appreciate you taking the time to talk to me, and for your thoughtfulness (and generosity) in answering these questions.

The Passing of All Things with Time

Gerry Sloan

My mother marvels in her diary
at the perfect saucer-sized
sugar cookies
her granny would bake
on a wood-burning stove.

When her husband died,
she moved into town
and learned to cook with gas,
but kissed by the wrong kind of flame
her cookies never tasted the same.

Daybreak
(for Katy)

Gerry Sloan

When you live among hills, tall trees
are the first to see the sunrise
emerging from shadows,
their dry leaves lit like banners
announcing retirement from the factories

of photosynthesis. Though all is not lost
if they can bed down as compost,
play midwife to upstart seedlings
who will repay their debt to the sun
by standing on tiptoe again and again.

Cemetery Plums

Gerry Sloan

We sensed the end of an era
when it vanished from the calendar
and folks showed up for the potluck
with boxes from KFC.

No store-bought fruit
tasted sweeter than wild plums
plucked from the fencerow
on Decoration Day

while our elders—some dressed
in Sunday finery, some in their best
overalls—strolled among headstones,
some leaving plastic bouquets,

some honoring the dead
the only way they knew:
with hugs and lingering
handshakes for the living.

The Vernacular *Ozark(s)*: Our Placename Revisited

Lynn Morrow

Ozarks enthusiasts speculate on the origin of the term *Ozarks*, its meaning, its boundaries, and its use. This essay primarily discusses its use over the past two centuries, but will include a few comments on other aspects of the term. The actual origin of the term, "Ozark," is lost within cultural processes of the eighteenth century in trans-Mississippi Arkansas, but we do have evidence for the larger context of its origins. As with many things described as "Ozark," outsiders began the use of the term in print.[1]

While millions of tourists travel to the Ozarks, it was not always so. Historically, the region did not attract large migrations for settlements, resulting in a lack of institutions, commerce, and society, which provides a context for writers to describe a "thin" society, one without complex or diverse social and corporate organization. But the Ozarks was "thick" with natural resources. It possesses a distinctive topography—upland prairie, park-like forests, deeply entrenched valleys, and widespread erosional features that geologists call karst, an Edenic environment so loved by market hunters, and later conservationists. The ubiquitous karst features include caves, springs, sinkholes, and natural arches, landmarks that modern tourists enjoy. It was Ozark game and minerals, and later timber, that were the region's defining early attractions for travelers and immigrants.

Amidst nineteenth-century visionary designs for the exploitation of Ozark natural resources, state government employees and scholars—usually scientists—marched forth to survey, study, and write about the Ozarks. Geologists and geographers provided the primary paradigms for understanding the distinctions of the natural Ozarks. Geologists termed the region the *Ozark Uplift*, geographers, the *Ozark Plateau*. Historians, coming very late to the study of this region (about the size of Tennessee) often refer to it as the *Ozarks*, or *Ozark Upland*. One general observation is that during the late eighteenth century *Ozark* was a noun that sometimes referred to Arkansas Post; in the nineteenth century, *Ozark* was normally a modifier or an adjective in a variety of two-word placenames until late in the century;

and during the early twentieth century, journalists and commercial tourism needed a short promotional term and the one-word *Ozarks* became common.[2]

Morris Arnold's groundbreaking work in colonial Arkansas explains the geographic origin of the term in the lowland forests of the Arkansas Delta, a land where camps of Indian families, adventurers, and backwoodsmen who hunted bear and deer for the regional economy of New Orleans traveled along the White, St. Francois, and Arkansas rivers.[3] Arnold's work indicates that "from the earliest times, the Frenchmen dated their letters 'Aux Arcansas' meaning at the Arkansas, i.e., where the Arkansas [Quapaw] Indians lived," located near Arkansas Post, a colonial entrepôt on the lower White River dating from 1686. There were at least three distinct locations for the Post in the Arkansas River Delta upriver from the confluence of the White River and the Mississippi. The location in the colonial correspondence was shortened to "Aux Arcs" and pronounced "Ozarks" in French. This linguistic precedent occurred in the decades prior to the French and Indian War, 1756-1763. The one-word *Ozarks* may well have been used in vernacular speech, but it is curiously absent in major writings on the region during the nineteenth century, giving way to two-word terminologies, such as, *Ozark Mountains*.[4]

When the Spanish assumed military control of colonial Arkansas, the term entered generic use by the European powers contending for the lucrative fur trade of colonial Arkansas. For a time, travelers referred to a *Spanish Ozark* (the traditional Arkansas Post settlement on White River) and a *British Ozark* (c. 1768-1779) at Concordia, an English trading post across the Mississippi from the mouth of White River. The British used the post to supply liquor to the Quapaw Indians to harass the Spanish. The Quapaw, however, remained friendly with the Spanish as they had been with the French. A fire destroyed *British Ozark* in 1779 and its hunting families joined *Spanish Ozark*. By 1780, the Arkansas Post was also referred to in Anglo correspondence as *Oasark* (from *Osark*)—a specific place on White River. Much later, in 1818, Thomas Nuttall wrote that the remnants of Quapaw Indians commonly referred to themselves as *Osark*.

The "Aux Arcansas" trade was much easier to pursue up the larger Arkansas River than its swampy tributaries to the north and the majority of Ozark trade came from the northwestern hinterlands. During the eighteenth century, hunters moved up the Arkansas River drainage, up the White River into the Little Red, the Black, and St. Francois rivers; a few men entered the White River uplands, above modern Batesville, during the late eighteenth century, most after 1790. By the close of the century, an undeclared "Ozark Region" included the Arkansas River and its numerous watersheds penetrated by adventuresome traders, while the specific applications for *Ozark* included the Arkansas Post, the Quapaw Indians, and the Arkansas River.

During the 1790s eastern Indians and Anglo Americans explored and settled further into the Arkansas uplands. Traders met, worked, and did business at easily identified natural settings — river bottom barrens or prairies that settlers named, such as Oil Trough Bottom, mouth of Big North Fork River, mouth of Bear Creek (modern Boone County, Ark., currently under Bull Shoals Lake), and more. It is easy to speculate that the hunters and settlers carried the term *Ozark* up White River as they entered ever deeper into the forests of Arkansas. Bear hunters, in particular, who camped to process lucrative bear oil and bear products in addition to associated forest resources, such as ginseng, deserve primary consideration as the cultural force who diffused the term *Ozark*. But, by 1800 there was no regional term commonly accepted by the literate for the uplands.

For a time, there were competing terms for the Trans-Mississippi interior uplands. They included usages of the *Black Mountains* and the *Masserne Mountains* in regions known to us now as the Ozarks; the origins of those terms are unknown to researchers, and their use was discontinued by the mid-nineteenth century. The older and more widespread use of *Ozark* remained current vernacular with traders, travelers and explorers, and finally settlers.

Explorers and writers continued using *Ozark* in a variety of ways. In 1801 Moses Austin referred to the Arkansas River as *Oas Arke* during his voyage down the Mississippi River.[5] Christian Schultz in 1807-1808 mentioned the "Ozark or Arkansas" Indians; Fortescue Cuming in his Trans-Mississippi tour of 1807-1809 referred to Arkansas Post as the "settlement of Arkansas or Ozark;" John Bradbury in 1809-1811 wanted to travel from St. Louis to *Ozark*, i.e., the Arkansas River; Thomas Ashe in 1816 wrote about the "Ozark or Orkansas

River" and the "post of Ozark on the Orkansas River;" and in 1818 Thomas Nuttall used "Osark" in referencing the Post and the Indians. Henry R. Schoolcraft was either unfamiliar or uncomfortable with the term *Ozark* and used instead "western country" as his geographic term in the title of his first book in 1819, and he used the "Interior of Missouri and Arkansas" in his second book in 1821.

The first official reference to the Ozark Mountains came from Major Stephen H. Long (1784-1864), who left St. Louis in 1819 in command of a military expedition to explore the West. After touring the Missouri and Platte River Valleys, he published a report in 1822 that gave us the terms "Great American Desert" for the Great Plains and *Ozark Mountains* for the Trans-Mississippi uplands. A result of his expedition was to permanently place the name *Ozark Mountains* on published maps depicting the highlands of Missouri and Arkansas. As indicated on their map, these mountains stretched from near St. Louis southwestward into what we know today as the Ouachita Mountains of southeast Oklahoma, or in the context of 1820 the *Ozark Mountains* extended from St. Louis to the Mexican territory of Texas. Major Stephen Long, an official of the historical antecedent of the federal Army Corps of Engineers, had finally named the Ozarks.[6]

For the next generation the status of *Ozark Mountains* as an official term employed by the Army Engineers in Stephen Long's formal account (written by Edwin James) continued to be found on maps and in publications. Gottfried Duden introduced the *Ozark Mountains* to Germans in his famous *Report of a Journey to the Western States of America* in 1829. George Featherstonaugh, another scholar in the Trans-Mississippi in 1834-1835, noted the penchant of French Canadians to shorten names. For example, he said that in going to the Arkansas Mountains they would go to "aux Arcs" and "thus these highlands have obtained the name *Ozark* from the American travelers." In 1836 Sen. Lewis Linn of Ste. Genevieve addressed the U.S. Congress saying that southeastern Missouri "is now better known under the appellation of Ozark," and promoters in Franklin County, Arkansas, named their new town *Ozark*. St. Louisan Alphonso Wetmore in 1837 published in his now famous *Gazetteer of the State of Missouri* that "the Ozark mountains are elevations of a reputable class." Scientist and physician George Engelmann (1809-1884) left St. Louis in 1837 for Little Rock, where he viewed the "Ozark forests" of the Little Red River. A commercial steamboat and barge, both named *Ozark*, plied the waters of the Mississippi River in 1838, and by 1842, the ferry *Ozark* operated at St. Louis. In 1841, politicians formed *Ozark* County in Missouri, and Josiah Gregg (1806-1850) in his famous *The Commerce of the Prairies*, 1844, wrote about the "craggy ridges about the Arkansas frontier—skirts of the Ozark Mountains." Settlers could read the *Ozark Standard* in Polk County, Mo., in 1840, and by 1853, when Schoolcraft published his revised and combined narratives on his journeys into the "western country" his new title included the phrase *Ozark Mountains of Missouri and Arkansas*. Ever after, the term Ozarks as a geographical term has not been questioned, only debated as to geographical extent.[7]

The late-nineteenth-century tradition of studying the natural and physical world of the Ozarks produced a literature that profoundly affected the use of the term *Ozark(s)* and the discussions about its geographic extent, conversations that continue today. In 1853 the Missouri General Assembly formed the first Missouri Geological Survey to study natural resources in the state. Driven by legends of great mineral wealth in the Ozark Mountains that permeated oral and written traditions, George C. Swallow, the first state geologist, directed most of the Survey's resources into southern Missouri. The scientists completed some mapping and a few reports prior to the Civil War—the war forced suspension of further work until 1870. Then, Swallow's peers resumed a short era of work that included Garland Carr Broadhead becoming state geologist in 1873. Broadhead's work in geology and as an author of Missouri and Ozark articles and reports for the next generation would be significant in state history, providing a popular and scholarly forum for the common use of the term *Ozark*.[8] In 1874 the legislature discontinued the Survey and turned its property over to the School of Mines at Rolla. Scholars continued their work from Rolla and at the University of Missouri-Columbia, until the Survey was reestablished in 1889.

Henry Rowe Schoolcraft came to the Ozarks to study minerals, make a name for himself, and secure a government position—a goal he eventually achieved in the Great Lakes Region. Others followed him to the Ozarks, often looking for the fabled riches of colonial lore. Travel in the interior Ozarks—whether for the Indian trade of the 1820s or "prospecting tours" of settlers and mineral exploration—resulted in the knowledge that the center of the region was elevated, or was a table land, while the outer edges sloped to lower altitudes. Explorers, traders, and later scientists and journalists became acquainted with this ridge land that ran generally southwest from St. Louis into southwest Missouri. Nathan Parker, state school superintendent and author of *Missouri, As It Is in 1867* called this ridge the *Ozark Chain* and the *Ozark Range*, relying upon Schoolcraft for descriptions. He found the term *Ozark Mountains* upon "some of the first [nineteenth-century] maps of the State" and quoted G. C. Swallow, state geologist, for more of his description of topographical Missouri.

Images on early and mid-nineteenth-century maps faithfully reflect this *Ozark Ridge* viewpoint; even the Lewis and Clark map of 1809 Louisiana contained the symbols—a southwesterly hatching—of the ridge. Cartographers placed hatch marks to represent mountains that followed the high ground into southwest Missouri and beyond and writers used the ridge to describe places, land or water, on either side of it. G. C. Broadhead in 1874 wrote about the "heavy growth of pine . . . south of the main Ozark ridge." In one of the numerous state promotional texts, John O'Neill in 1877, writing for the Missouri legislature, described Greene County extending "over the highest summits of the Ozark Mountains" while Douglas County lay on the "south side of the Ozark Mountains" or on the south side of the ridge.[9]

The Ozark sub-region we now know as the St. Francois Mountains in southeast Missouri, home to Missouri's fabled granite rocks, atop the Ozarks' highest elevation, was the location of historic mineral lands and became the *Ozark Center*. It was a "center" from the view that all other Ozark lands were lower in altitude. The proximity of this area to Ste. Genevieve and St. Louis, and the lucrative profits from minerals over a long period of time, made the geographical area much better studied and generally known than the lower Missouri geography.

Beginning mid-century, mineral investors in southwest Missouri stimulated the interest, survey, and exploration of Ozark topography. The federal Government Land Office survey contracts led to fairly accurate representations of Ozark drainage patterns, but the last GLO survey contract in Missouri was in 1852. Then it was up to private investors to examine the land more closely—particularly railroad and mining. In 1857 the Granby Mining and Smelting Company in Newton County led by state Sen. Henry Blow (1817-1875) and brother Peter Blow, Jr., and Mayor Ferdinand Kennett, all of St. Louis, became a sensation. By 1859 with its some 8,000 population, Granby was by far the largest settlement in southwest Missouri.

Interrupted by the Civil War, Peter and Henry Blow reorganized their company in 1865 with engineer James B. Eads and two others. This new company specifically targeted their business operations for the counties of Jasper, Newton, McDonald, Lawrence, Barry, Stone, and Taney. The Blow family and their associates included scientists working in and out of government who discussed the nature and location of Ozark minerals. The speculations of the St. Louisans led them into the White River country, where they became principal voices for the promotion of the Pacific railroad from Rolla through Springfield—along the *Ozark Ridge*—and westward toward their mineral deposits in Newton County.

Ozark caves, because of their karst erosion, were good places to search for veins of ore; caves also became enormous attractions among "curiosity-seekers," i.e., early tourists who sought wilderness adventure. The Granby survey teams explored many square miles of southwest Missouri. During one outing in 1869, they visited a locally known sinkhole in Stone County – finding only high quality marble or limestone deposits, not commercially viable ore. Later, this karst opening became Marble Cave, while Stone County became known in state literature for its numerous caves to be explored. Promotional and scientific literature began to include "Ozark marbles" and Ozark lead deposits in their general descriptions.[10]

The southeasterly axis of mineral surveys from Granby to Lead Hill, Arkansas, became known as the "Ten O'Clock Run"—a large region wherein St. Louis mineral interests, and others with venture capital, speculated in "mineral lands" for a generation. Investors were encouraged by the Joplin area mineral strikes on the northwest and later by the 1880s diggings on the southeast in Marion County, Arkansas. Surely, they thought, as the century wore on in a wake of discoveries of caves and natural bridges, a great strike lay in between.

During the 1880s, the combined efforts of the United States Geological Survey, the Missouri Geological Survey, and private capitalists began to produce the first systematic maps of the Ozarks. Railroad corporations promoted the *Ozarks* in their pamphlets for commercial and tourist excursions, and in Rolla, a scholarly home for geologists. Locals watched the Rolla *Ozarks* baseball team and attended performances of the *Ozarks Minstrels* at the opera house. Former state geologist, G. C. Swallow, and the current state geologist, G. C. Broadhead, and others discussed the sandstone and limestone stratigraphy in the region, formalizing the vernacular "cotton rock" term used in construction, calling the strata collectively the *Ozark Series* in the larger region of the *Ozark Highland*. The scientists, by looking inward at Missouri's resources, took an increasing inventory of natural benefits.[11]

This scholarly introspection increasingly used the vernacular *Ozark* term to modify concepts. Two Ozarkers who contributed significantly to the geological discussions were Curtis F. Marbut from Barry County—who distinguished himself in statewide studies at the University of Missouri and later internationally—and Edward M. Shepherd from Greene County—professor and later president at Drury College. Geologists conceded in their scholarly reports that *Ozark Mountains* "has clung to the district ever since its earliest explorations," but geologists preferred to use the more recent and more expressive term, a "domeshaped" *Ozark Uplift,* sculpted by erosion; scholars noted what travelers had long observed—"nearly all the ridges rise to about the same height," giving view to an ever-level horizon.

The scientific search for well-defined districts within the *Ozark Mountains* of Major Stephen Long, stretching nearly to Texas, resulted in the recognition of smaller upland regions. The Ouachita Mountains of Arkansas became recognized in state and national journals as "materially distinct" from the hilly regions to the north, while the Shawnee Hills of southern Illinois were considered geologically kin.

In the 1890s scholars walked across the Ozarks to study "ridges and knobs" and mineralized spring waters. Scientists representing the Missouri Geological Survey and the Missouri World's Fair Commission in 1893 conducted an exploration and published an article about Marble Cave in *Scientific American* that brought more attention to the White River Hills. In June 1896 Missouri's talented Luella A. Owen explored the cave and gave it and the region notoriety in her *Cave Regions of the Ozarks and Black Hills*, 1898. Owen's book suggested that the Marble Cave area become a national park and her writing became the standard text on Ozark caves, caves "centered in southwest Missouri," for fifty years. Expanded articulation about the sub-regions of the *Ozark Highland* led to recognition of several *Ozarks*, i.e., similar but different natural or physical expressions found throughout the greater region.

By the end of the nineteenth century, journalists adopted the geologists' terms with great frequency. Railroads touched most Missouri counties, allowing travel, commerce, settlement, and easy access to towns. Newspaper stories included "local color" tales, especially dialect stories, which imitated themes in recent Appalachian writings about these rustic realms, often becoming Sunday features in the urban papers. Vernacular use of the term *Ozark* led to an extension in ever-widening commercial, ethnic, and cultural descriptions and in naming new civic organizations. Examples included the *Ozark Range Mining Company* in Lawrence County and the *Ozark Battalion*, a Union veteran's organization created from south-central and southeast Missouri counties that began holding reunions in Rolla, Salem, and Cuba. Using *Ozark* became fashionable and was already a complimentary sobriquet proclaimed by 1870s promoters in Greene County for the county seat—the *Queen City of the Ozarks*.[12]

South of Greene County, journalists and promoters, seeing opportunities in the embryonic White River tourism of the early twentieth century, placed newspaper stories throughout Missouri and the Midwest. With the impoundment of White River and the creation of Lake Taneycomo in 1913, the traditional geographic descriptions that used two words, e.g., *Ozark Uplift, Ozark Plateau, Ozark Mountains* etc., gave room to a shorter, punchier term more palatable in promotion— the *Ozarks*—embraced by the *Ozarks Press Association*. Meanwhile, a rash of new organizations using the modifier *Ozark* appeared, e.g., *Ozark Power and Water Company* (for electric transmission from Powersite Dam), *Ozark Trails Association* (forerunner to Route 66 promotion), *Ozark Plan* (promotional real estate), the *Ozark Bankers Development Committee, Ozark Dairy Association, Ozark Fruit Growers Association*, and by 1919, the influential *Ozark Playgrounds Association*.

The rapid appearance of these commercial organizations in southwest Missouri kept the public imagination focused upon a "Heart of the Ozarks" in the White River Hills. Government publications reinforced the "Heart of the Ozarks" location in southwest Missouri with phrases like "This is in one of the Ozark counties" when discussing White River drainage areas in Barry, Douglas, and other counties. In 1916 the statewide agricultural magazine, The *Missouri Farmer*, said plainly that Branson was in "the heart of the Ozarks" where Harold Bell Wright found the setting for his story, *Shepherd of the Hills*. Specific new place-names enlivened the usage with the appearance of *Camp Ozark* and later *Ozark Beach* along Lake Taneycomo.[13]

While dramatic events in literature and industry applied common usage for the term *Ozarks* in the White River Hills, scientists increased their analysis and comparison of the Ozarks with other regions and began publishing more definitive statements about the Ozarks. Fundamental were Curtis Marbut's path-breaking studies, *Soils of the Ozark Region* in 1910, and his *Soil Reconnaissance of the Ozark Region of Missouri and Arkansas* in 1914. Marbut simply said, "The Ozark region of Missouri is unique. It is the only region of its kind in the world." Marbut's summaries of the natural and cultural Ozarks stimulated Missourian Carl Sauer to publish *The Geography of the Ozark Highland of Missouri,* 1920, the most influential monograph for academic study of the Ozarks in the twentieth century. Sauer's benchmark examination was immediately used by journalists and scholars who wrote of the region and the sub-regions. Well before Sauer's book, the term *Ozark Mountains* had even found its way into legal decisions of Missouri's higher courts when discussions of economics, transportation, waterways, and so on were in order. By the end of the 1920s some journalists, such as May S. Hillburn in southwest Missouri, began to claim the title of an "Ozark feature writer."[14]

The upper White River country was the first Ozark sub-region to become culturally associated with the *Heart of the Ozarks* because of the immense popularity of the *Shepherd of the Hills,* the new access via the Missouri Pacific railroad, and the recreational catalyst, Lake Taney-como. The widely touted "Galena to Branson Float," primarily a wilderness adventure for affluent urban tourists in the early twentieth century, received broad coverage in newspapers. The Arcadian image developed in the White River Hills, c. 1910-1930, established the area as synonymous with the *Ozarks*. During the Depression Missouri automobile road maps reinforced this view when labeling *Ozark Mountains* across the White River Hills. In 1935, the Kansas City *Star* published a quilters *Ozark Trail* pattern.[15] A generation later when I questioned Missouri senior citizens during the late 1970s about "where is the Ozarks?," from as far away as Miller County to as close as Lawrence County the summary answer was always "down there on White River." The promoters had made their point, and still do.[16]

Since the Lake of the Ozarks came into being in 1931, there has existed some debate over where the "true Ozarks" lie and continuing discussion over the boundaries of the Ozarks. The arguments concern the distinctions in geology or ethnic origin or local pride in a particular place. These questions are not likely to subside as long as vigorous Ozarks tourism continues.[17] But the term *Ozark* is also one of feeling, not precise boundaries. When talking with each other, residents do not agree exactly where they mean by the *Ozarks*, but they may assert that they live in the best part of it!

We have *Ozarks* and *Ozark Mountains* that parallel *Adirondacks* and *Adirondack Mountains* in usage. In Missouri, we have Lake Ozark and Lake of the Ozarks. Residents also refer to the Osage, not Osages, and to the Delaware, not Delawares, when talking or writing about historic Indians. Moreover, the late Ernie Deane, placename specialist for Arkansas, commented about the widespread and diversified use of *Ozark* and *Ozarks*. He, too, recognized the legacy from regional history that gave the Fayetteville area the *Ozark Barber Shop* to *Ozarks Electric Cooperative*. Dan Saults wrote about the *Ozark Highland Trail*, a wilderness journey across southern Missouri and northern Arkansas. The University of Arkansas Press published *Ozark Vernacular Houses* studied in the *Arkansas Ozarks*. Silas C. Turnbo's stories about the *Ozarks Frontier*, and Henry Schoolcraft's *Ozark Journal* about the interior of the Ozarks make contributions to Ozarks history. We moderns read about the *Ozark* big-eared bat and the blind *Ozark* cavefish. By March 2000 Missouri businesses had chosen the adjective *Ozark* to describe 3,658 enterprises and *Ozarks* for 312 more.[18] Vernacular culture in the Ozarks will likely expand its use of *Ozark* and *Ozarks* to describe entities that we cannot yet imagine.

Endnotes

[1] A version of this paper was delivered at the national conference of the Council on Geographic Names Authority held at Springfield, Missouri, on October 8, 2010. The author is a former vice-chairman of the Missouri Board on Geographic Names and a long-time member.

[2] Interested readers should consult E. Joan Wilson Miller's "The Naming of the Land in the Arkansas Ozarks: A Study in Cultural Process," *Association of American Geographers* 59 (1969): 240-251 who lists six variants on the naming of the Ozarks in her wide-ranging case study that included other terms, as bald, bayou, barren, bottom, branch, hills, hollow, knob, prairie, and more, and the excellent survey, "Who Named the Ozarks and When?" in the Missouriana section of the *Missouri Historical Review* 32 (1938): 523-533.

[3] See Morris S. Arnold, *Unequal Laws Unto a Savage Race: European Legal Transitions in Arkansas, 1686-1936*, 1985, and *Colonial Arkansas 1686-1804: A Social and Cultural History*, 1991, both from the University of Arkansas Press, Fayetteville.

[4] A Union soldier who had just encountered the Ozarks early in the Civil War used a two-word term, *Ozark hills*, when writing home about his adventures in 1861. See Council Bluffs *Nonpareil*, Nov. 30, 1861, "From Rolla." This source was supplied by John Bradbury, Western Historical Manuscripts Collection-Rolla, Missouri University of Science and Technology.

[5] See Moses Austin Papers, *Annual Report of the American Historical Association*, Eugene C. Barker, ed., 1919. Thanks to Walter Schroeder for this citation.

[6] For decades many Ozarkers have referred to B.C.E., Before the Corps of Engineers, in describing life prior to the construction of the great reservoirs. It is ironic that Major Long's crew, representing the Army Corps, was here almost before anyone else and provided the report that formalized the lasting regional name. Moreover, Schoolcraft, upon leaving Missouri in the Spring of 1819, met several members of Long's expedition at Herculaneum, Mo. One wonders whether they used any Ozark term in their conversations.

[7] Additionally, in 1858, a newspaperman on the first Butterfield Overland Mail trip noted their "team of four mules crossed the much dreaded Ozark range, including the Boston Mountains."

[8] By 1905 Broadhead's wide-ranging intellect had produced some 168 reports, articles, and newspaper stories about the natural and historic past of Missouri; many included themes about the Ozarks. G. C. Broadhead Papers, Western Historical Manuscripts Collection, University of Missouri-Columbia, f. 16.

[9] In the twentieth century, one writer, wanting something different than the image of the hatching, or the term *ridge*, used the metaphor "an irregular vertebra column" that stretched southwesterly across Missouri. See *The Missouri Yearbook of Agriculture* (Columbia: State Board of Agriculture, 1915), 601.

[10] In 1866, local exploration in Greene County led to the discovery of Knox or Lincoln Cave, now known as Fantastic Caverns. In 1868, G. C. Broadhead reported in the *Third Annual Report of the State Board of Agriculture* the "large cave a few miles south of Ozark," the site now known as Civil War cave. Then Broadhead noted that "Missouri has no such large and noted caves" in comparison to Virginia and Kentucky – the

reports of the Granby surveyors were not yet in. In 1869, the discovery and workings of the Alma mines in Christian County signaled continued interest in the mineral future of the White River region. By 1874, G. C. Broadhead revealed in the *Report of the Geological Survey on 1873-1874* that "in southwest Missouri very extensive caverns" exist.

[11] The Ozarks sedimentary rocks are by far the most important rocks in the modern economy. For a readable and scholarly narrative see A. G. Unklesbay and Jerry D. Vineyard, *Missouri Geology* (Columbia: University of Missouri Press, 1992) and G. C. Swallow's, "Ozark Highlands" essay in the *Fifteenth Annual Report of the State Board of Agriculture ... for the Years 1880 and 1881*, 309-314.

[12] Springfieldians had used the Queen City term from at least the mid-1870s following the arrival of the railroad in 1870.

[13] See Raymond A. Young, *Cultivating Cooperation: A History of the Missouri Farmers Association* (Columbia: University of Missouri Press, 1995), 29-30, and the Missouri Red Book or *Thirty-Third Annual Report of the Bureau of Labor Statistics ...* (Jefferson City: Hugh Stephens Printing Co., 1912). This popular series was the Red Book of state economics to distinguish it from the Blue Book, the state manual of politics and bureaucracy. Out-of-state real estate companies contributed to the currency of the term *Ozark,* such as the Ozark Plateau Land Company of Buffalo, New York.

[14] Highlands and their highlanders were popular terms in the early twentieth century. They were brought into prominence by several books including Horace Kephart's *Our Southern Highlanders,* 1913; Carl Sauer's *Ozark Highland,* 1920, and John Campbell's *The Southern Highlander and His Homeland,* 1921. In the Ozarks, "Highlander" clubs or associations were popular until World War Two.

[15] Kansas City *Star,* April 17, 1935.

[16] See Champlin Oils, *1936 Official Motor Trails Map Missouri,* copy at Missouri State Archives.

[17] In 1967 the Missouri General Assembly enacted Senate Bill 216 that made the rock Ozarkite, commonly called chert, the official rock and lithologic emblem of Missouri.

[18] Missouri Secretary of State, Business Services database search by author, March 1 and 24, 2000.

Swallowhole

Amy Wright Vollmar

I'm near the creek
at my own risk,
the signs tell me—

banks could collapse
into the deep,
currents may take

me beyond reach
of hackberry root
down the swallowhole—

where the creek veers
from its safe path
to plunge beneath

the soft clay bank
below my feet,
carrying sky,

tearing a way
through coils of stone,
pulsing down hollow

when it vanishes,
making a cave
I want to see.

Smallin Cave

Amy Wright Vollmar

The arch trembles
with droplets
nearly ice

but lets us through,
twines stalactites
all around us,

folds us in
with pipistrelles
to the throat of a cave

that sings with flow,
where in rimstone
above a pool

that never dries,
the Osage chipped
a winter sun

that follows us,
piercing the dark,
lighting our way

toward the spring.
We listen,
the cave breathes—

one long exhale
down the ravine—
her waterfall.

Traverse

Amy Wright Vollmar

To make a trail
along the bluff—
where all is rock

chained to moss,
young chinquapin oak
and raspberry vine—

you begin with a blade,
maybe a pick,
and some idea

of whether you'd like
the trail to meet
the waterfall

or the old mule road
gouged by hard rain
that slants up

to the blufftop glade.
You may pass
through cedar woods

where the barred owls call
all the afternoon,
you might cut

stairs of stone
or wind a while
through hickory dusk

where the rain lingers
like spiderwebs
in the long leaves.

You could trace your way
around snailshells
and beetle husks,

turn at the call
of the blufftop crow,
only to find

you are not now
where you believed
your path might lead —

you have only followed
one way
through the woods.

On the Greenway

Amy Wright Vollmar

Along this trail
people tell me
what they believe
barred owls discuss

and what they think.
They say the creek
will surely be
too high to cross,

today is nice,
without a wind
but gnats are bad,
the creek could be

a photograph,
and a live snake
just crossed the path
before the bench

beside the spring —
but when deer graze
the hawk's prairie,
people I meet

hold their fingers
to their lips
and cannot say
what I might see.

Evenings with Betty Dine

Victoria Howerton

In the 1930s there was no West Plains Civic Center. In its place sat a record store owned by a local couple. There was a modest sound-proof room in the back where customers could take the records for a trial run. They had a lot of repeat business, at least browsing business, in part because of that room and in part because they were just nice friendly folk who made visitors feel welcome.

They're gone. Their store's gone, swept along in the tidal wave of change which constantly overlays one reality with a newer one. It requires conscious effort to distance ourselves from the present in order to see it and the past more clearly. Perhaps the best we can do is place the present on a timeline. Because what is the impact of modernity if we have no past to compare it to? We can feel neither the glow of superiority nor the twinge of poignancy without an historical baseline. Often our only points of reference are black and white photographs carefully lining a modern space, whether in a restaurant chain or a bank.

For the past nine months, my point of reference has been my 88-year old neighbor, Betty Dine. Every night at eight o'clock, I cross Shuttee Street to 204 West Maple to put in one drop of medicine in Betty's left eye to stave off glaucoma. Then we chat for a while about things old and new. Elizabeth Aldine Briscoe lives in the home where she and her eight siblings were raised (and some born). She embodies the complexities and contradictions of modernity, having lived through two of the greatest catalysts for change in the 20th century: the Great Depression and World War II, both pivotal events which are now four generations behind us. In 1946 she hitched her wagon to the rising star of the modern American woman, moving from West Plains all the way to New York City, where she spent decades working as a supervisor in the Hartford Insurance Company.

Yet now she's my window into the past. Her tales of independence are as quaint as they are exciting. She makes going to the opera sound both trendy and enviable. (The first record she ever bought was a production of Boris Godunov, acquired in the friendly music store mentioned earlier). During her time in New York she spent her surprisingly meager salary on helping her family back home, singing lessons for herself, season tickets to the New York City Opera, and a piano for entertaining her friends who loved music as much as she did. My so-called sense of adventure, nurtured on a fast food diet of documentaries from around the world, stands quaking at the thought of traveling to the hulking metropolis of New York not ever having seen it. "My first big puzzle," Betty Dine once told me when I asked her about NYC, "was where are all those people going as they disappear into the ground?"

The summer of 1942 Betty Dine worked at Eades Cash store on the square. One day a young woman about Betty's age came in to buy a graduation dress. Betty Dine remembers the encounter for two reasons: 1) The girl wasn't allowed to try on any hats because she was black; although Betty Dine doesn't remember if the same rule applied to the dresses, and 2) it was the first time Betty Dine stopped to consider where black teenagers in the area went to high school.

At that time there was an all-black elementary school for children living in "Lincoln Town" — the residential area reserved for black workers and their families — but there was no high school open to them. The West Plains high school wasn't integrated until the 50s, so any black student wanting to continue past eighth grade went to Springfield. Betty Dine herself is surprised she had never thought about these inequities until confronted with a girl wanting to shine for her graduation ceremony more than two hours away. In defense of the Betty Dine of 1942, in her day fewer than half of all Americans, regardless of color, continued studying beyond eighth grade. In the 40s that was to change, along with practically everything else.

The Briscoes were an educated lot: four of the nine children became teachers. Lindsay Briscoe, Betty's father, was a West Plains mail carrier. His neighbor, Guy Buck — original owner of the home where my husband and I live — was the other mail carrier. Lindsay was generous, affable, and known for his wonderful singing voice. I cannot speak to his inner thoughts concerning race, but several of his actions speak for him. Betty Dine mentions how he castigated one of his sons for calling a black boy, who was his son's friend, a nigger. Another time Lindsay took a very young Betty Dine on a Good Samaritan expedition to the home of the Lincoln schoolteacher. Betty Dine had hatched the idea of donating a stack of surplus Sunday school material to the Lincoln school children, and her father willingly obliged her.

Our conversation on this topic, by the way, came about after Betty Dine had browsed a newly published book of old West Plains photographs. I asked if anything in it had surprised her. "Well," she says. "I never knew Lincoln Town had a name. Everybody just called it Nigger Hill." Inexplicably that nugget of information didn't make it into Images of America. Betty Dine was also disappointed the book didn't mention the weekly Saturday night concerts put on by the school band down on the square.

For someone like me, who comes from a background of restless folk who don't put down roots of significant length and keep the neighbors (and quite a few of the family) outside the fence where they belong, even a housebound Betty Dine seems more connected to her family and the West Plains community than I. She still has an older sister, age 91, who occasionally visits and writes. Her brother and sister-in-law, both in their 80s, sometimes roll into West Plains from Colorado to catch up on news and police the yard. She got a letter a while back from the youngest in the family, Priscilla, 74, who lives in New York, and my heart almost stuttered at the tenderness in her voice as she ripped open the envelope. "I wonder what the baby has to say."

The house reverberates with echoes of family: The many beds upstairs where Lindsay used to sing the children lullabies; the doorway where sickly baby Bob (nursed back to health by the entire family and spoiled in the process) would bellow for his mother to come back when she left on an outing with Daddy; the same doorway where poor Angie suddenly collapsed, never to awaken.

Yet the present, the modern reality, isn't shunted to one side. Betty Dine cuts out articles from the *Quill* about my husband's activities and projects, which I at least read and sometimes hang on my refrigerator, and there's rarely a person involved in community events of whom she hasn't heard. I earnestly try to provide her details, but she is usually the one who fills in the blanks for me, like the day I was telling her about the extraordinarily helpful organizer of the West

Plains Music Festival, Paula . . . somebody . . . "Speraneo?" inserts
Betty Dine. Oh, yes. Speraneo.

Sometimes Betty Dine carries her eye for detail a bit far. Like the
day I told her about the MSU Springfield Theatre Troupe which per-
formed for my elementary school in 1972. I remember being awestruck
by the young man who performed "Greensleeves" on our cafeteria
stage. I was in kindergarten at the time. "Do you remember his
name?" she asks.

She is a little demanding, my Betty Dine, at least when it comes to
places, names, and correctly adding columns of figures. I have to smile
when she repeats what one of her co-workers in New York had to say
on the matter, slowing her speech into a Long Island drawl, "Betty, the
trouble with you is you're too goddamn particular." My gut feeling is
that Betty Dine sees that as a great compliment.

Well-known children's author Madeleine L'Engle wrote *The
Summer of the Great-Grandmother*, which chronicles the last months
before her mother's death. Madeleine, Sr., had been a modern, vibrant
woman who lived life large, but by age 90, only vestiges of her earlier
life remained. L'Engle, at age 50, wrote, "[Mother] strode casually
through a world which is gone and which I will never see except
through her eyes."

Our frightfully modern world has sloughed off the outdated
fashions and ideas of the past, and we casually stride through it, as
oblivious to our impending obsolescence as a grasshopper is to winter.
We must understand that modernity is an illusion doomed to crash
into the barrier of time; perhaps we can salvage our humanity from the
wreckage. Betty Dine most surely has.

House Hunting, Bee Branch, Arkansas

Paulette Guerin

Beneath the flaking green
lay the previous peach.
The tin roof looked like pie pans
Grandma tied to posts in her garden,
counting on wind to bang crows away.
I unlocked the attic with a skeleton key
for a view of the whole town—its waxy trees,
church steeple, trailer of watermelons.

We passed on the place; but I wonder
how things would have been different
if the doll house had become our home,
heavy wooden doors wheedling on their springs,
days reading in the tall weeds,
falling asleep in the shadow of a tombstone.

Mountain Air

Paulette Guerin

Mornings, air filtered through window screens,
heavy with moisture

that wakes the grass. In winter,
the air was thin; in drought, alive

with dust and pine. The smell descending
with dusk told us the time,

that our minutes were being swallowed
into the blue glow along the horizon,

where, in summer, we stayed under the stars,
sky blacker than coffee or tar.

Owl

Paulette Guerin

After Grandma hit the owl with her truck,
a vet removed the dangling wing.

She raised rats for him to hunt
in the seven-foot cage. Sometimes dinner

was a slab of cold, raw meat.
We watched him click his beak,

lids slide over glassy eyes.
Autumn nights I prayed

into the darkness of shivering leaves,
cricket-song, and flightless cries.

The People Living There Even Drank Rainwater from Cisterns

Benjamin G. Rader

We children loved Mahans Creek. True, in the 1930s and early 1940s, we had to live without a lot of comforts—electricity, a gas-burning cook stove, basic privacy, and a telephone. And, there must have been times we didn't eat well, though I have no memory of those. What we did have front and center was the magic of Mahans Creek.

Fed by springs, the clear-water creek rushed from one side of the narrow, steep-sided hollow to the other, in some places carving out limestone bluffs and caves along the way. Dense stands of willows and towering sycamores grew along its banks. Pools usually no more than three feet deep emptied into stretches of fast-running water that ran only a few inches above the gravel and sand that formed its bottom. Less accessible to predators, it was in these stretches that each year the yellow suckers spawned. During spawning season, the creek-bottom farmers gigged the suckers, and their wives fried up messes of them for dinner.

By digging wells of only ten feet or so deep in the hollow's floor, the farmers tapped into a water-filled aquifer. Not only did the rock-lined wells furnish fresh, clear, cold drinking water, but the farm families also cooled and stored their milk, butter, and watermelons in them.

In the summers, Pap, his clothes soaked with sweat from farm work, would finish his day by stripping off his overalls and under-clothes and taking a dip in the always-cold creek. Whenever we could, we boys (my brother Mike and I) lollygagged naked in the creek. "There was always something to do on the creek," explained my first cousin, Jerome Rader.

For children, the creek's attractions even trumped the popular Saturday afternoon Western films of the day. Another cousin, Arch Pummill, who like me spent his early years on the creek, recalled almost ninety years later (in 2010) that he "bitterly resented leaving the creek" and to that day had never forgiven his parents for moving to

Pittsburgh, Kansas, in the early 1920s. For us children, without going to heaven, living on the creek was as close to paradise as we could get.

Little did we understand that like Adam and Eve in the Garden of Eden after they tasted fruit from the Tree of Knowledge, we were about to be thrust out of our idyllic homeland. (Not by God . . . at least not directly). We didn't know that it had been hard enough to earn a living on the creek in the best of times, but that these were the worst of times. Not only was there the Great Depression of the 1930s but there was also the worst drought in the history of Shannon County. World War II brought a brief and limited respite from the hard times. In 1944, Pap finally gave up; he took a job as an electrician in West Plains, Missouri, and bought a little hilltop farm six miles northeast of town.

The "goat farm," so named because it was fit only for raising goats, was nothing like Mahans Creek, at least to us children. There was no year-around clear water creeks, no springs, no steep ridges or narrow hollers. Except for scattered, muddy-watered ponds, it was a dry, red-clay country.

The people living there even drank rainwater from cisterns.

Mahans Creek as it looked in 2009. In the immediate years after World War II, the creek changed a lot. Beaver, restocked by the Missouri Conservation Service, stripped the creek's banks of much of its former vegetation, and bulldozers, employed by the local farmers, straightened and otherwise altered its natural course. In some respects, it came to resemble a drainage ditch. Schools of yellow suckers no longer made the annual migration up the creek to spawn. Photo: Courtesy of Benjamin G. Rader

Born in a Veil

Benjamin G. Rader

My Mom believed in omens. She was not alone. Just about everybody secretly does. If pressed, most folks are likely to feel uneasy about a black cat crossing their path or rain falling on their wedding day. There are also good omens, such as meeting a cow on a country road or having a bird doo-dooing on your head.

That my Mom was especially receptive to signs arose partly from her childhood experiences. She was born in an extraordinarily secluded place, McHenry Holler, deep in the woods of Shannon County's Missouri Ozarks. No neighbor's house or farm was within sight. The unpredictable forces of nature were ever-present. But, that was not all; her father, "Raz" Eddings, was something of a shaman. Said to have native ancestry and abetted by his extensive knowledge of roots and herbs, Raz served as the neighborhood's medicine man.

He delivered babies as well, including my mom and her nine sisters and one brother. When the time came for a birth by his wife, Florence, Raz would instruct his children to go down to the creek and play. He then hung the kitchen table "oil cloth" on the clothesline. When the birth was completed, he took down the cloth and the children returned to the house.

Raz concluded that one of his daughters, Iva, had in effect murdered her twin sister by denying her food in the womb. Iva was therefore a "witch," and hence he refused to permit her baptism. When I learned about this as a senior citizen, my mind unaccountably leapt to the conclusion that this had something to do with Iva never having had children of her own, although she had three different husbands. By the way, upon leaving home, Iva forthwith sought out a preacher who happily baptized her. Still, perhaps needless to add, the accusation left a scar that Aunt Iva never forgot.

Having grown up in this world of signs and spirits, my Mom attributed great importance to my birth, for not only was I her firstborn, I was also born with a veil (a thin birth membrane covering my face). Such is a rare phenomenon indeed—about one in every 80,000 births, I learned from Google. Cultures extending at least as far back as the ancient Greeks and Romans have attributed to such children great wisdom, foresight, and luck. At birth, according to legend, Jesus Christ himself had a hood or caul over his face. Not only this, but such babies were reputedly far easier to rear than their less fortunate counterparts.

Almost at once doubts about the ages-old prophecies surrounding born-in-a-veil babies must have arisen in my mother's mind. For I was NOT a tranquil baby with a smiling disposition. Far from it! Rather than welcoming entry into the world of the Great Depression of the 1930s, I yearned for the comfort of the womb. The log cabin in which we lived had no air conditioning, no electricity, no running water, and no indoor toilet. The heat that summer and the following one broke all local records. Sleeping haphazardly and given to colic, I made life miserable for both of my parents.

Still, somehow Mom survived my trying infancy and continued to look for portends that I was something special. I had a competitor, one who made invidious comparisons possible: a cousin, Catherine "Kitty" Pummill, my age, who lived on the other side of the ridge separating our two farms. As a preschooler, Kitty—effortlessly it seemed—memorized dozens of nursery rhymes, her numbers, and, as I recall, even the alphabet. Maybe she could read a little as well.

My mom, perhaps reluctantly, joined in the competition. After all, her baby had been born with a veil. But, it was a mistake. While Mom hammered me relentlessly, I exhibited virtually no aptitude for mastering the subjects that came so easily for my cousin. On one occasion, mom and I both broke down in tears together. Or maybe it was just me.

I am guessing that at that point in her life, Mom must have lost virtually all faith in the baby-born-in-a-caul prophecy. It was not easy, however, for her to dismiss it completely. Throughout her later life, she would at least jokingly say that she expected great things from me.

Last of the Good Ol' Days

Jim Hamilton

News that the world's population has reached seven billion confirms what I've believed for years: I grew up in the last of the proverbial good ol' days.

No doubt, every generation thinks the same, recalling the joys, simplicity, and innocence of childhood more than the state of the world. Whatever they believe, it's true for them.

I believe, though, my childhood years were the last good ol' days for generations beyond mine.

Born in late 1947, I was a child of the 1950s and 1960s. Marred by drought, wars, racial turmoil, assassinations, and all sorts of social upheaval, they were tumultuous decades; yet, for my brother Russell (born in 1950) and me, they remain the last of the good ol' days for what we enjoyed that now is gone.

Much of what we treasure from those years was there because of what we did not have; that is, we did not have as many people in this area as we do today.

The population of the world in 1950 was 2.5 billion—less than 36 percent of what it is now. Missouri's population of 3.9 million was just 65 percent of the 6 million counted in 2010. More important to a couple of Ozarks country boys was the sparse inhabitation of Dallas County. In 1950 the county had 10,300 people; by 1960 the count had dropped 1,000 to just 9,300 people—the lowest census total for the entire century. That's in contrast to about 17,000 today.

Just 9,300 people were scattered across 537 square miles of the county, and a good many of them clustered in small towns. We had elbow room. Fewer people meant:

• Lots of idle land for hunting. Old farms overgrown with buckbrush and dewberry vines were havens for cottontails and quail. Large parcels of timber were open to 'coon and deer hunting.

• We knew all our neighbors, whose place we could hunt on, and which ponds we could fish. That was most everyone's, as long as we respected their gates, fences, and livestock. And we did.

• We knew every car or truck that passed by the house, and we could generally predict when. Not many passed.

• Fewer pole lights on the horizon. From our back steps in the early 1960s we could see one light in the west, at a house near Olive. Hunting at night we could orient ourselves by distant house lights.

• Creeks now dry or stagnant ran deep and clear. Springs fed upper Greasy Creek near our place. We filled milk cans with drinking water there when the well pump went out. The Pomme de Terre and Niangua rivers teemed with fish. I learned to fly-fish for bass on the Pomme near Fair Grove. We filled tow sacks with suckers from the Niangua near Hog Eye. The rivers are but whispers of what they were.

You may note my definition of "good" ol' days" is mostly a measure of freedom to hunt and fish. I might add to that the simple freedom to wander at will across Ozarks hills and wade Ozarks streams.

Population growth, for all its economic benefits, makes us poorer. I can no longer walk out the back door on the old farm with a couple of hounds without soon being in someone's back yard. I tried deer hunting there a couple of years ago, but found too few directions I could safely shoot. Most of the places I used to fish the rivers are posted today. The old fishing holes at Potter's Ford, where Dad and countless other folk beat paths to the water's edge have long been fenced off. I suppose they're hardly worth fishing, anyway.

The Ozarks I knew as a boy has passed into history. I'm thankful, though, that I was able to experience the last of the good ol' days.

Turn Right at Mohawk

Jim Hamilton

Giving directions once was an art form best demonstrated by old men in overalls, a dialogue serving for both their amusement and the utilitarian purposes of wayfarers.

As often as not, it better served for amusement than for traveling instructions.

Interrupted from his spittin' and tale spinnin' on the bench in front of the local Farmers Exchange, the "director" might find his own amusement more important than the utilitarian objective of sending a city-born wayfarer in the right direction.

It would not be uncommon to provide directions incomprehensible to the "directee." The said wayfarer, too proud to admit his relative ignorance of the geography, would simply nod, point down the road, and respond, "Thataway, you say?"

"Yup."

It's not hard to imagine such exchanges on the front steps of the Elkland MFA in 1965 sending a stranger to Beach or St. Luke, rather than Marshfield—or to imagine the ol' boys out front watching tailfins disappear and commenting, "Figured he'd miss the turn; reckon he'll soon figure it out for hisself . . . or mebbe not."

Now, I don't know that the reg'lars on the MFA bench ever purposely sent a traveler astray, but I do recall the confusion of a young reporter lady at Bolivar sent to do a story out north of Polk some years ago.

"You go past Polk town a mite, then turn right at the Mohawk store," she was told. Several trips up and down that road, though, revealed no right turn at any such store, so she came back and asked a merchant at Polk.

"The Mohawk store? That's been gone for years. Nuthin' there now. You was at the right place, though. Just turn there where the store used to be."

Of course. "Everyone" knew where Mohawk was in those days—just like they knew Jugtown, Hogeye, Dogtown, Redtop, Spring

Grove, Wood Hill, Thomasville, Tilden, and any number of other communities either extinct or misnamed.

Even directions to my home place could be made confusing: "Coming north of Fair Grove on 65 you cross the Pomme de Terre and go a ways to AA, then turn east. You keep goin' over a few hills and a creek, but be sure you stay on the blacktop at Goss Schoolhouse corner (of course, a hobo burned it down years ago). Headin' north you go mite more 'til you come to a big white barn at the top of the hill (it burned down years ago, too), and you turn right there, too. Don't keep goin' straight at the barn or you'll soon come to a square corner where the Olive store used to stand (it burned when I was a boy) and the pavement turns back west and comes out at Carter's store and station (used to be Floyd McCurry's) on 65. All that's on OO, which takes off at the big white barn. You oughta be goin' east on AA (take it easy on the hills and a rolly stretch just past Gerald Tracy's place—there's been wrecks there)."

Reckon I'll stop there; don't need anyone visiting nohow. Main thing to remember is to take a right at the big, white barn.

Finding and following directions these days ought to be a lot easier, thanks to 911 and new county road names, but it ain't necessarily so, as the ol' song goes.

Prior to 911 we had a logical road numbering system. County roads were given a number with a prefix linking them to the state or federal highway they connected with—65-100, for example. That prefix at least gave us a place to start looking on the county map.

The cutesy road names assigned by 911 offer no such clue.

I live on Truman Road, so-named for no apparent reason, at the corner of Broken Bow, also so-named for no obvious reason.

Nearby Bassett Drive, I suppose, was named for the dog at the last house on the road, and I assume Kelly Road a couple of sections south led to Kelly School; but I've no idea who Griggsby was to get a name-sake road within walking distance of Bassett. Sometimes the road names make sense, more often they don't.

I reckon it would make no difference to a stranger if a road was named or numbered, and I'll confess a 911 address comes in handy when a mail order store won't take a post office box number. It also makes UPS and FedEx happy. Most official forms have no place for

"The place with a willow tree in the field a half-mile west of the new bank."

My main complaint with road numbers is when the TV news people use them to locate crashes on the interstate. The recent snow brought that to the forefront when they reported a truck crash at "the 84 mile marker" on I-44.

We may memorize county road names, but most of us don't count mile markers.

Between Springfield and Strafford would give me a general location. "Mile marker 84" might as well have been "the Mohawk store."

Reviews

A History of the Ozarks, Volume 2: The Conflicted Ozarks. **By Brooks Blevins. (University of Illinois Press, 2019. Pp. 297).**

Reviewed by D. Matt McGowan

Imagine this scenario: A band of misfits show up in your front yard. They raid your closets and refrigerator. They steal your car. Then, depending on your politics, they kill your father and maybe an older brother before torching your house and leaving with all your cash and credit cards.

Hard to fathom. And yet it happened on a frequent, if not routine, basis in the Ozarks during the Civil War. You can read about it in Brooks Blevins's *A History of the Ozarks, Volume 2: The Conflicted Ozarks.* Blevins is the Noel Boyd Professor of Ozarks Studies at Missouri State University and author or editor of several books about his homeland, including *A History of the Ozarks, Volume 1: The Old Ozarks*, published in 2018. Its sequel, *The Conflicted Ozarks*, second in Blevins's trilogy of Ozarks history, covers the last half of the 1800s, only 50 years, but this half-century is undoubtedly the most complex in the region's post-European-settlement history.

Though less action-packed than subsequent chapters focused on the war and Reconstruction – though no less well-written – the first chapter of Blevins study is seminal because it sets the stage for the drama and massive conflict that follows. We learn that slavery, that "peculiar institution" so central to the agricultural economy of the Deep South and unequivocally the pressing political issue of the day, barely existed in the Ozarks. There are notable exceptions to this, in Greene County, for example, home of Springfield, and especially in the more fertile border counties along the Missouri, Mississippi and Arkansas rivers. But, compared to Virginia, the Carolinas, and Deep South states, the Ozarks had few slaves, especially in the rugged and sparsely populated interior, which was not conducive to plantation farming.

This is the great irony of Ozarks history during this period, for no region of the country suffered more during the Civil War. That is not to say that it wasn't about slavery, that combatants did not choose to fight based on abolitionist principles (see John R. Kelso below) or a desire to preserve the republic – or, on the other side, to perpetuate a way of life based on the economic advantages of servitude. But, as Blevins carefully explains, there were other forces at work, including a precedent, if not propensity, for violence established by the Kansas-Missouri border wars of the previous decade; the strategic, geopolitical importance of another border – that separating Missouri and Arkansas – a breakdown of civil law and dissolution of local government, and, most importantly, a frontier culture defined by so-called honor and punitive revenge and retribution.

The Ozarks, Blevins says, "hosted two wars: a conventional affair of competing military powers that largely played itself out by the end of 1862 and a borderland guerilla war that took its place for the remainder of the conflict." The conventional affair consisted of the three major battles – Wilson's Creek, Pea Ridge, and Prairie Grove – and Blevins skillfully explains the circumstances and execution of each without focusing too much on military strategy or the personality of the generals. Readers may have to work to keep track of the dizzying number and names of units and regiments, but this really cannot be avoided, and readers will sense that Blevins will not sacrifice accuracy for convenience.

Despite Confederate success at Wilson's Creek, the Union, by the end of 1862, has control of Missouri and the borderland with Arkansas. But this a tenuous hold and almost constantly under Rebel attack, either by regular army units, irregular partisan units or bands of guerillas – called Bushwhackers at the time – whose aims often had more to do with settling a score than winning a war. The Union established a string of garrisons to patrol this vast area, but it remained "unpacified" and devolved into a "no man's land," where there was no rule of law and no safety, especially for civilians.

As guerrilla attacks intensified and Confederate raids into Missouri became more desperate, the Ozarks unraveled. More and more civilians simply moved out, with those sympathetic to the Union going to Springfield or Rolla or points farther north, and those supporting the Confederacy to Fort Smith, or somewhere else along the Arkansas River valley, or even Texas. What they left was a scorched and shattered land where civilians suffered at the hands of foraging soldiers and guerillas ranging from unscrupulous to criminal.

The early years of Reconstruction were no better. Radical Republicans swept into office and quickly enacted legislation intended to punish and disenfranchise Democrats and Confederate sympathizers. Hostilities persisted, with old combatants and partisans exacting revenge, leading to more violence and destruction of property. Blevins expertly documents how this milieu spawned vigilantism (the Bald Knobbers, a Taney County, Missouri, group were organized initially to establish local law and order) and, as was the case with one Arkansas county, near insurrection. The emergence of the Ku Klux Klan, who focused on fighting Republican political control more than terrorizing ex-slaves, caused Arkansas's Radical Republican governor to declare martial law.

There is so much turmoil within these pages that the reader's heart is still pounding when the dust settles and the region finally gets serious about economic reconstruction. It almost feels anticlimactic as Blevins finishes out the century by focusing on the development of railroads and new industries, such as mining and timber. Not that these pages aren't interesting, especially the speculative, decentralized nature of mining operations in southwest Missouri, but it is difficult to compete with the drama of the war and its immediate aftermath.

Like all excellent historians, Blevins understands that people make history, and his writing is especially piquant when he describes the remarkable lives of people like John R. Kelso, the ardent abolitionist and Union soldier and spy who said all Confederates deserved to die, and Sempronius "Pony" Boyd, no less passionate than Kelso about the Union cause but nevertheless willing to work with his ex-Confederate brother-in-law, founder of the *Springfield Leader* newspaper, to rebuild Springfield.

Great surveys of history imbue readers with a burning curiosity for the smaller stories within, and Blevins's *The Conflicted Ozarks* is the perfect example. There are so many events and people you will want to know more about that you'll find yourself paging through the footnotes for ideas for further reading.

The Guestroom Novelist: A Donald Harington Miscellany.
**Edited by Brian Walters. (University of Arkansas Press, 2019,
Pp. 319).**

Reviewed by Mark Spitzer

In the interest of full disclosure, I should first mention that I am a
University of Arkansas Press author and a die-hard convert to the
Unorthodox Church of Donald Harington, who is my all-time favorite
novelist. After picking up his knee-slapping *The Architecture of the
Arkansas Ozarks* (1975), it didn't take more than a few years to plow
through thirteen more of his novels. Each riveting storyline incorp-
orates a revolutionary innovation in storytelling; like framing the
narrative voice as a lesson in architecture in *TAOTAO*, or narrating
from the POV of animals and apparitions in *With* (2004), or shifting to
the future tense to end with a mind-blowing magical postmodernism
in *Lightning Bug* (1970). However, I'm not so indoctrinated by the
genius of this iconic Ozark author that I can't offer an objective critique
of his new, posthumously published *The Guestroom Novelist*, which is
his very first nonfiction book.

"Sacrilege!" I can already hear the cries. "You can't say that! He
won the prestigious Porter Prize for literary nonfiction!"

Okay, let's clear this myth up right now. *Let Us Build Us a City:
Eleven Lost Towns* was published in 1986 and has been commonly
billed as "nonfiction" by booksellers, but that's not what Harington
received the Porter Prize for the following year. According to the
Encyclopedia of Arkansas, he received that award for "literary excel-
lence." And as the Porter Prize website clearly indicates, that
"excellence" was awarded for "Fiction." And as Harington states in
The Guestroom Novelist, "Let Us Build Us a City is . . . a novel in the form
of a nonfiction travelogue" (183). As for Harington's other alleged
nonfiction book, *On a Clear Day* (1995), that's really a limited print-run
art book of less than one hundred pages by George Dombek in which
Harington only wrote 29 partial pages of text. Hence, *On a Clear Day* is
not really a genuine, full-size, single-authored book.

So on to what types of nonfiction this miscellany covers. As the subtitle's subtitle explains, *The Guestroom Novelist* is a collection of "Interviews, Essays, Articles, and Reviews." Still, there's more diversity to these selected works than the book cover suggests. Let's start with Part I: "Essays, Articles, and Speeches," in which the problematic essay "The Guestroom Novelist in America" kicks off the collection and introduces its thematic concept. Why is this problematic? We'll get to that in a bit.

The second essay, "Let Us Become Arkansawyers," is a brief and enlightening study of a phased-out word that Harington argues should be brought back since it hinges on a linguistics of labor ("sawyer" meaning someone who saws timber) from which Ozark culture and heritage evolved. Other essays include an overview of Arkansas "cities" that basically went bust, one of the most articulate and visually rich reviews of an artist and his art (William McNamara) that I've ever read, some commentary on the mythology of the historical Arkansas hero Albert Pike, an homage to chicken and dumplings, a disappointingly thin history of the Porter Prize, and a memory of a first date. Some of these "lost works" are colorful gems that will sparkle for lovers of Harington's prose, but a few, I hate to say, were lost for the main reason why minor works of celebrated authors are meant to stay lost; because they're not strong enough to add substance to the conversation.

On to Part II, "Reviews," which consists of reprinted intros to other artists' books, including books on art and architecture, and novels by Nabokov, Mark Twain, Kevin Brockmeier, Daniel Woodrell, and Stephen King. In two of these "reviews" Harington reverts to his signature move of flipping things on their heads. By suddenly interviewing his subjects (author Peter Straub in one case, poet Miller Williams in another), Harington shifts the focus 180 degrees, which works to add an intriguing, imaginative context to a highly cerebral format that just doesn't speak in the playful language us lovers of Stay More (Harington's fictional Ozark setting) have come to expect. Still, it's unfortunate that the artists Harington chose to write about in this section were all male and white, especially in the age of the #MeToo movement, which could work to further pigeonhole him as part of the old school literary patriarchy he was definitely part of.

But now we get to the meat of the book: "Part III: Interviews," which makes up two-thirds of the collection. This is where most readers will find the most value, because let's face it: many readers who gravitate to *The Guestroom Novelist* will do so because they've read all the novels so now they're looking for anything they can get by Harington. And since those readers, like me, are addicted to Harington's prose, they have questions about the author, his craft, influences, back stories, relationships, development as a writer, and so on. This is the section that provides that context, and it will interest readers ranging from those who've just discovered the novels to hardcore Harington scholars.

In fact, in this series of in-depth interviews, Harington, in his own Haringway, creates himself into even more of a character in the legend he created of himself. The persona he assumes is that of a provocatively comic curmudgeon, sometimes getting testy with his interviewers. To a question asking if his novels "have nothing to do with the outside world," Harington responds, "That's a lot of crap" (110). Harington then goes on a semi-rant before turning the tables on Linda Hughes, who is suddenly the interviewee. Harington does this as well with Larry Vonault by abruptly becoming the director in a bizarre theatrics which challenges what the camera sees and questions who is really sitting where. Brian Walter's final interview is also switcherooed, which allows for the firing of some surprise afterburners at the book's conclusion.

There are also plenty of paradoxes and contradictions to be seen in these interviews. But that's the thing about Harington: he's all about duality, doppelgangers, bigeminality (having two penises), coming up with the unexpected, playing with time, and reversing things—which is one reason he's been referred to as "the court jester of the Ozarks" (x). At one point, Harington explains how he designs characters by combining qualities that actual people don't combine (my paraphrase) to explode stereotypes. Harington also says, "A novelist should not—ever—have the teaching of writing as a career. Teaching of writing interferes too much with one's own writing" (168). But then Harington goes into detail about how he got his "first teaching job, at a small college in New York called Bennett" (169), where he was provided the opportunity to dive into the novel-writing process, finish his book, and make friends with William Styron, who helped launch his writing career. In fact, Harington later states, "I like teaching" (273), thereby complicating his insistence that it's not in the writer's interest to teach.

Now back to the problematic theme of *the guestroom novelist* in *The Guestroom Novelist*. The idea of this essay, which is the cornerstone of the entire book, is that you (and yes, Harington approaches this piece from the second person) are in a typical guestroom filled with typical guestroom novels. You've got your Sir Walter Scott, your Thackeray, your Margaret Mitchell, your Edith Sitwell, your Robert Louis Stevenson, and a bunch of authors you never heard of—because that's what ends up on the back burners of home libraries. These are the books that aren't displayed in *living* rooms. The guestroom is where the midlisters and forgotten authors go—and especially those ignored by *The New York Times*.

Harington then aligns himself with these writers by making arguments about how they should've received more attention, but the industry left them in the dust. For example, in a letter to the editor of the *Arkansas Democrat Gazette* appearing right after the essay, Harington notes how his agent tried to "peddle [it] to the *New York Times Book Review, Atlantic Monthly,* etc., without any luck, probably because the author is himself the epitome of the guestroom novelist . . . worthy but unknown" (24). The result is that Harington's stance comes off as privileged whining as he blames his lack of recognition on factors outside himself.

That essay, however, was written back in 1990, before Harington's novels took off. After writing that essay, Harington worked with some powerful New York literary agents and was eventually picked up by quite a few New York publishing houses representative of the Parthenon of presses he desired to be published by: Little Brown and Co., Harcourt Brace Javonovich, Delacorte, Vintage, and Holt. Some print runs surpassed twenty-five thousand. Those books didn't bring in much in royalties, and their lack of sales often made publishers hesitant to publish more. Still, Harington was reviewed in *The New York Times, Time Magazine,* and plenty other high-profile publications. Sometimes he got good reviews, sometimes he didn't—but that's not anything to complain about when all publicity is good publicity and the most powerful literary machinery in the world is putting your name in lights. Additionally, Harington had short stories published in *Esquire*, he was featured in several national Book of the Month clubs, he won the *Oxford American* Lifetime Achievement Award, the Robert Penn Warren Award, and the Porter Prize. And when several of his books were re-released by Toby Press, Harington stated, "I could not be happier with the situation" (263).

So again, it's that contradictory nature of the character Harington created of himself reflecting on himself through a craft in which creating convincing characters depends on reflecting consistent patterns of behavior. Thus, if Harington would've changed his character from a snubbed underdog to a satisfied and accomplished writer, he would've undermined the character he created of himself. And as Walter's interviews clearly show, nearly twenty years after creating himself into the character of the overlooked outsider, court jester Harington was ultimately satisfied with his publishers and reviews. Just take a look at his own words: "*With* is steadily amassing a respectable series of fine national reviews" (160); "[*With*] sold well" (263); "[Publisher] Matthew Miller has made me known after all these years of obscurity. Without Matthew Miller, I would be nobody" (266).

But Harington wasn't the only creator of his own character. *Entertainment Weekly* had a hand in labeling him as "America's Greatest Unknown Novelist," a title Harington enthusiastically embraced. This moniker matched the initial character he created for himself and perpetuated the premise that he was being held back, that an injustice had been done unto him, and because of this, he was deserving of sympathy.

So that's why I'm calling timeout on the *guestroom novelist* theme of *The Guestroom Novelist*—because the sentiments at work in this framework hark back to an angst that Harington later overcame. Still, it's an angst that Harington held on to, so perhaps there's a certain degree of logic for this theme. But whatever the case, this is why Donald Harington's first true nonfiction book (with a good amount of fiction in it) earns a mixed review. This is also why I'd advise most readers to stick with the novels instead (which is what Harington does best), and why I'd recommend this miscellany to those who want to know more about the artist behind the art. Because as Harington says in his own words (no doubt obliquely referring to his own inescapable modus operandi), "really, it's all fiction" (209).

Follow. By Amy Wright Vollmar. (Cornerpost Press, 2020, Pp. 105).

Reviewed by Craig Albin

Amy Wright Vollmar's distinguished book *Follow* is a double first, a debut collection by an estimable poet and the initial poetry offering by Cornerpost Press, an independent publishing company founded by Ozark writers Phillip and Victoria Howerton. The pairing between Vollmar and Cornerpost Press is fortuitous, since both Vollmar's poetry and her book as object display the high, bright sheen of excellence, a quality enhanced in no small part by the inclusion of photos by the author's son, Jake Vollmar.

The three titled sections of *Follow*—"Traces," "Field Guides," and "Passages"—each detail the speaker's alert, preternaturally observant forays into the natural world. At first the reader may be reminded of Annie Dillard's essay collection *Pilgrim at Tinker Creek*, which was awarded the 1977 Pulitzer Prize, but the guiding voice in *Follow* is distinct from Dillard's, less laden with science and more musically attuned to the notes one may discern when alone in woods or near creek or cave.

The poems comprising *Follow*'s opening movement abound in images of entrance, a fitting pattern since "Traces" is essentially an invitation to follow the poet into increasingly intimate encounters with the natural world. The book opens with the poem "Signs," which announces the speaker's choice to venture beyond "the place / where the gravel path / washes out with every storm" in order to spy "trillium's unfolding heart, / and mayapple's / hidden flowering" (3). By forging beyond the path domesticated by human hand, the speaker enters a world of wildness and discovery. In "Verge" she follows a path "one hoofprint wide" that takes her "past a gate of thorn," a lovely image suggesting either entrance or exclusion, depending upon the speaker's determination, although the inclination here is all on the side of resilience (5). In "Switchback," for instance, the speaker announces "the way to the waterfall / is not easy" and then proceeds to slide, draw, clasp, and grab her way nearer the desired destination. She confesses she would "like to chop / a path," "clip poison ivy," and pile rocks "in cairns / that point the way," but were she to do so "the waterfall / could not surprise me / every time I arrive" (23). As if to punctuate this point, Vollmar closes "Traces" with "A Map of the World," a sly poem in which the speaker laments the inadequacy of a paper map "made so / far above Earth / that these bluffs / are only shadows." Instead, she practices a cartography of immersion, trusting "a secret / branch of flow" that "traces its way / to the river / where my map starts" (26).

"Field Guides" forms the middle of the book, a grouping of poems with darker, more foreboding notes, as if to forestall lazy criticism that *Follow* belongs to the sweetness and light school of nature poetry. An early poem titled "The Ridge Runners"—a phrase rich in reference to Ozark outlawry—declares "the bobcat, my neighbor / is avoiding the law, / shotgun pellets in his thigh" (32). The title poem, "Field Guide," contains quiet allusions to threat or violence, for the speaker finds "a flint knife" before tracing "a deep scar / where a bear slid in mud" and finally witnessing a mayfly "vanish, / become part fish" while a squirrel laps "from the bitter lake" (31). Likewise, in "Beware," the speaker's journey "darkens" during a seemingly playful encounter with a fox whose "perfectly white teeth / are sharp as chert" (38), and "Stone County in Winter" opens with ominous portent embedded in the lines "they say a cougar / walks these woods" (41).

"Passages" marks the final movement of the book, with poems limning the now established theme of exploration and discovery. In "Reconnaissance," the speaker attests to an increasingly earned fluency with the natural world, declaring that "the creek is / a way I think / through the dark layers / of the bluff" and later conceiving of the creek as metaphor, "a map for owls / And sycamores / I can follow" (56). "Noland Hollow" continues the speaker's argument with man-made maps as she chafes at their efficient artifice versus the necessarily messy guideposts of actual terrain: "On my map / this river / is a gooseneck in blue / on an even page, / but inside / the map / the river is green / and thick with seeds" (60). At the end of the poem she even eschews the map to follow "only / the geese, / who leave a trail / of feather curls / as they veer / into autumn" (61), a decision reminiscent of Ike McCaslin's choice to discard his compass in Faulkner's *The Bear*. Finally, in "Shift," the book's closing poem, Vollmar invokes individual drops from a waterfall to craft a last metaphor of exploration and discovery, "each drop finding / its own path / for the first time" (79).

To be sure, *Follow* is evidence that Amy Wright Vollmar has found her own path as a poet. Whether a debut or not, the book is surefooted, mature, and wise. It deserves to be read in solitude and savored, but it should also be the focus of discussion in university classrooms, community book clubs, and local libraries. Vollmar has created a significant artistic achievement, and *Follow* should be recognized as such.

Beautifully Grotesque Fish of the American West. By Mark Spitzer. (University of Nebraska Press, 2017).

Reviewed by Henry Hughes

Fish maniac, Mark Spitzer, devotes insane hours and energy to piscine pursuits with the rod and notebook studying various species, interviewing anglers and biologists, catching lots of fish, letting most go and keeping a few to prepare using his mouthwatering recipes. He also thinks deeply about our cultural and biological relationship with fish and water. A dynamic writer with an original voice, Spitzer's books range from experimental poetry on hellbender salamanders, novels, and literary translation to a suite of sterling nonfiction that includes *Season of the Gar* (2010*), Return of the Gar* (2015), and *In Search of Monster Fish* (2019), which features a chapter on gar fishing in the Arkansas Ozarks. He has also appeared with Jeremy Wade on *River Monsters*.

Spitzer lives and teaches in central Arkansas, and *Beautifully Grotesque Fish* opens with the elusive American eel—"yep, they're actual fish"— on the Caddo and Ouachita Rivers. The author reminds us how eel mysteries have inspired work by Aristotle, Pliny, and Sigmund Freud, who spent weeks dissecting eels "in hopes of writing the seminal study on their testicles. Unable to find these, he moved on to psychology. Go figure." Freud may have had a hard time because young eels are intersexual, "meaning they can go either way," and environmental factors influence their ultimate gender. In one of the most fascinating stories of fish behavior, all American and European eels migrate as much as 10,000 miles to the Sargasso Sea to spawn. But eel populations are in jeopardy and Spitzer joined biologist Casey Cox to help study their life cycle. Using electrofishing, the two collect only one specimen from the Caddo, but they meet a self-proclaimed "redneck" mother sporting tattoos and cutoff camo. The woman had caught a bunch of eels and she advises them to use chicken livers for bait. Casey hands her a research survey, and "She accepted it like a pamphlet from a Jehovah's Witness, then hit the gas and drove away."

The Ozarks are also highlighted in a lively chapter on paddlefish. Combining his astute and sometimes wry descriptive skills with a respect for science and natural history, Spitzer gives a playful, insightful and thoroughly readable profile of Missouri's state fish: "That crazy flat spatulated nose is so unlike anything we've ever seen on any other fish that our imaginations naturally picture this fish as some sort of alien life form."

Spitzer's human associates are often as fascinating as the fish he meets. On this outing in late March, the author picks up Hippy, once a "goofy, gangly, wild-bearded longhair with stinky feet and overalls" who now has "a respectable haircut and a relatively clean shirt." Spitzer and Hippy drive up to Warsaw, Missouri— "Paddlefish Capital of the World"—and connect with a local guide to troll Lake of the Ozarks and Truman Reservoir, "home to the healthiest paddle-populations in the world."

As plankton grazers, paddlefish don't take bait or lures like most fish. Hippy says they are "gentle, ancient . . . swimming around looking like blimps." But their flesh is delicious and snagging them is a local sport. Spitzer and Hippy don't hook any paddlefish on Lake of the Ozarks, yet Spitzer provides an exposé on the overdevelopment of the lakeshore and on poaching rings involving Russian demands for caviar: "It could be argued that due to the lack of true sturgeon roe—which is the purest cocaine of the caviar trade—paddlefish eggs are synonymous with a cheaper-grade street crack."

Humor aside, a single large female paddlefish with 20 pounds of eggs could be worth $4,000 on the black market. Missouri and other state agencies have cracked down on these destructive trades, and Spitzer praises paddlefish hatchery programs that have successfully raised these precious creatures for restocking and for their meat and delectable eggs. While writing this review, news arrived that the Chinese paddlefish has been declared extinct. Biologists in the People's Republic were never able to successfully rear paddlefish in captivity, and overfishing and habit degradation in the Yangtze River killed them off. Spitzer is optimistic about the future of Ozark paddlefish, however. Fishing Truman Lake the following day, Spitzer and Hippy snag and land a few catfish and two keeper paddlefish over thirty pounds.

Like noodling, trotlining, gigging, and bow fishing, all popular in the Ozarks, snagging is a questionable practice by some sporting standards. Spitzer always tackles these controversies with open honesty that can be humorous, self-admonishing, and sincerely remorseful. In talking with Hippy at the end of the fishing trip, Spitzer admits, "it's a weird way to fish. I still don't know how I feel about snagging those catfish by accident, and I keep wondering if this sport is really a sport. I mean, we didn't burn one calorie trolling out there for two days straight." Hippy acknowledges his friend's comments and they conclude that everything about paddlefish and catching them is weird: "There's just nothing *not weird* about paddlefish."

Beautifully Grotesque Fish is an intelligent, energetic, slightly gonzo adventure across the West's great waters, from the Ozarks through Oklahoma, Texas, Kansas, and Nebraska, up to Minnesota, and across to Idaho and Oregon where Spitzer wrestles with white sturgeon, the largest freshwater fish in North America. He also wrestles with environmental and personal crises. Spitzer's narrative voice is strong and daring but also reflective and humble, and at times his casual style almost sounds careless. While alligator gar fishing in Texas, he writes: "I was thrilled to be psyched and psyched to be thrilled like I hadn't been in years—no doubt due to some personal crap I'd recently gone through, which I won't go into." In the next paragraph he says, "No, I take that back. I will go into it," and he opens up about a painful divorce "eating at me like battery acid" and the death of his mother— "it was about as sucky as a year can get." You might expect this phrasing from a pop star's memoir, not a professor's book on fish, but Spitzer's unaffected voice succeeds in telling us a richly informed, compelling, and honest story. "These fish provided transcendental moments," he writes in the conclusion, "that reassure our chromosomes that Nature can save us from ourselves." Spitzer's devilishly good writing helps minister this salvation.

Ozarks RFD: Selected Essays, 2010-2015. **By Jim Hamilton. (Cornerpost Press, 2020, Pp. 270).**

Reviewed by Steve Wiegenstein

The newspaper column is a surprisingly difficult genre: strict word count limits, inflexible deadlines, and the necessity to be both original and familiar to a broad spectrum of readers. Jim Hamilton is a master practitioner of the form. For more than forty years, he wrote columns for the *Buffalo Reflex*, and a collection of his early columns, *River of Used to Be,* holds a valued place on my bookshelf. Now comes a new collection, taken from the most recent decade and published by a new press.

Readers of a certain age will remember when writing a newspaper column was a prestigious perch reserved for those who had proved themselves to be exemplary reporters and writers. On the national scene, Mike Royko, Molly Ivins, Jimmy Breslin, and others swayed political debates. In the Ozarks, Jean Bell Mosley and Thomza Zimmerman, Leonard Hall, and Sue Hubbell reported from their homes and farmsteads on the rhythms of life in nature and community. Hamilton's columns are in that vein – observant, nostalgic, rarely offering comment on current events.

That doesn't mean they are shallow, though. The columns regularly steer through emotional shoals. Hamilton writes with painful honesty about losing a wife to cancer and a daughter to a car crash, and about the more general disasters that befall a nation and a community. Faithful dogs and treasured fishing holes inhabit these pages, but so do wars and calamities.

I suspect, though, that the columns most readers will respond to are his reminiscences of childhood in the Ozarks. Hamilton has a gift for memory that reveals itself through precision; the word pictures in these columns are detailed, vivid, and evocative. Perhaps one of the signs of love is noticing, and if that's the case these columns are just about as loving as one can get these days. Jim Hamilton seems to have noticed, and remembered, everything that ever happened to him.

Is there repetition among them? Sure. One of the pitfalls of a newspaper column is the obligation to produce material on deadline, again and again, week after week, and no columnist escapes the repetition trap forever. But even when he's returning to a familiar subject or theme, Hamilton finds a way to approach it in a different way, shedding light from a different angle. Still, as with all collections of columns, these are best read in modest amounts. A newspaper column is literature in bite-sized form; as with all bite-sized things, they are better enjoyed when consumed at a moderate pace.

Hamilton's columns capture a moment, dig deep into a memory, and analyze an emotion. Each column is a finely crafted exploration of an experience or recollection, and although you can see their origins in the deadline-driven world of newspaper production, they transcend those origins and offer us lasting insights. There's both sweetness and precision in these columns, a combination that is hard to pull off and even harder to sustain. This collection of work is a real joy.

The Pain Trader and Other Poems. By James Fowler. (Golden Antelope Press, 2020, Pp. 77).

Reviewed by Terrell Tebbetts

James Fowler writes poems about his state and region, the little postage stamp of a world that he knows well. He succeeds when he offers apt descriptive and narrative portraits of characters and settings and then leads readers into new understandings of them.

Sometimes Fowler uses historical events as settings for his narratives. In "Revelation," for example, he follows a wandering hunter, a man without ties, free to keep moving through the world as he pleases. But then he finds the world itself moving as the New Madrid earthquake shakes up his world. Having seen and felt the instability of the world, this character ends up "set / on gaining himself a wife and child," settling down in an unsettling world.

In "Aftermath," Fowler uses the 1865 explosion of the Sultana riverboat as his setting. The first-person narrator, a Southerner seemingly fresh from the just-ended Civil War, spots the blue-clad bodies of Union soldiers killed in the explosion as they float past on the Mississippi River. Acknowledging that during the Civil War he and his buddies "might of whooped and seed / the hand of Providence" in such a death-dealing accident, he comes to realize that "a floatin' charnel house / like this don't count for good." He is as changed by this event as is the character in "Revelation," ready after years of war for death to be "draint out of the works" of man and nature.

Fowler gives readers another Civil War poem in "Brown Study in Blue and Gray," set as the battle of Shiloh looms. He is less successful here, for instead of focusing on a central character changed by historical events, he creates an omniscient narrator who looks with askance at the boys ready for battle, their sights set "on incomparable feats / Of staunch derring-do-or-die." He thus stays too close to the well-worn observation that untried soldiers are frightfully naïve.

He does better in "Elaine," one of his metrical poems. Here Fowler comments on the 1919 Elaine Massacre in which hundreds of African Americans were killed by whites determined to maintain white supremacy in the face of union organizing among black sharecroppers. Fowler gives the piece power not by providing a changed central character but by tying the massacre to the blues emanating from the African American community of the region, specifically that of B. B. King. This poem is one of the truest to the title of the volume, as a bluesman, like a writer, can indeed be a pain trader, creating great art out of great pain.

Moving away from historical settings, Fowler also gives readers a more intimate world in which he depicts characters in their ordinary lives, often seeking new understanding of the lives he depicts.

Sometimes he paints broadly. In "Mountain Airs" his first-person narrator is an 80-something Ozark widow who summarizes the ups and downs of her married life. In "Gayne Preller Takes Stock," the title character does the same. These poems try to cover too much to be detailed enough to put readers inside these lives. Thus they may lack power.

When he paints more narrowly, however, Fowler hits home, excelling in observing and describing specific behaviors of men and women at work or leisure in specific settings and then pondering their significance.

In "The Striper," for instance, Fowler depicts a man repainting stripes in an empty asphalt parking lot and then imagines a life that might have led the man to such an occupation. In this case, he imagines a misspent youth lived outside the lines accumulating a "slate of misdemeanors" and "a mess of low-wage jobs" and ending in a Dantean twist, a punishment, it seems, in which he is sentenced to "spend whole days / toeing, walking, hell, laying down the line."

In "Goat" Fowler gives readers not a man beat down by life but a boy experiencing its sorrow. The first to find himself unseated in a game of musical chairs in his church's Fellowship Hall, too young to put this defeat into perspective, the boy cannot see beyond "the present catastrophe" and so "chokes on the pain / as on something / too large to swallow, / impossible to stomach."

In poems like these, Fowler puts readers right into his subjects' experiences and draws out sympathy for our fellow human beings.

In other poems on daily life, Fowler elicits not sympathy but understanding. One of the best of these is "Threads." Fowler describes a quilting bee, a circle of women "arranging scraps" and "piecing patterns" as they chat about "husbands, children, / household tasks, and prizes at the county fair." Having put readers into that circle, Fowler goes on to picture the bee as much more than a stitching together of pieces of cloth:

This is how time gets stitched, the fabric
adorned with scarcely traceable designs

encompassing the most disparate swatches of life. Here, as in many other poems, Fowler measures up to Robert Frost's observation that it takes a true poet to get out of a poem well.

In a few of his poems on ordinary lives and ordinary places, Fowler goes for humor. In his treatment of Hot Springs' one-time attraction, he imagines "I. Q. Zoo" animals being trained not just to put on shows for tourists but to carry out covert operations. What if, he asks, the invasion of "the Bay of Pigs had included a couple of / our porkers?" And wouldn't Mr. Gorbachev be surprised to learn that when he "was being exhorted to tear down that wall, / our moles were already on the job." What a fine play on words to exit that poem on!

In "Original Sin" Fowler has fun depicting a boy in Sunday School deciding that merely eating a forbidden apple couldn't possibly be bad enough to condemn the whole human race. He wants to find out what Adam and Eve really did, maybe by doing the same thing himself, whatever it was. He yearns to tear off his "clip-on tie / and stiff dress shoes" and "scuff up his soul" a little. Alas, there's "no chance in heck" for that.

As deft as Fowler is at such observations and insights, as apt as he is in exiting poem after poem, some readers will want a little more from him by way of prosody and language. Though he uses rhyme and blank verse occasionally, much of the poetry in this volume lacks the rhythms and fresh language many expect from poetry. Some of the imagery seems stale: a road is "snaking through" a neighborhood. A boat is packed "stem to stern." A town needs "relief from suburban malaise." A man lives in a "ranch house in suburban hell." The language here, in short, is not as consistently fresh as the depictions of characters and settings.

On the whole, Fowler gives readers a well-realized, insightful tour through his native country. Though no character speaks from the grave, the volume reminds me of Edgar Lee Masters' tour through Spoon River country. Though it's a volume of poems, not short stories, it also reminds me of Sherwood Anderson's *Winesburg, Ohio*. Readers who enjoy those works will surely enjoy this volume.

Hipbillies: Deep Revolution in the Arkansas Ozarks. **By Jared M. Phillips. (The University of Arkansas Press, 2019, Pp 138).**

Reviewed by Tim Nutt

The settlers of the Ozark Mountains continue to have a reputation for a spirit of independence and what could be considered unconventional lifestyles with their reliance on the land. The "back-to-landers"—derisively called "hippies," "free spirits," and "longhairs"—were often viewed with suspicion, but as Jared Phillips shows in *Hipbillies*, they made lasting societal and political contributions.

From the late 1960s to the early 1980s, the Arkansas Ozarks became a destination for those wanting to escape the consumer-driven world and create a new utopian society. Phillips documents the lives of the individuals who moved to the hills of Northwest Arkansas to cast off the ties of consumerism and to live off the land. The phrase "deep revolution" in the title reflects the migrants' deep desire to generate change through a return to nature. The change was not easy, and for all the successes, there were a number of failures. In some cases, the back-to-landers did not prepare or research as deeply as such moves required, which resulted in setbacks. Phillips, a historian and assistant professor in international studies at the University of Arkansas, weaves the personal stories of these modern-day pioneers into the larger Ozarks story. The dynamics between the newcomers and the old-timers are particularly fascinating and Phillips does an excellent job of describing the uneasiness and distrust felt by both sides. Phillips has done Ozarks history a service by bringing this topic and these names to the forefront. Those interested in the history of this region should know of Edd Jeffords and his *Ozark Access Catalog*, a resource guide for newcomers. Jeffords, of course, is just one of many important names in the "back-to-land" movement. It is interesting to note that some of the migrants to the Ozarks are still familiar today to Northwest Arkansas residents.

Hipbillies is more than a purely academic work; it is an invaluable contribution to the social history of the Ozarks. Phillips is an outstanding historian and writer. The research Phillips did for this book is extensive and evident. The early chapters give the readers context for the "back-to-land" movement, setting the stage for the move to the Arkansas Ozarks. His narrative flows easily, making *Hipbillies* a highly readable and enjoyable work. His writing makes it easy to get caught up in the lives of the subjects.

Though the volume is relatively slim at 138 pages, it is packed with information and detail. We have seen a rise in publications on Ozark histories in recent years, which speaks to the significance of and interest in this region. As society grapples with its impact on the climate and the effects of capitalism, a review of such environmental movements will become ever more valuable. Phillips has produced an important and timely work in the Ozarks historiography, and everyone who cares about the Ozarks and our planet should read *Hipbillies*.

Arkansas Travelers: Geographies of Exploration and Perception, 1804-1834. By Andrew J. Milson. (The University of Arkansas Press, 2019, Pp. 277).

Reviewed by Jason McCollom

"Mapping the perceptions of the travelers has illustrated the places experienced and perceived by these men rather than simply the spaces they traversed. This geographical focus on the history of these spaces yields a deeper understanding—a deeper map—of the Arkansas past" (222). So argues Andrew J. Milson in *Arkansas Travelers: Geographies of Exploration and Perception, 1804-1834.* Milson, a geographer and historian at the University of Texas-Arlington, came to this conclusion by analyzing the cultural and environmental perceptions of four early-nineteenth-century travelers in Arkansas—William Dunbar, Henry Rowe Schoolcraft, Thomas Nuttall, and George William Featherstonhaugh—and then applying a unique methodology to visually and geographically map those perceptions. Though not all the explorers traversed large swaths of the Ozarks, their observations, and

Milson's analysis, provide a glimpse into the region's formative years of European settlement.

Dunbar explored the Ouachitas and Hot Springs immediately after the Louisiana Purchase. Schoolcraft made his way through the Ozarks, and Nuttall along the Arkansas River Valley, in 1819 during Arkansas's territorial period. Featherstonhaugh traveled across northeast Arkansas towards Little Rock in 1834, on the cusp of statehood. Milson has a keen eye for discerning four layers of "landscapes" and "places" in the travelers' reports, or, their observations, geographically bound, on culture and the environment. First, Milson teases out their perceptions of native culture and land use; then those of hunters and settlers of European extraction; next, observations on the commercial potential of the land; and finally, the natural environment.

The first chapter provides excellent biographies of the four men. In chapters two through five Milson utilizes each explorer's travel reports to reconstruct their journeys, with highlights of their cultural and environmental perceptions. Mississippi plantation owner William Dunbar headed a group along the Ouachita River to the hot springs of Arkansas. During his 1804-1805 trek his observations homed in on the commercial and settlement potential of this area. Dunbar encountered French and Spanish settlers in Louisiana and Arkansas and various Native tribes, such as the Caddo, Quapaw, and Osages. He commented on several natural resources with the potential to produce gunpowder and dyes and noted modest deposits of coal and iron ore as well as numerous animals.

From 1818 to 1820 Thomas Nuttall made his way down the Mississippi to the White River, en route to the Arkansas River. He characterized the Mississippi and White River basins as unsuitable for settlement or farming, owing to constant flooding and the shifting of the rivers. Once on the Arkansas River, Nuttall became more optimistic about commercial development, and had mostly amiable contact with the Quapaw and Cherokee. Near present-day Fort Smith, he projected a bright agricultural and settled future for the Arkansas River Valley.

Arriving in St. Louis in 1834, Englishman and Geologist to the United States George W. Featherstonhaugh headed a mission to survey the lands between the Missouri and Red Rivers. Traveling south through the eastern Missouri Ozarks, Fenston, as he was known, found few redeeming qualities in the settlers and hunters he encountered. He envisioned this region of the Ozarks as separate from the progressing civilization of St. Louis, and as an area in which agriculture and commercial development was stunted and stagnate. Moving into the Arkansas Ozarks he evinced disgust at the local culture, describing, for instance, a settler woman's face as "extraordinarily dark, bony, [and] hairy" with "trimmings to match" (158). In contrast, Fenston found the natural Ozarks landscape fascinating and aesthetically pleasing. Once in Little Rock, moving towards the hot springs like Dunbar before him, Fenston could not help but to denigrate American cultural frontier norms, such as gambling, drinking, and superstitious religion.

"Greenhorn" explorer Henry Rowe Schoolcraft and his companion Levi Pettibone arrived in Potosi, Missouri, in 1818 with a design to survey the mining potential of the region. A New Yorker looking to make his career and fortune, Schoolcraft was ill prepared for a 90-day, 900-mile trek through the Ozarks of Missouri and Arkansas. Of all the travelers in Milson's book, Schoolcraft spent the most time in the Ozarks and provides a wealth of cultural and environmental perceptions of the region. Schoolcraft started traveling southwesterly from Potosi and linked up with the North Fork River in present-day Ozark County, Missouri. He found little commercial or agricultural potential in the rocky, barren landscape, though the waterways merited his praise. He reached the White River and then the James River near Springfield, where several settler families assisted him with supplies, food, and advice. At the James River, Schoolcraft's tune changed: he foresaw vast, productive farms and economic development in southwest Missouri. By early 1819 Schoolcraft was back on the White River, which he also predicted could harbor flourishing farms and settlement, going into the Arkansas Ozarks near present-day Batesville, and then back north to Potosi.

Milson brings his analysis together in chapter six, "Deep Mapping the Arkansas Past." The methodology involved mapping the journeys via GoogleEarth, and adding for each traveler place-marks indicating positive, negative, and purely descriptive perceptions on environmental and cultural features. Finally, a cartographer illustrated 18 maps with corresponding symbols along the travelers' routes. Taken together, the maps and the written journals provide a more holistic interpretation. Mapping reveals that the four journeyers generally praised areas they deemed already or potentially commercially or agriculturally developed, and disparaged poorer, non-agricultural, and non-white cultures (though there are individual exceptions, which Milson discusses).

Arkansas Travelers is a unique, interdisciplinary study of the cultural and environmental landscapes of the state. The numerous maps provide a welcome accompaniment to Milson's shrewd reading of each party's journey. For the field of Ozarks Studies, the author's breakdown of Schoolcraft's time in southern Missouri and northern Arkansas and his accompanying maps are unrivaled. From this first methodological step, future research would do well to investigate broader questions. Can these travelers' perceptions be considered unique among their early-nineteenth-century counterparts in other regions of the U.S.? Apart from merely positive and negative perceptions, what additional significance can be derived from mapping travelers' paths? It will be exciting to see to what conclusions similar historical geographic studies lead scholars.

Contributors

Craig (C. D.) Albin is a professor of English at Missouri State University–West Plains. In 2009, he became the founding editor of *Elder Mountain: A Journal of Ozarks Studies*. His fiction, poetry, essays, and reviews have appeared in a number of publications, including *Arkansas Review, Big Muddy, Cape Rock, Cave Region Review, Georgia Review, Harvard Review, Natural Bridge, Philological Review*, and *Style*. Ten of his short stories were collected in *Hard Toward Home*, published by Press 53 in 2016, a collection for which Albin received the Missouri Author Award from the Missouri Library Association in 2017. His poetry collection, *Axe, Fire, Mule*, was published by Golden Antelope Press in 2018.

Karen Craigo was appointed by Gov. Mike Parsons as Missouri's fifth poetry laureate in 2019. Her work has appeared in numerous journals, including *Atticus Review, Indiana Review, Prairie Schooner*, and *Poetry*, and she has published three chapbooks and two full-length collections of poetry, *Passing Through Humansville* (2018) and *No More Milk* (2016). She is the poetry series editor for the Missouri State University-based Moon City Press and the nonfiction editor for the literary journal *Mid-American Review*. As a journalist, she is editor and general manager of *The Marshfield Mail*, a 128-year-old weekly newspaper based in the Webster County seat.

Faith Collins is a student at Missouri State University-West Plains and is a beekeeper.

Charity Gibson earned her PhD in literature and criticism from Indiana University of Pennsylvania. She is an assistant professor of English and teaches undergraduate courses in literature and composition in Southwest Missouri. Her doctoral and teaching area of specialization is contemporary American literature. In much of her research, she explores issues related to motherhood, the mother-daughter relationship, and parenting in contemporary culture. She is raising four children with her husband. She enjoys walking, playing the piano, traveling, and reading.

Paulette Guerin earned an MFA from the University of Florida, and she now lives in Arkansas where she works as a freelance editor and teaches English at Harding University. Her poetry has appeared in *Green Briar Review, Cantos, Concho River Review, The Main Street Rag, Summerset Review, The Tishman Review,* and the *2018 Best New Poets* anthology. Her chapbook, *Polishing Silver*, was published by Finishing Line Press in 2011.

Jim Hamilton was brought up on a small dairy farm in southern Dallas County near Elkland, Missouri. He began his journalism career as his FFA chapter's reporter in 1964 and was editor of the Southwest Missouri State College *Standard* in 1970-71. He served as a U.S. Air Force journalist and base newspaper editor and worked as a news editor at the *Bolivar Herald-Free Press*. In 1978 he began a 24-year stint as editor and publisher of the *Buffalo Reflex*. He subsequently served as managing editor of *Springfield! Magazine,* then returned to newspapers in 2004 and served as a regional writer and columnist until retiring in May 2015. He continues to freelance columns and features. A collection of his columns, *The River of Used To Be*, was published in 1994, and a second collection, *Ozarks RFD: Selected Essays, 2010-2015,* was published by Cornerpost Press in 2020. Hamilton was inducted into the Missouri Southern State University Regional Media Hall of Fame and the Missouri Press Association Hall of Fame in 2016.

Brian Hardman is associate professor of English at the University of the Ozarks in Clarksville, Arkansas, where he teaches classes in American literature and a variety of other courses in the Humanities and in the Environmental Studies program. He was born in Willard, Missouri, and, besides a few years living in the West, has lived most of his life in the Ozarks. He holds a BS in communications from Missouri State University and an MA and PhD in English from the University of Arkansas. Outside his professional interests, he spends his free time exploring the mountains, lakes, rivers, and hollers in the Ozarks with his wife (a native of Cabool, Missouri) and two children.

Kimberly D. Harper, a native of McDonald County, Missouri, earned a BA in history at Missouri Southern State University and an MA in history at the University of Arkansas. She is a seventh generation Ozarker and the author of *White Man's Heaven: The Lynching and Expulsion of Blacks in the Southern Ozarks, 1894-1909* (University of Arkansas Press).

Phillip Howerton is professor of English at Missouri State University-West Plains. His essays, reviews, and poems have appeared in several journals and books. He is a co-founder and co-editor of *Cave Region Review*, an associate editor of *The Heartland Journal*, general editor of *Elder Mountain: A Journal of Ozarks Studies*, and owner of Cornerpost Press. His poetry collection, *The History of Tree Roots*, was published by Golden Antelope Press in 2015, and his *The Literature of the Ozarks: An Anthology* was published by University of Arkansas Press in 2019, a project for which he received the Missouri Literary Award from the Missouri Library Association.

Victoria Howerton holds a BA in Latin American Studies, a BJ in journalism, and an MA in Spanish, all from University of Missouri-Columbia, and she is also a registered nurse. While living in Washington, D.C., she worked as an HIV/AIDS educator for La Salud, as a housing coordinator for Adelante Advocacy Inc., and as coordinator of HIV/AIDS outreach at National Council of LaRaza. Victoria has served as a Spanish interpreter in courtrooms, hospitals, and police departments, and she interpreted for former Ecuadorian president Rodrigo Borja when he visited Columbia, Missouri, in 2005. She has taught Spanish at MU and at North Arkansas College, and her journalism, editorials, translations, book reviews, and interviews have appeared in a variety of newspapers and journals, such as *The Columbia Missourian, The Missouri Folklore Society Journal*, and *Cave Region Review*.

Henry Hughes grew up on Long Island. After completing an MA in Creative Writing at Purdue University in 1990, he spent five years working in Japan and China. He finished a PhD in American Literature at Purdue in the spring of 2002 and began teaching at Western Oregon University where he teaches a variety of literature and writing courses. Hughes is the author of four poetry collections, including *Men Holding Eggs* (2004 Oregon Book Award), *Moist Meridian* (2011 Finalist for the Oregon Book Award), *Shutter Lines* (2012, with photographs by Paul Gentry) and *Bunch of Animals* (2016). His poems and essays have appeared in *Antioch Review, Carolina Quarterly, Shenandoah, Seattle Review, Southern Humanities Review, Gray's Sporting Journal,* and *Harvard Review,* and he is a regular book reviewer for *Harvard Review Online*. His fishing memoir, *Back Seat with Fish: A Man's Adventures in Angling and Romance,* was published in 2016 by Skyhorse. He is the editor of a *Journal of Melville Studies* special issue, "Melville in the Marquesas," and the Everyman's Library anthologies, *The Art of Angling: Poems about Fishing and Fishing Stories*.

Robert Lee Mahon has been teaching composition and literature at East Central College, in Union, Missouri, for the past 44 years. Since ECC is a community college, the teaching is pretty basic, which, he says, suits his rather basics-oriented personality, and which he hopes informs his poetry. He has been published in numerous literary journals over the years, and, at 74, is flattered that his poems still see the light in journals like this one.

Jason McCollom is associate professor of history at Missouri State University-West Plains. His book, *Political Harvests: Transnational Farmers' Movements on the U.S. and Canadian Plains, 1905-1950,* will be published by University of Nebraska Press in 2021.

D. Matt McGowan grew up in Webb City, Missouri. He attended Missouri Southern State College (now University) and the University of Missouri, where he earned a bachelor's degree in history and a master's degree in journalism. He was a newspaper reporter, and for many years he has worked as a science and research writer at the University of Arkansas. His stories have appeared in *Adirondack Review, Deep South Magazine, Concho River Review, Hawaii Pacific Review, Arkansas Review,* and others. He lives with his wife and children in Fayetteville, Arkansas.

Lynn Morrow, MA, Missouri State University, served as research historian for the Center for Ozarks Studies, managed the historic preservation consulting firm Kalen and Morrow, and administered Missouri's national model in public records preservation at the Missouri State Archives. Lynn has published widely in the *Missouri Historical Review*, *Gateway Heritage*, *Missouri Folklore Journal*, *Ozarks Watch*, *Big Muddy*, and in other serials, dictionaries, and anthologies. He co-edited two documentary histories, co-authored *Shepherd of the Hills Country: Tourism Transforms the Ozarks, 1880s-1930s* (University of Arkansas Press), and edited *The Ozarks in Missouri History: Discoveries in an American Region* (University of Missouri Press).

John Mort's first novel, *Soldier in Paradise* (1999), was widely reviewed and won the W. Y. Boyd Award for best military fiction. He has published seven other books, including two readers advisory works, two novels, and four collections of stories. His short stories have appeared in a wide variety of magazines, including *The New Yorker*, *Missouri Review*, the *Chicago Tribune*, the *Arkansas Review*, and in *Sixfold*. He is the winner of a National Endowment for the Arts literary grant, the Hackney Award, and a Western Writers of America Spur for the short story, "The Hog Whisperer." In 2017 he was awarded the Sullivan Prize for his short story collection, *Down Along the Piney*, which was published in 2018 by the University of Notre Dame Press. Mort served with the First Cavalry from 1968 through 1970 as a rifleman and RTO. He attended the University of Iowa, from which he earned a BA in English (1972), an MFA in writing (1974), and an MLS (1976). He has worked as a librarian, editor, and teacher. He lives in Coweta, Oklahoma.

Tim Nutt is director of the Historical Research Center at the University of Arkansas for Medical Sciences. Previously, he was Head of Special Collections at the University of Arkansas-Fayetteville and founding Deputy Curator of the Butler Center for Arkansas Studies at the Central Arkansas Library System. He also served as the founding Managing Editor and Staff Historian of the award-winning online *Encyclopedia of Arkansas History & Culture*. A native of Bigelow, Arkansas, Nutt received a BA in history from the University of Central

Arkansas and a master's in library science, with an emphasis on archives, from the University of Oklahoma. He is a past president of the Arkansas Historical Association and a certified archivist.

Benjamin G. Rader is the author of *Down on Mahans Creek: A History of an Ozarks Neighborhood* (2017) and five other books and is James L. Sellers Professor of History *emeritus* at the University of Nebraska—Lincoln. Born and raised in the Ozarks, he lives in Lincoln, Nebraska.

Molly Bess Rector lives in Fayetteville, Arkansas, where she co-curates the Open Mouth Reading Series—a community-based poetry series that hosts monthly readings by visiting writers, as well as workshops and retreats. Molly earned her MFA in poetry from the University of Arkansas, and she offers writing and editorial support for artists developing professional materials (artist statements, CVs, project descriptions, and so on). She is the recipient of residencies from the Edward F. Albee Foundation and the Vermont Studio Center, as well as a grant from the Artists 360 program to pursue her interest in the intersection of the human emotional landscape with physical landscapes impacted by nuclear science. Molly served as the inaugural poetry editor for *The Arkansas International*, for whom she still occasionally writes reviews. Her work has appeared or is forthcoming in *Hayden's Ferry Review*, *The Collagist*, *Ninth Letter*, and *The Boiler*, among others.

Gerry Sloan is a retired music professor living in Fayetteville, Arkansas. He has published four chapbooks (one translated into Mandarin) and two poetry collections: *Paper Lanterns* (2011) and *Crossings: A Memoir in Verse* (2017). His work has appeared in such literary magazines as *North Dakota Quarterly*, *The Kansas Quarterly*, *The Nebraska Review*, *Nebo*, *Slant*, and the *Anthology of Magazine Verse & Yearbook of American Poetry*. He received the WORDS Award for Poetry in 1990 from the Arkansas Literary Society. More recently his "Poem for Palestine" won first place in the Gaza Freedom Flotilla Literary Contest.

Mark Spitzer, novelist, poet, essayist, and literary translator, grew up in Minneapolis where he earned his bachelor's degree at the University of Minnesota in 1990. He then earned his master's in creative writing from the University of Colorado. After living on the road for some time, he found himself in Paris as writer in residence for three years at the bohemian bookstore Shakespeare and Company. In 1997 he moved to Louisiana and earned an MFA from Louisiana State. He taught creative writing and literature for five years at Truman State University and is now an associate professor of creative writing at the University of Central Arkansas. Author of more than 30 books, he has published nonfiction fish books, memoirs, novels, poetry collections, plays, articles on creative writing pedagogy, and books of literary translation. Spitzer has also been the official Nebraska state record holder for the yellow bullhead.

Douglas Stevens is a seventh generation Ozarker and has taught history and English at both the high school and college level. A sometimes poet, he is currently completing a second obscure volume of poetry and is researching the exponential growth in the number of administrators in Missouri's institutions of higher education and the exponential growth of their salaries.

Terrell Tebbetts holds the Martha Heasley Cox Chair in American Literature at Lyon College. He has published over three dozen articles on American literature in several books and in journals such as *Philological Review, Southern Literary Journal, The F. Scott Fitzgerald Review, The Steinbeck Review,* and *The Faulkner Journal.* He regularly co-leads the Teaching Faulkner sessions at Ole Miss's annual Faulkner and Yoknapatawpha Conference.

Jim Vandergriff is a rural Ozarker by birth and genealogy, having been born in Laclede County, Missouri, in 1942, with six generations of Ozarkers behind him, and having lived in Laclede, Pulaski, and Phelps counties until his seventeenth birthday. He then joined the Navy, where he served until age 21. After the Navy, he returned to Missouri and attended the University of Central Missouri. Soon after receiving a master's degree in English in 1972, he began his career as a college professor. He earned a doctorate in teacher education in 2001 from the University of Arizona. He retired to Arizona in 2008. He has been a Missouri Folklore Society member since 1977 and has served as editor, director, and president for the organization.

Denise Henderson Vaughn has been passionate about the Ozarks ever since she bought forty acres near Ava, Missouri, during her senior year of high school. She built a cabin there, gardened, and within a few years adopted a mission: environmental education in the Ozarks. During twenty years with the *West Plains Daily Quill,* her coverage of natural resource issues earned several awards for investigative reporting. She completed a master's degree in journalism and conservation biology from the University of Missouri (2014), has taught journalism there and at MSU-West Plains, has served as writer or media specialist for a half-dozen science and environmentally focused non-profits, and has produced two documentaries available online, *Karst in the Ozarks* (2010) and *Karst in Perry County* (2020). Her work has also appeared in the *St. Louis Post-Dispatch* and *Forest History Today.*

Amy Wright Vollmar began writing poetry as a child in Alton, Illinois, while she explored the wooded ravine behind her subdivision. Deeper in southern Illinois, with her father's family, she learned how to sing Appalachian folk songs and where to find the sweetest hickory nuts. At Monmouth College in Illinois, Amy majored in English, but also wrote a few poems during botany labs. After graduating she lived in Texas, where she worked for the Fort Worth Museum of Science and History, helping museum visitors touch interesting things: a live opossum or an Apollo astronaut's glove. With her family, she chose to move to Springfield, Missouri, near the woods of the Ozarks. Hiking, kayaking, and writing followed, along with a job creating curriculum and teaching first graders at Phelps Center for Gifted Education in Springfield. Now retired, Amy volunteers with students, writes, and hopes to show people the beautiful fragility of the wild places she loves through poetry. Her poetry has previously appeared in *Cave Region Review* and *Elder Mountain.* Amy's first book of poetry, *Follow,* was published by Cornerpost Press in March of 2020.

Steve Wiegenstein holds a doctorate in English from the University of Missouri-Columbia, and he has taught at Centenary College of Louisiana, Drury University, Culver-Stockton College, and Western Kentucky University. Wiegenstein's nonfiction and short fiction have appeared in numerous literary journals and magazines, and he maintains a blog on which he discusses Ozarks-related topics. He is the author of *Slant of Light, This Old World*, and *The Language of Trees*. *Slant of Light* was an honorable mention for the David J. Langum Historical Fiction Award in 2012, *This Old World* was a finalist for the M. M. Bennetts Award for Historical Fiction in 2014, and *The Language of Trees* received the Missouri Writers Guild's Walter Williams Major Work Award in 2018. His short story collection, *Scattered Lights*, will be released by Cornerpost Press in the fall of 2020.

Steve Yates is the author of two novels from Moon City Press, *Morkan's Quarry* and *The Teeth of the Souls*, he is also the winner of the Juniper Prize in fiction, and University of Massachusetts Press published *Some Kinds of Love: Stories* in 2013. His novella, *Sandy and Wayne*, won the inaugural Knickerbocker Prize, and Dock Street Press subsequently published *Sandy and Wayne* in 2016. His *The Legend of the Albino Farm* was published in 2017 by Unbridled Books. Yates is associate director/marketing director at University Press of Mississippi. He lives in Flowood, Mississippi, with his wife, Tammy.

CPSIA information can be obtained
at www.ICGtesting.com
Printed in the USA
BVHW090025161020
591040BV00005B/313